For Ellen and Tom Broadbent

Just ~~the~~ ... will have an official ... you in it. It's not a textbook, but it ain't bad. Hope you enjoy it.

Cordially,
Stu Hirschberg

# Myth in the Poetry of Ted Hughes

*By the same author*
At the Top of the Tower: Yeats' Poetry Explored Through 'A Vision'

# Myth in the Poetry of Ted Hughes

## A guide to the poems

STUART HIRSCHBERG

**Barnes and Noble Books**
Totowa, New Jersey

Published in the U.S.A. 1981 by
Barnes and Noble Books
a division of Littlefield, Adams & Co., Inc.
81 Adams Drive, Totowa, New Jersey, 97512
in association with Wolfhound Press, Dublin

ISBN 0-06-492883-7
Library of Congress Catalog number: 79-55-697

Typeset by Lagamage Co. Ltd.,
Printed and bound in Great Britain
by Billing and Sons Limited
Guildford, London, Oxford, Worcester

# Contents

# Dedication

*Don té a mbíonn an ceart aici
i gcónaí*

# INTRODUCTION

Edward James (Ted) Hughes was born in Mytholmroyd, West Riding of Yorkshire, England on August 17, 1930. He was educated at Mexborough Grammar School, Yorkshire and went up to Pembroke College, Cambridge in 1951. In 1953, Hughes changed his course of study from English to Archaeology and Anthropology and thereby came under the 'Cambridge School' of Anthropology indebted most prominently to Sir James Frazer, author of *The Golden Bough* and including Jane Harrison, Gilbert Murray, Francis Cornford and A. B. Cook.[1] Through this course of study, Hughes first became acquainted with the enormous inheritance of myth and folklore which would later provide him with the materials and framework out of which his poetry evolved.

The poetry of Ted Hughes is bound to occupy a central place when the history of twentieth-century poetry comes to be written. Yet, even the most casual reader of Hughes's poetry is soon aware of depths beyond which he cannot go, mysteries that can only be guessed at but never fully understood. Hughes's 'frame of reference', as A. Alvarez has remarked with his customary insight, is 'different'.[2] As we shall see much of what is different about Hughes's poetry stems from a succession of self-adopted masks that, in turn, create the boundaries we have called the poetry of the Shaman, Trickster and Scapegoat.

Yeats once wrote that 'to me all things are made of the conflict of two states of consciousness, beings or persons which die each other's life, live each other's death'.[3] Ultimately, the poetry of Ted Hughes and the poetry of Sylvia Plath (the American poetess, now deceased, whom Hughes married in 1956) are reciprocals of each other; each moves toward the condition of the other. In Hughes's recent work we see the tentative self-questioning so characteristic of Plath's early poetry, while in Hughes's first animal poems we can fully observe an absolute certainty achieved through imaginative fusion with universal forces that Plath finally attained only in her very last poems. The full implications of Plath's self-transformation are outside the scope of the present study, but readers

7

should be aware that the exact same process we will outline and explore chronologically operating in Hughes's poetry is duplicated, in reverse form, in Sylvia Plath's work.

For Hughes, in his earliest animal poems, the process of writing the poem recreates the rite of blood brotherhood between the Shaman and his animal Helper. Whether hawk, bear, jaguar, or pike, among others, Hughes establishes a mystical alliance and 'exchanges blood' with his animal familiars. Hughes makes contact with a feral energy at the heart of the cosmos, mindless, luxuriant, capable of bringing death and revitalizing the dead, a terrible power to be both summoned and feared. This force is vastly superior to anything he sees working in man. In fact, it is totally alien and indifferent to man's welfare. How best to cope with this force, to channel it, if possible, becomes his preoccupation. Hughes's style at this point is still basically rigid, modelled on the quatrain, without that emphasis on the single line as stanza that will emerge later. The closed form is a reflection of his desire to push back into manageable limits the forces, Faust-like, he has evoked.

In *Wodwo,* Hughes explores the implications, in a premonition of victimhood, of psychic vulnerability, dissociation and dismemberment and seeks unsuccessfully to embrace the path of self-surrender where nothing is held back and everything is put on the line. Yet, while provoking Hughes's fear and admiration and bringing into focus the exact nature of the necessary sacrifice, he cannot yet bring himself to this point. He draws back and in the process of drawing back summons into existence the grotesque grinning figure of Crow, the Trickster. While Crow prides himself on his ability to escape punishment (in the first half of the Crow sequence) we see him at last looking down on the suffering victim which, in some mysterious fashion, he has been responsible for creating. The hatred of Crow for the suffering victim, a hatred close to tears, projects the hatred of one part of the self watching the other part that has been mutilated and is waiting to die. At last, in *Prometheus on his Crag, Cave Birds* and *Gaudete* Hughes writes poetry from the point of view of the victim, the Scapegoat, scorched, held in suspension, subjected to withering scrutiny: the poetry, so to speak, of The Hanged Man whose mysterious smile suggests that his present agony is the necessary precondition to enlightenment.

This book is addressed to the interested student as well as the general reader who is curious to discover how a major contemporary poet has drawn on ancient myths and the folk-lore of many cultures. Through a detailed analysis of how Hughes brought myths and legends into his poetry we are able to understand how he rooted his personal feelings in the context of universal archetypes while at the same time enriching these omnipresent themes with the personal drama of a life touched by startling and tragic events. This reciprocal trans-mutation is undoubtedly the main determining event moving Hughes into the forefront of contemporary poets.

First, we see Hughes as self-sufficient, self-centered Shaman, then as misfit Trickster and lastly as tormented Scapegoat. We see Hughes advancing through a series of self-assigned roles, wearing masks derived from his acquaintance with Sir James Frazer's *The Golden Bough* and Robert Graves's *The White Goddess*. But, remarkably, each of the poems and works that we will discuss on a chronological basis, transcends the personal incidents that motivated it to achieve all the liberated, permanent, fully articulated, aesthetically objective dimensions of true art.

Throughout his career as poet, Hughes's continuing absorp-tion with the psychological, moral, social and religious sym-bolism derived from ancient mythologies bespeaks a mind trying to re-establish touch with the heritage of a long vanish-ed past. These ancient archetypes reverberate in his poetry with an evocativeness, continuity and power that makes much of contemporary poetry seem bloodless by comparison. Without question, Hughes's poetry possesses, as the present study endea-vours to show, qualities which cannot help but invigorate the tradition of twentieth-century poetry.

Stuart Hirschberg
New Jersey
U.S.A.

# Part I    Shaman

'When I began to sing', said the shaman Semyonov
Semyon, 'my sickness usually disappeared.' In Joseph
Campbell, *The Masks of God: Primitive Mythology*
(New York: Penguin Books, 1976), p. 265.

## Chapter One
## PRIMORDIAL ANIMAL TOTEMS

### *HAWK ROOSTING*

Shamans believe that by identifying oneself with an animal,
an animal charged with the whole mythology of the species,
a man could become 'something far greater and stronger than
himself'.[1] For primitive man, the act of donning the skin of
an animal was important because it allowed a feeling of magical
transformation, a 'going out of the self'.[2] Thus, shamanism
basically is not a regression into animal life, but is instead an
acquisition of a 'superhuman mode of being'.[3] By contrast,
human characters within Hughes's work are often drastically
reduced, limited and dissociated. For Hughes the significance
of shamanism, that is, the fusion with the mythical life of certain
animals, is the sense of power it offers, communion with cosmic
life and force, and a recentering of the personality and a corresponding sense of the renewal of the universe as an ecstatic and
euphoric experience. As Hughes has said of his animals, 'their
reality seems less questionnable than ours'.[4] Thus, what Hughes
admires about animals is their single-mindedness and self-
centredness. For him, they have a substantiality, a realness about
them that conveys qualities of security, stability and permanence
that human beings simply do not have. His sense of human
beings, on the other hand, is of creatures so shot through with
spaces and existential openings that to believe in them would
be like putting one's faith in shifting sands. People wobble
in and out of existence, waver between being and non-being;
animals do not. Moreover, poems for Hughes have a life like
that of animals, a life quite separate from even Hughes himself.

11

Poems in which animals fly, swim, or crawl live perpetually in exactly the same way without change or alteration; the existence of the poems themselves about animals are for him a shamanistic participation in a realm whose existence is unquestionnably stable, permanent and exempt from change. Beyond this, Hughes's animal poems are his reaction against a rationalistic demand for civilization carried so far that everything around one is habitually humanized, tainted with the rationalistic self. To counter this trend, these poems enlarge the scope of existence from the private to the archetypal realm. Through his animal poems Hughes immerses himself in the dark, irrational forces around and within him in order to purge himself of the artificial social construct, the personality.

Although based on shamanistic rites, these poems serve a personal, psychological function so that through violence, primitive contact with suppressed hatred and repressed aggression and even a kind of psychic self-mutilation, the sterile personality created by society is destroyed and the instinctual suppressed self can emerge liberated. In many cases, Hughes's need to liberate the forces symbolized by these animals is revealed in the fact that they are often shown constrained by situations and environments that limit them. The jaguar is caged, the bear is in hibernation, the hawk is seen at the end of a day of hunting. Hughes seeks, as did ancient shamans, an alignment with the unknown forces governing the universe. His work is a journey beyond the rational to the primitive depths of experience to liberate the self. In a way his emphasis on violence, death and brutality is a ritual submergence and submission to the inevitable death of the old self that must precede the liberation and emergence of an authentic self, to gain access to the power habitually held in check by society. The relationship between Hughes and the terrifying predators he describes is like that of the shaman to his totem animal. Eskimo legends and myths, for example, speak of an animal 'that wounds the candidate, tears him to pieces or devours him then new flesh grows around his bones. Sometimes the animal that tortures him becomes the future shaman's helping spirit'.[5]

All of these elements come together in 'Hawk Roosting',[6] one of Hughes's most complex and compelling poems. Perched high atop a tree, like a king on his throne, a hawk appears to be sleeping in a vast wood. From his mighty body and powerful beak to his vice-like talons which can crush his victims effortlessly, he is the embodiment of lordly grandeur. He exults in his domain; he fits perfectly into his environment. The high trees, the air that lifts him, the sun that warms him, the earth that lies upward for his inspection are made so that he may function perfectly. Each single feather that covers his body is the product of countless millenia of evolution and adaptation. His life goes on because others die for him. He dispenses death into the world. To his victims the death that he brings is comprehended as fate. The path from his treetop perch to the bones of his victims is straight and true; when he kills, he kills quickly.

Throughout the poem we see everything through the hawk's eyes in the first person. The hawk's eye is the centre upon which everything in the poem pivots — the world itself revolves at his bidding. Each of the last four stanzas of the poem is interlocked so that the last sentence of each preceeding stanza flows into the first sentence of the following one. Each last sentence makes a claim that the next line justifies and supports. As the sun slips down behind the woods in a blaze of red and orange signalling a time for the hawk to rest after a day of hunting, Hughes describes the hawk as 'roosting', his eyes closed. Each detail of the poem convinces us of the integrity of Hughes's vision. Animals, for Hughes, are the apex and most compelling of life forms. The thoughts we overhear are devoid of wish fulfillment characteristic of the dreams of men; the hawk's dream and his achievement are one. In his sleep the hawk enjoys contemplation of his kills ('Or in sleep rehearse perfect kills and eat' — a play on 'hearse', a carrier of the dead). Hughes defines nature within the framework of predator and prey; predators are irresistibly powerful, victims are powerless, constantly forced to adapt to environments that change to their disadvantage. It is inevitable, of course, that one should come to be at the mercy of the other. There is no middle ground in Hughes's poetry; one either identifies with the predator or with the victims who exist to be the prey. In a January 1971 interview (in *London Magazine*) Hughes responded to a question about the significance of his choice of the hawk by saying, 'what I had in mind was that in this hawk Nature is thinking. . . I intended some Creator like the Jehovah in Job but more feminine.'[7]

At a later point, Hughes identifies the hawk with 'Isis, mother of the gods',[8] although *The Egyptian Book of the Dead* tells us that the hawk is not Isis, but the son of Isis and Osiris whose name is Horus, a masculine deity. From the first, says E.A. Wallis Budge, the editor and translator, 'The visible emblem of the sun-god was at a very early date that of the hawk, which was probably the first living thing worshipped by the early Egyptians.'[9] Isis, on the other hand, was 'the wife of Osiris and the mother of Horus . . . her commonest names are "the great goddess, the divine mother, the mistress of charms or enchantments"; in later times she is called the "mother of the gods", and "living one". She is usually depicted in the form of a woman . . . the animal sacred to her was the cow . . . .'[10] Hughes's reinterpretation of the hawk as feminine and identification of Nature with the hawk's characteristics as a malevolent, controlling, devouring force is more significant for his poetry than the original choice of the hawk itself. The implication for Hughes's poetry cannot be overestimated. His view of nature as a terrifying, unforgiving feminine force this early in his work underlies his profound ambivalence and yet deep attraction to Robert Graves's comprehensive archetype, 'the White Goddess'.[11] This obsessive theme permeates Hughes's work from his earliest poems and unites works as apparently diverse as *The Wound* (where revengeful female furies, the Bacchae, assail the hero), his 1967 translation of Seneca's *Oedipus, Orghast* and the associated Prometheus poems (where the vulture embodies the revenge of the creatress) and his 1977 work *Gaudete* where the Reverend Lumb outrages and is in turn pursued and destroyed by incensed female worshippers of a love-cult he has created. Whether called the White Goddess, the vulture, the Anima or the eternal feminine, it is clear that nature, for Hughes, does have the character of an overwhelming, devouring, demonic maternal force — the principle of nurturing gone terribly wrong, as it were.

It must be remembered that this conception is unique to Hughes himself; no Egyptian, Indian, Scandinavian, Germanic or Hellenic myths identify the hawk as a feminine principle. Hughes's ambivalence stems from a mixture of fear and admiration. What he admires about the hawk and by extension, all predators is their ability to exercise total and complete control over their environments. The hawk, simply stated, will not permit things to change: 'I am going to keep things like this.' When Hughes has his hawk say 'there is no sophistry in my body' he is emphasizing the fact that the hawk is not subject to self-doubt, it has no capacity nor desire for casuistry, elaborate ratiocination, or self-deception. In contrast, Hughes's human characters are frequently assailed by self-doubt, they are undone by aspects of themselves they but dimly perceive to exist and are victims of dissociation and inner schisms within their personalities (e.g. the narrator in *Snow,* Ripley in *The Wound,* the unnamed human victim in *Crow,* Rev. Lumb in *Gaudete*). Whereas human characters in Hughes's work are frequently portrayed as being powerless, the hawk is an image of enormous strength and unity. The more of Hughes's animal poetry one reads, the more one becomes aware of his sense of the ultimate, untouchability of Nature. We feel that Hughes is speechless with admiration, intimidated with respect for what he both loves and fears. He forces us to pay attention through an effort of intense poetic concentration. He creates the object for us. His grasp is unerring, at once spontaneous and studied. His animal poems fuse an almost naive vision with the power, always grounded in an immediate perception of his animal subjects, that convinces us of the integrity of his vision. His selection of language is concise, vivid, enormously controlled, and yet filled with spontaneity and a sense of discovery.

Hughes's awareness of the hawk as totem animal permeates and creates the imagery and structure of the poem at its most basic level. The hawk is not a symbol of any supra-sensual reality; it is that reality. As such, it is a unifying, holistic and mystical centre that transmits an ideal that Hughes clearly feels offers a far more profound truth than the shattered, pluralistic and morally bankrupt truths offered by political, economic, social and religious systems within contemporary society. Taken in perspective, Hughes's response to the disorder of his age is analogous to although plainly different in kind from W. B. Yeats's complex synthesis of Irish folklore, occult thought and esoteric gnosticism. What is startling about Hughes's poetry is the absolute literalness, concreteness and achieved visual depth of realization of which he is capable. His poems never centre on generalized abstractions but begin and end with startling images, clear visual and perfectly augmented marvels of concentrated power.

## AN OTTER

Among the Ojibwa Indians the otter has the first importance. Their myths tell us that a messenger of the great spirit 'seeing the miserable state of sick and enfeebled humanity reveals the most sublime secret to the otter'[12] and makes it immortal so that it can 'initiate and at the same time consecrate men'.[13] The otter has such an extraordinary importance as an animal sacred to both the Ojibwa community and its shamans that the seashells shamans use to revive persons whose souls have been lost or 'strayed'[14] are kept in otter-skin pouches called Mide. Significantly, this is the term by which shamans of the community are called. And it is an article of belief among the Ojibwa's (as strange as it may seem to us) that otters act, as Eliade says, as both 'healing shamans and serve to a certain extent even as priests'.[15] This is so because the otter, as tutelary animal, not only enables the shaman to transform himself but it is in a manner his 'double',[16] his alter ego. This alter ego is one of the shaman's souls — the 'soul in animal form'.[17] The shaman, it is widely believed, not only has the ability to change into the animal and understand its language but more importantly he shares its 'prescience and occult powers'.[18]

As Hughes describes him, 'neither fish nor beast is the otter';[19] he is a creature that moves easily in two worlds, land and water. Yet he is 'of neither water nor land', he is at home nowhere. He does not 'take root like the badger'. The mysteriously bifurcated double existence of the otter provokes Hughes's admiration as an emblem for the existence of the secret self, submerged but always there. The uncaught and uncatchable, secret primordial self exists side by side, yet invisible with the visible land-held self of the otter. The odd, undulating movements made by the otter over land are duplicated and evoked by the curious humped-back fluctuations of the verse within part I. By contrast, the more thoughtful and static form in part II simulates the otter's ability to remain at the water's surface for hours, waiting, watching; as Hughes says 'so the self under the eye lies, attendant and withdrawn.' Hughes's heart evidently goes out to this creature whom he compares to a 'king in hiding' (like Hopkins's response to the 'windhover', or Lawrence's reaction to the 'snake'). Hughes centres on the otter's elusiveness, its ability to submerge without leaving a trace. He stresses its solitary nature, its loneliness, in forced exile, that is at once pathetic (the otter 'wanders cries') and noble. He 'gallops along land he no longer belongs to', a rootless detached nomad capable of covering extraordinary distances by land or, as Hughes says, 'from sea to sea crosses in three nights'. Although he can be caught and killed, the real archetypal self of the otter lives forever, always escaping, manoeuvering with extraordinary ability, submerging and reappearing, suspiciously eyeing the 'tainted and necessary' air that he must breathe, yet resentfully superior.

While the otter, for Hughes, is a symbol of the soul in hiding, the deep soul, his split existence makes him particularly suitable as a projection, in the form of a totem animal, of the shaman's habitual mental state of being conditioned to allow his soul and body free movement in different realms. In modern terms, the shaman clearly has a psychotherapeutic function. He comes into the picture when the soul has either left the patient's body, or has been stolen by demons and sorcerers. The shaman is needed when there is severe psychic dissociation, as Eliade notes 'all through Asia and North America . . . the shaman performs the function of doctor and healer. He announces the diagnosis, goes in search of the patient's fugitive soul, captures it, and makes it return to animate the body that it has left.'[20] What is this after all but the reintegration of the self expressed in the context of primitive religion. Yet the dangers to the shaman's own psychic life are very great and demand a 'constant equilibrium between ordinary reality and the supernatural realm'.[21] His psychological life often becomes as precarious, of necessity, as those of his patients whose souls he may descend into the underworld,  in trance, to retrieve. Thus, the otter's extraordinary ability to live a double existence, as well as the well known belief among the Ojibwa of the shaman-as-otter, make him an ideal totem animal to dramatize the 'shaman's psychic life'[22] as a 'constant balancing act, as though he were a psychic tightrope walker on the razor's edge between the external world and the bizarre, magical, often terrifying "world within" '.[23] With this in mind we can understand why Hughes chose the otter for the Reverend Lumb's totem animal, as a creature with whom he literally exchanges his blood-soul. Lumb, too, is in much the same situation as the otter in this poem, 'seeking some world lost when he first died that he cannot come at since'. He is tormented with the memory of a 'world lost' which is so closely intertwined with his own nature that any attempt to separate them is experienced as a profound self-mutilation and indeed this is what does happen to Lumb in Gaudete.[24] The enormous importance the shaman archetype has for Hughes, and the value accorded to it within Hughes's poetry, reflects a corresponding need to restore the balance of spiritual forces. The principle function of the shaman is 'magical healing',[25]  the need to reunite body and soul. The dissociation of personality that is so characteristic of Hughes's

protagonists is answered by the shaman's ability to reinte-
grate what we would term split personalities, although primi-
tives would put the case in terms of possession 'by evil spirits'.[26]

## NOVEMBER

Into the cold, death-like atmosphere of a bleak November day
enters the solitary narrator whose boots echo 'on the lanes
scrubbed stones'.[27] The visual imagery suggests a cold, wet,
winter landscape where trees harbour no life: 'treed with iron
and birdless'. The skies are leaden and overcast, the landscape
is barren and a penetrating rain seems to fill up every pocket in
the ground leaving no dry place to rest, 'the month of the
drowned dog. After long rain the land was sodden as the bed of
an ancient lake'. The rain beats down into the ground so hard
that it splashes back into the air, creating the illusion that
the ground itself is smoking, 'in a moment/The fields were
jumping and smoking.' Making his way across the muddy
countryside, the speaker comes across a tramp, curled up
motionless and silent in a water-filled ditch 'made brown
foam' by the thrashing downpour. Apparently oblivious to
the bitter rainstorm enveloping him, the tramp reminds the
narrator of an animal in hibernation, his head buried in his
beard, his arms folded tightly and his knees drawn up to his
chest trying to shut out the harsh weather. 'I took him for dead',
says the speaker but a cold blast of wind proves the tramp to
be alive as he struggles, in his sleep, to warm his hands and feet
in the driving downpour of wind-blown water that 'smudged
the farms'. After watching the tramp for a few seconds and
marvelling at the 'strong trust' that allows him to not only
brave the elements, but to be unconcerned as to possibly
being drowned in the ditch by a sudden flood of water (a fate
alluded to in the image of 'the drowned dog'), the speaker
runs for cover into the woods. Taking shelter under a
'black oak', the speaker comes across a gibbet and is confronted by a collection of dead animals that the groundskeeper has
caught and hung from a wooden beam:

> The keeper's gibbet had owls and hawks
> By the neck, weasels, a gang of cats, crows:
> Some, stiff, weightless, twirled like dry bark bits
>
> In the drilling rain. Some still had their shape,

Had their pride with it; hung, chins on chests,
Patient to outwait these worst days that beat
Their crowns bare and dripped from their feet.

Although bound and hung by their feet and spinning around
in the driving rain, the speaker observes that the animals appear
to be hanging from the gibbet differently from each other;
some hang shapelessly 'like dry bark bits', while others hold
their shape in death and despite the driving rain 'had their
pride'. The comparison between the 'strong trust' of the tramp
and the speaker's acute awareness of his own vulnerability
as he runs for shelter from the heavy rainstorm establishes
the poem's central meaning. Hughes then underscores the
contrast between the speaker and the tramp by linking them
to the different postures of the dead animals. The tramp lives
in the open and like a dog sleeps upon the ground; he is at the
mercy of the natural elements and must lie down and make his
bed wherever he happens to be. To underscore the comparison
Hughes describes the tramp's face 'tucked down into his beard'
the way the animals have their chins on their chests. Like the
animals bound and hung by their feet, the tramp's feet are
bound with 'sacking and hairy band'. At another point Hughes
refers to the tramp as a 'hedgehog'. Yet the tramp's marvellous
ability to sleep a deep and trusting sleep, to stay curled up like
an animal, to patiently outlast the worst weather, communicates a 'secret trust', a basic acceptance of the cycles, purposes
and direction of nature that the speaker simply does not possess.
His lack of secure attachment, his avoidance of natural processes which ironically results in having his life controlled by
his fear of nature is paralleled by the carcases that aimlessly
twirl in the wind 'like dry bits of bark', without 'pride' of
selfhood. What the speaker lacks and by contrast the tramp
possesses is a basic understanding and patience to realize and
work with the processes of nature. This is what Hughes means
by 'secret trust'. Having this gives the tramp a kind of animal
pride and power to endure an existence that throws man into
a diminished and defensive role. While the speaker is defeated
by the cold gloom and the sudden drenching rain forces him
to retreat, to run and to hide, the tramp has powers of endurance that make him less like a human being and more like
the thorn roots gripping the dark earth. Projected through the
tramp is Hughes's attitude toward an inhospitable environment which can only be endured if one possesses oneself the

qualities apotheosized through the tramp's unconscious acceptance of the natural world. What the tramp can endure and what the speaker cannot is an environment too harsh for plants and ordinary men to survive in.

Each detail of the poem conveys Hughes's feeling about a time of year, where things survive only in proportion to which they become like inanimate objects. To convey this environment, Hughes blurs the equilibrium between life and death, just as tangible objects, trees, men, the landscape itself become indistinct and seem to merge on gray rainy November days. What is alive appears dead and what is dead takes on the quality of life. The dark, somber climate quickly becomes more than a physical condition. In November, too, one cannot truly say where autumn ends and winter begins. Hughes's imagery is tactile and vivid and through phrases like 'the rains' 'dragging grey columns' and verbs which include quivered, riddled, clenched, plastered, hammered and drilling he presents a striking picture of an unstable threatening land where only non-living things like the metallic trees can survive the season's turbulence. Indeed the imagery of metal emphasizes the lifelessness of the scene; trees stand black and leafless as if they were made of iron, the land shines like hammered lead and mist silvers drops of rain. With the lifeless, black and cold silhouettes of trees starkly projected against an overcast November sky as a background, the speaker's first sight of the tramp suggests that the tramp, too, is dead. Like the tramp the land itself has the appearance of a drowned dog with damp, dead brown grass lying flat and sodden like fur. Each of the poem's ten quatrains extends into the subsequent stanzas to further strengthen, through a metrical equivalence, Hughes's conception of blurred boundaries. Each detail, image, and the total form of the poem carries Hughes's reaction to existence in a way that is comprehensive while not explicitly dogmatic of any one philosophy. In the larger cycle of the year November is projected as a transition time, a necessary initiation into death within the larger regenerative process when men as well as the land wait to accept the burden of winter. How best to do this is dramatized in the distinction Hughes draws between the tramp's 'strong trust' and consequent powers of endurance and the speaker's acute awareness of his own vulnerability and consequent inability to survive.

Hughes's mastery of narrative elements in verse form has the effect of creating a communal ritual into which his readers are drawn as partakers in and co-creators of the ritual that is the poem. The effectiveness of poems like 'November' and, as we shall see, 'Pike' is due in no small part to Hughes's ability to create an impersonal yet intense pantomine, instilled with rhythmical, chant-like repetitions to create an environment in which the subliminal mind is released from conscious control. This in truth is what the shaman does as studies of the oral poetry sung by shamans have clearly shown. Incantation and rhythmic repetition of selected sound patterns, echoing and re-echoing amongst themselves, in powerful, fluent and subtle ways, draw us into the heightened state of perception which shamans themselves achieve and sustain.

## PIKE

Mircea Eliade tells us that the narratives of shamans are filled with accounts of the shamans' encounters with 'pikes'[28] and other animals; the shaman 'pursues them'[29] and mimics his epic encounters with them. In 'Pike'[30] Hughes focuses on one such meeting in order to dramatize the presence of dark, irrational forces at the edge of man's awareness. Moreover, as Eliade says, the more powerful the shaman, the more powerful are the creatures with whom he must come to terms. For Hughes, the universe presents a predatory visage of irrationality and violent death for which the cannibalistic pike are an apt symbol. Hughes proceeds for eight stanzas to give precise naturalistic details concerning the various pike he has observed (e.g., 'The jaws' hooked clamp and fangs'). Primarily, he relies on exact numerical descriptions ('Pike, three inches long') to stress that he is an accurate observer; throughout the imagery is very concrete. Hughes meticulously records the various colours ('green tigering the gold') and types of vegetation ('last year's black leaves'). His careful choice of verb forms ensures that the pike are presented in characteristic actions from birth to cannibalism:

> Three we kept behind glass,
> Jungled in weed: three inches, four,
> And four and a half: fed fry to them —
> Suddenly there were two. Finally one
>
> With a sag belly and the grin it was born with.
> And indeed they spare nobody.

With the shift to more generalized images in the final three
stanzas of 'Pike', this rationalistic response to natural phenomena
fails. The pike transcend scientific classification and become
symbolic of a malevolent universe. The narrator's view of nature
as subject to human standards and circumscribed by human
concepts cannot be maintained before his intuitive perception
of nature as a vastly superior and essentially inscrutable force
totally alien and indifferent to man. These characteristics are
already apparent in the first stanza of 'Pike'. The rest of the
poem extends these qualities in proportion to the increasing
uncontrollable dimensions of the pike. The poem's central
metaphor is drawn from the idea expressed by Angelo de
Gubernatis in his *Zoological Mythology*. One feature common
to a number of legends associated with the pike is a belief that
the 'pike . . . is now a form assumed by the devil . . . and now
an enormous fish with great teeth, which slaughters the little
fishes'.[31] Moreover, the 'greenish pike may represent the
moon'[32] and the 'luminous pike, like the moon, can expand
and contract.'[33] De Gubernatis relates one story which makes
this clear. In the Mahabharatam,[34] the great Indian epic work,
'Manus receives the little fish in a vase of water in which he
performs his ablutions . . . in one night (evidently in its character
as the moon) the fish grows so much that it can no longer
remain in the vase; Manus carries it into a pool, afterwards
into the Ganges; finally, the fish increases so much in size
that Manus, recognizing Vishnus in it, is obliged to give it
entire liberty in the sea.'[35]

Immediately at birth, the pike are 'killers from the egg'.
These voracious predators rise to the surface of the pond
in a dance of death 'among the flies'. The mention of flies
not only extends the image of death, but also magnifies
the diabolic element of this world which, by association, is
possessed by the pike as surrogates for the lord of the flies.
In the second stanza, Hughes adds another disturbing, yet
fascinating dimension to the myth he is creating. In the pond,
the pike are four-hundred times as destructive ('A hundred feet
long in their world') as their actual size ('three inches long')
suggests. If a similar scale holds to the end of the poem where
the pikes are 'too immense to stir', the corresponding power
they embody would be of a satanic and overwhelming proportion.

Since man's role, for Hughes, is diminished and his efforts
are futile and weak when compared with the malevolence of

the universe, the speaker's 'I' appears only in the eighth stanza ('A pond I fished') and plays a very limited role. To convey his sense of a hostile universe of brute power, Hughes employs stark, terse phrasing in a staccato rhythm ('perfect/Pike in all parts') reminiscent of primitive incantations. He augments this atavistic quality by using numerous one-syllable words ('For what might move, for what eye might move') and entangles the entire poem in a heavy net of assonance and consonance ('that past nightfall I dared not cast'). Hughes sees the mystery in the pike as revealing a dynamism of the natural world which forms a barrier against man's egocentric and rationalistic tendencies. And, although the universe revealed by Hughes is an alien and terrifying one characterized by incessant violence and sinister permanence, he calls upon the reader to face the hellish nature of existence without faltering.

Critics, from time to time, have called Hughes to task for what has appeared to them as an unnecessary exhaltation of violence and, by implication, an utter disregard for those values, ideals and virtues by which society is always reaffirming its own validity. Yet it is clear that these values, for Hughes, are simply unreal; he is not surrendering to the irrational but merely returning to those ritualistic patterns celebrated, for example, in 'Lupercalia', that have been and must be again unearthed, affirmed and shared if the onrushing apocalypse that 'social consciousness' has been helpless against is to be averted.

## *LUPERCALIA*

Each of the four parts into which 'Lupercalia'[36] is divided refers to one aspect of the protocol followed in the sacrificial feast of Lupercal, an ancient Roman festival celebrated to insure the fertility of the populace, its fields and flocks. The god of the feast was Faunus, or Pan as he was often known, a spirit who supposedly kept wolves away from flocks (*Lupus* means wolf, hence, *Lupercus*).[37] In addition, each of the four sections describes one of the necessary participants within this Roman fertility celebration, whose main purpose was to restore fecundity to barren women through an elaborate ritual. Athletes/priests from the city were sanctified using the blood of dogs and the milk of goats that had been previously sacrificed. They then raced through the streets striking the waiting women with strips of goat-hides. Dog bitches were chosen because of their

connection with the fertility symbol of the she-wolf that was
reputed in legend to have suckled Romulus and Remus, the
founders of Rome. Although a tattered and crude shadow
'declined' from its heritage as a noble wolf, the dog Hughes
describes is still 'good enough/To double with a bitch' — it
still goes wild after a bitch in heat. Barren women look to and
worship this dog's 'brute's quick'. The goat, too, is used as a
symbol of sexual activity because of its connections with Pan,
the satyr, giver of fertility. A current of strong sexual imagery
underlies Hughes's descriptions of the goat whose 'bent horns,
stamp, sudden reared stare startle women'. The goats which
have been slaughtered to complete the sacrificial offering are
'goats, black, not angels' — the imagery has demonic overtones.
Yet, the light in their eyes is no 'brute light' but a 'golden
element' — a regenerative sexual force. Pan's lower extremities
appeared in the form of a goat and he was often depicted
wearing an ivy wreath (Hughes alludes to the 'spirit of the ivy')
on his horned head. The animal and sexual features of Pan came
into prominence at the consummation of the festival when the
priests, called *Luperci*, ran through the streets of the city swing-
ing thongs of goat-skin. A blow from one of the thongs was
reputed to have the power to cure sterility, a fact referred to
in the poem's last lines:

> Fresh thongs of goat-skin
> In their hands they go bounding past,
> And deliberate welts have snatched her in
> To the figure of racers. Maker of the world,
> Hurrying the lit ghost of man
> Age to age while the body hold,
> Touch this frozen one.

The woman who waits for the ritual of the feast is described as
living a meaningless life, 'the past killed in her, the future
plucked out'; a living death has 'stripped her stark'. In contrast,
the goats are portrayed in imagery that is both sensual ('bellies
round as filled wine-skins', 'a rank thriving') and supernatural
('their eyes golden element'). A touch of the gods shines through
their eyes. In some mysterious manner, these qualities will
pass to the women touched by the strips of goat-skin held by
the racers who themselves are more than human instruments
('nothing mortal falters their poise') of the gods; they are a
'theorem of flung effort'. The racers, 'wet with blood: the dog

has blessed their fury', successfully reconnect the earth and sky, man and gods, and the poem ends with a prayer for life to the powers of nature that control the cycles of fertility and birth.

In this poem we have an intuition of Hughes's conception of an energy at the heart of creation that is both divine and destructive, a power that is indistinguishable from the 'rank thriving' of goats or the 'blood heat' of dogs, a feral energy which Hughes perceives as an effloresence of the blood. Hughes compares the animals to be sacrificed with tinder since their deaths 'spark . . . the blood heat' and act as a catalyst to make women fertile. Both the dog and the goats have a primal physical force, a 'rank thriving', that the *Luperci* hope to pass on through the ceremony to the waiting women. The nature of this force, demonic, violent, yet fertilizing, underlies Hughes's characterizations of the sacrificial animals. The dog is a snarling mongrel, a scavanger with bitten ears and glistening sharp teeth in a large 'grinning mouth' to suggest a kind of devilish implacability. The goats, too, are rendered as self-satisfied and rather sinister. Significantly, the goats are black. Whereas white animals were sacrificed to the gods of the upper air, only healthy physically perfect black animals could be sacrificed to a deity who ruled over the underworld. After the animals were killed a feast was held on February 15 in a cave on the Palatine Hill; young men comprising two teams of *Luperci* would run a race along a course marked out at the bottom of the Palatine Hill. Accordingly, the fourth section begins with the description from the point of view of the onlookers who hear the sound of 'thudding feet' powerfully approaching and then see the runners 'wet with blood' dressed only in the skins of slaughtered goats striking those whom they pass with thin strips of goat-skin. The runners are 'wet with blood' since after the sacrifices each man's forehead was smeared with the blood of the victims and then wiped off with a piece of wool dipped in goat's milk.

Hughes's mastery of technique is everywhere present. Initial words of stanzas tend to be weak stressed prepositions or conjunctions ('over sand', 'though wet', 'to the figure of racers'); moreover, thoughts begun in previous stanzas are broken on lightly stressed words at the weakest points. The cumulative effect of this technique is to create a sense of uncertainty which chimes in perfectly with the onlookers' sense of anticipation and hopeful expectancy. The short clipped lines and harsh imagery suggest that the world itself is a desolate dry place ('over sand that the sun's burned out') in need of renewal.

The barren sun-scorched land is the physical correlate of the woman burdened by a sterility that has plucked her out from 'the wheel of the living'. By contrast, the bodies of the racers at the orgiastic festival are 'brass bright' and annointed with oils that transmute the 'golden element' into human form. At the close, the poem shifts to examine one of the barren women who has been struck by the fresh thongs of goat-skin that raise 'deliberate welts'. She is 'snatched into the figure of the racers', and although she had perhaps come to the festival because of its religious function, she is now drawn up, rapt, absorbed and transported into the wild unrestrained frenzy engendered by the spell of the moment. The poem ends with a prayer to the 'maker of the world', a ritual petition asking the gods for an acceptance of this poem as an offering to imbue 'this frozen one' with the 'blood heat' that alone brings power, strength and energy. Thus, for Hughes, the rankest most sensual element offers a path to a principle of vitality that is akin to a divine 'golden element'. Yet, carried to its ultimate conclusion, this mindless yet luxuriant force which is alone capable of revitalizing the dead is a power to be feared. Why this should be so is implied within the poem. The terrible dilemma is not simply that Hughes glories in instincts on a purely animal level or that he sees literally everything beyond these instincts, and that includes all human history and past civilizations, as inaccessible to him ('the dead are indifferent underground./Little the live may learn from them—/a sort of hair and bone wisdom,/a worn witchcraft accoutrement') but that this force once summoned is irresistible. For him the only value of the past is the scant records of spells and rituals it holds to enable one to contact the powers that govern the world. Yet while he profoundly desires to align himself with this force as a remedy for 'barrenness' at all levels, natural, psychological, social, etc., he fears that those whom it touches it destroys. This complex set of reactions underlies Hughes's ambivalence toward the archetype of the White Goddess and describes exactly the consequences of the fearsome energy, divine and destructive, that the White Goddess brings to the 'barren poet' who beseeches her favours. In effect, this same matrix prevails in Hughes's early and later poetry, although under different guises. The dynamics are startlingly similar to those in *Gaudete* where the 'frozen', sterile Reverend Lumb literally needs an infusion of bull's blood to make him live. And this in turn extends one of Hughes's main themes —

the split between soul and body and the consequent polar opposition of frozen powerless self and senseless yet demonically powerful universe.

The practice of using myth to organize poetic utterance, the persistence of certain patterns of imagery, recurring with increasing frequency, alerts us to the fact that these patterns of imagery coalesce in instinctively sought archetypes that are tantamount to basic modes of perception for Hughes. One such archetype, as we shall see in 'Cadenza', is that of the shaman which is no mere mythical motif but the poem's very heart's blood, animating it and bringing it to life.

## CADENZA

In 'Cadenza'[38] we see Hughes assuming the role of shaman in order to guide the soul of one newly dead through the regions of the world after life. This has traditionally been one of the shaman's most important responsibilities since without his aid those who have just died might become disoriented and lost. As Mircea Eliade observed, one function of the Altaic shaman is to 'symbolically escort the deceased into the beyond'[39] because he alone knows the 'roads' of the afterlife. In fact what distinguishes the shaman from the ordinary priest is that to the shaman alone is given 'power to consort with the dead with impunity, search for the soul of a sick person in the underworld or accompany a dead person there'.[40] The shaman's ability to guide the soul is all the more necessary when the dead person is a suicide. Variations of this myth appear in the descent of Orpheus to Hades to redeem the soul of his wife, Eurydice (a legend Hughes dramatized in his work *Orpheus*) as well as in the Polynesian myths of descent into the underworld of the 'Maori hero Hutu' who goes down 'to the underworld in search of the princess Pare who had committed suicide for his sake'.[41] Everywhere the vocation of the shaman is inseparable from his ability to divorce his soul from his body and project it on a magical flight through the topography of the world beyond in order to reorient, cure and guide the souls of the newly dead. 'Cadenza' is a vividly realized account of shamanic ecstasy and a reaffirmation, through shamanic ritual, of Hughes's incorporation of shamanic technique. His function is that of an intermediary between this world and the next. Like 'Cadenza' 'shamanic ritual' is an 'epic narration of mythical scenarios';[42]

we should remember, however, that the shaman does not merely 'recite the myths or express the religious symbolism in making the ritual artifacts, the shaman lives the myth'.[43] Above all, the shaman's function, as Lommel observes, is to 'adjust, avert and heal defects, vascillations, disturbances, of the soul'.[44] The shaman has nothing to do with the ordinary ceremonies of birth, marriage and death. He only comes into the picture when something unusual has occurred, when the natural order has been displaced and endangered, as a kind of exorcist. His role, as Eliade says, is one of 'magical defence'.[45] Keeping this in mind we can understand the intent underlying the mysterious and powerful imagery in 'Cadenza'. The title refers to a virtuoso solo performance, often at the end of a concerto movement or aria where the soloist either freely elaborates on the melody or performs improvisations that have been previously composed. The soloist quite literally takes off from the given melody, rising through a series of elaborate flourishes of the most complicated and intricate kind before rejoining the orchestra. For Hughes, the violinist in the poem is both the symbol of the artist and a shamanic figure as well (the shaman often takes on the role of 'an active artist — a singer, dancer, decorator and stage manager').[46] He launches into a series of free improvisations which 'separate him' from the orchestra until he rejoins it, apocalyptically, at the end of the poem, 'Blue with sweat the violinist/Crashes into the orchestra, which explodes'. Hughes is above all an incredibly visual poet and from the outset he transforms the violinist, in full orchestral dress with the tails of his tuxedo moving wildly, into an image of a dissociated body and soul. The swallow tails of the performer become first the long side wings and legs of the grasshopper's 'husk' and then quite literally the swallow is suddenly transfigured, flying in attendance to accompany a coffin:

The violinist's shadow vanishes.
The husk of a grasshopper
Sucks a remote cyclone and rises.
The full, bared throat of a woman walking water,
The loaded estuary of the dead.
And I am the cargo
Of a coffin attended by swallows.
And I am the water
Bearing the coffin that will not be silent.

It is characteristic of Hughes's work that he interweaves threads of ancient myths in order to bring them into relationship with his own life. This is one reason why his poems are such extraordinarily complex achievements. The relationship of the image of the 'husk of the grasshopper' carried away by rising wind and the flight of the swallows bearing the coffin away works to extend the theme of the violinist's shadow separating itself from the performer, even as the shaman projects his soul outside his body in order to begin his journey to the other world. In antiquity Greeks poured oil on swallows and 'let them fly away apparently for the purpose of removing ill luck in the household'. Moreover, as Frazer tells us in *The Golden Bough*: 'The Bataks of Sumatra have a ceremony which they call making the curse to fly away . . . the sacrifice is offered to the gods of three grasshoppers . . . then a swallow is set free with a prayer that the curse may fall upon the bird and fly away with it.'[47] The expiatory symbolism is obvious and is clearly meant to underscore the exorcism of evil and restoration of spiritual health and psychic integration that is the shaman's paramount function.

All of the ancient Greek stories in which the swallow is mentioned have in common one feature that is apparent in 'Cadenza' as well: a woman believed to be dead is not — she's not in the coffin where she is expected to be. As Robert Graves relates the story in *The White Goddess*[48] a work with which Hughes is obviously familiar, Philomena is told that her sister is dead. Later, Philomena and her sister whose name is Procne escape, becoming a nightingale and swallow respectively. In the story, they are fleeing from Tereus who has 'caught up an axe'. Hughes transforms this into an image of the sky 'full of surgery and collisions', from which 'the coffin escapes'. It is characteristic of shamanic technique that the shaman cures the injured soul by taking onto himself the crisis which is preventing the person who is dead from passing successfully to the other world. He is able to cure because he re-enacts within himself the crisis that is afflicting the dead soul. With this in mind we can understand both the predicament described in the lines 'the full, bared throat of a woman walking water,/The loaded estuary of the dead' and the resolution, 'and I am the cargo/Of a coffin attended by swallows'. The violinist-shaman has substituted himself for the dead woman in order to resolve a situation that has gone terribly wrong. An easy passage from this world to the next has been blocked. There's no room for the dead woman's soul. The river (both the river Styx and the Thames — following the pattern of the elegy in 'Lycidas', e.g.) is literally choked with the dead. The woman's soul cannot be accommodated. The coffin 'will not be silent'; the rites of passage are unresolved. It is only through the intermediary of the shaman that the urgent unexpressed needs of the soul of the dead woman can be facilitated to create an easy journey from this world to the next. The two line stanzas carry the poem forward like two swallow wings. The geometrical outlines of the swallow tails become the 'black diamond' of the coffin, transfigured amidst clouds that are 'full of surgery and collisions' — an image suggesting the pivoting and wheeling of thousands of migrating swallows. All the while, back on earth, everything seems tranquil: 'the sea lifts swallow wings and flings a summer lake open'. But the tension between the apparent calm with which the woman's death has been received and the unresolved anger and turmoil set the stage for the violent apocalyptic collapse at the end when 'the whole sky dives shut'. Two ideas are in urgent conflict, that which is apparently resolved and that which truly needs to be resolved. In fact the extraordinary surrealistic power of the poem lies in the mental anguish and wrenching torment projected with the power of as yet unresolved emotions. Just as swallows persistently return to the exact point from which they migrated and will often wait outside a door they have left the previous Spring, so 'Cadenza' returns to the point from which it started. This too is what the shaman as well as the violinist does after his travels have taken him over an immense distance. Throughout, in the guise of the shaman, Hughes has followed, accompanied and even facilitated ('I am the water bearing the coffin') the migration and final journey of the soul of the dead woman into the netherworld.

The hallmark of Hughes's poetry is its intensity, whether elaborated through the intricate associative technique that cumulatively creates our sense of the poet's 'voice', as in 'Cadenza', or the controlled, closed world in which Hughes circumscribes and presents various animals. If the personality of the speaker provides the core of Hughes's associative poetry, uniting indirect images, in an almost musical flow, heightened by a technique very close to stream-of-consciousness, then in poems like 'Jaguar' and 'Second Glance at a Jaguar' we can see Hughes working securely within the Imagist tradition of purely objective presentation.

## THE JAGUAR

In Hughes's first poem on the jaguar, he joins the crowd of curious onlookers who rush quickly past the cages that contain apes, parrots and even the tiger, lion, and boa-constrictor to stare 'mesmerized,/As a child at a dream, at a jaguar hurrying enraged/Through prison darkness after the drills of his eyes/ On a short fierce fuse'.[49] Jaguars are seen less often than are tigers or lions and they are harder to track and catch. Hughes focuses on the jaguar's rage as an abiding condition, in contrast to the boredom emanating from the caged tiger and lion who are 'fatigued with indolence' and 'lie still as the sun'. Even after he's been captured, the jaguar, suggests Hughes, seems oblivious to the fact of his having been caged, 'he spins from the bars, but there's no cage to him/More than to the visionary his cell.' The jaguar's rage protects him, engulfs him and provides the real environment within which he moves, 'the eye satisfied to be blind in fire,/By the bang of blood in the brain deaf the ear.' His rage not only makes him oblivious, but it frees him from the necessity of coming to terms with his caged environment. He carries the wilderness with him.

## SECOND GLANCE AT A JAGUAR

When we come to Hughes's 'Second Glance at a Jaguar'[50] we are immediately struck by the obvious increase in power and complexity and a significantly altered viewpoint. Hughes dispenses with the theatrical framework of someone strolling down a line of cages, mentally distinguishing the jaguar from the other animals. In this poem, the jaguar is not merely an emissary from a primeval world, he is a world in himself. The verse pattern conveys the gait of the jaguar through the sliding motion of run-on lines with a restless movement that pivots, turns and mimics the jaguar's distinctive motion. Hughes evokes perfectly the low-slung body, the sense of odd misalignment produced by the too high ball joints of the hips and shoulders, the impossible yet liquid movement:

> Skinfull of bowls, he bowls them,
> The hip going in and out of joint, dropping the spine
> With the urgency of his hurry
> Like a cat going along under thrown stones, under cover,

Glancing sideways, running
Under his spine.

The way it flings its head forward and the roundess of its head
and joints suggests an English bowler which modulates into a
picture of the jaguar being just a large cat pelted by stones.
The odd carriage of the head, the pale yellow surface covered
by black spots, becomes in turn the focus of the metaphor
'carrying his head like a brazier of spilling embers'. Each aspect
comes to life in turn: the fiery rage in the eyes, the spotted
coat, the open mouth filled with sharp devouring teeth. As the
jaguar turns back on itself, coming to each corner, the beautiful
pattern of spots reminds Hughes of a 'butterfly'. Thus far, the
reader will note that the poem is but an extension of the earlier
treatment, even taking Hughes's greater skill and subtlety in
description into account. But beginning with the line 'at every
stride he has to turn a corner/In himself and correct it' we
become aware that Hughes has significantly altered the poem's
viewpoint and added a previously missing dimension to his
portrayal. 'The Jaguar' displayed the animal quite literally
housed within his rage and presented his stride as a 'wilderness
of freedom'. But in the 'Second Glance at a Jaguar' the jaguar's
fate of outer imprisonment is nothing compared to his predicament of trying to purge himself from within, to burn
through the constraints of his own nature. Hughes's emphasis
on aspects of the jaguar — its ability to kill, its fastidious low-
slung movement, its odd disjointed powerful body and its
too thick tail and too solid legs — are part of an invocation to
bring the jaguar into focus. His reference to an 'Aztec disem-
boweller' evokes the jaguar's method of killing its prey by dis-
embowling it with a flip of its powerful paws and relates it with
the bloody sacrificial rites in Mexico, Central and South America.
Not only is the jaguar theme particularly pronounced in Olmec
Mexican Art, in the context of ritual sacrifice by disembowelling,
but even today, says Joseph Campbell, there is a 'were-jaguar
concept among North and South American Indian tribes'.[51]
Among these tribes, 'it is thought that a shaman can turn into a
jaguar at will and that he can use the form of this animal as a
disguise under which he can act as a helper, a protector, or an
aggressor.'[52] Among the Paez Indians it is believed that 'the
jaguar-spirit, or jaguar-monster, has shamanistic qualities and
is a shaman's guide and helper . . . . in preparation for ritual
actions the shaman must establish contact with the jaguar-

spirit and transform himself into a jaguar.'[53] The unusually elongated heads so prominent in archeological finds in Central and South America have led some researchers to believe that the heads of young boys were 'deformed artificially in such a way as to suggest the features of the jaguar'.[54] Professor Peter Furst of the University of California has put the case succinctly, 'Shamans and jaguars are not merely equivalent but each is at the same time the other.'[55] It is commonly believed that both shamans and jaguars are believed to have 'supernatural powers'[56] and among these tribes there is a fundamental belief that there is a 'spiritual bond and identity'[57] between the shaman and the jaguar. Thus Hughes not only widens the poem's field of vision by drawing on the tradition of jaguar worship among Central and South American Indians, but is consciously exercising a shamanic technique of identifying himself with an animal that is charged with the whole mythology of the species. The power of the earlier poem is still evident, but it is being used for an altogether different purpose. The jaguar's rage is no longer directed outward but against itself. For this reason Hughes swings the poem away from Aztec tradition and into the context provided by another pre-eminently shamanic work, *The Tibetan Book of the Dead.*[58] Taking his cue from the jaguar's ceaselessly repetitive pacing motion, 'swivelling the ball of his heel on the polished spot' and the unusual, sub-vocal coughing grunting sound of the jaguar's voice, 'muttering some mantrah', Hughes shifts the poem into a different but related context. In *The Tibetan Book of the Dead,* a mantrah, explains W. Y. Evans-Wentz, is a sequence of syllables or a word of power which has its own 'vibratory rate'.[59] Yet, power, once evoked, can destroy as well as save, 'if the adept be . . . a black magician he can by mantrahs call up and command elementals . . . because to each belongs a particular rate of vibration and this being known and formulated as sound in a mantrah gives the magician power even to annihilate by dissolution the particular elemental or spirit to whom it belongs.'[60] Hughes draws on this ancient concept and suggests that the jaguar calls up his rage to wear himself out from within to annihilate and free himself from his condition of enslavement — not to the bars but to his condition of 'jaguarness' which imprisons him:

He's wearing himself to heavy ovals,
Muttering some mantrah, some drum-song of murder

To keep his rage brightening, making his skin
Intolerable, spurred by the rosettes, the cain-brands,
Wearing the spots off from the inside,
Rounding some revenge. Going like a prayer-wheel,
The head dragging forward, the body keeping up,
The hind legs lagging.

The most visible marks on the jaguar's flanks are what Hughes
calls the 'cain-brands'. Cain, of course, is the first murderer,
the first to be overpowered by the rage to kill. These 'cain-
brands' are the jaguar's 'rosettes', the spots on the flanks and
underside arranged in clusters of four or five spots around a
central one (the leopard's 'rosettes' are identical except they
lack the central spot). What the jaguar wishes to wear out by
turning his rage against himself is the mark of Cain that he is
'spurred by' literally branded into his coat. And significantly
according to Indian tradition certain mantrahs that are chanted
over and over again are intended to release the personality from
control by irrational terror, from a bestial perspective and from
the whole delusionary rage of existence itself. Hughes's shift
within the poem away from Aztec mythology into Indian
mysticism is extraordinary since the Aztec culture had no
concept of release from bloody-minded sacrifices through
inner liberation using the power of rage against rage
itself. Only in the Indian tradition of mysticism do we see the
insatiable hunger and ravenous all-consuming rage of 'Vishnu
in his incarnation as the man lion'[61] turned against itself as an
image of liberation, an image implicit in Hughes's description
of the jaguar 'going like a prayer wheel'.

After reading Hughes's 'jaguar' poems and being reminded
that Hughes, as Sagar notes, 'changed from English to Archaeology' in his third year at Cambridge, I find myself in agreement
with Sagar that Hughes's 'grounding in these disciplines has
proved of immense and growing value in his creative work'.
It is certainly true, as Sagar observes, that Hughes's 'imagination is at home in the world of myth and folklore'.[62] But
combined with this is the enormously intuitive, sensuous and
direct grasp of the way in which the animals he writes about
actually appear, communicated in a manner that seems ineffably
'right'. In 'The Bear' we see Hughes immersing himself and
identifying himself with the natural force that is far greater and
deeper, that is paradoxically terrifying and liberating at once, a
state where fear and awe are one.

## THE BEAR

Hughes's poem 'The Bear'[63] is a great mythic evocation based on his personal encounter with the bear when he and Sylvia were camping in Yellowstone National Park, in the United States, in 1959. In a letter writen from Yellowstone Park, Montana, dated July 29, 1959, Sylvia wrote to her mother and brother, Warren:

> . . . in the blue weird light of the moon, not 10 feet away, a huge, dark bear-shape hunched, guzzling at a tin. . . . we lay there for what seemed years, wondering if the bear would eat us, since it found our crackers so interesting. . . . we heard a heavy shuffling tread. The bear, back from its rounds, had returned to the car. . . . it had discovered our oranges. From then until sun up, we lay listening to the bear squeeze the oranges open and slurp up the juice.[64]

From the first stanza Hughes paints a picture of a gaping mountain cave, like a great dark eye in the side of a mountain. Deep in the recesses of the cave the rays of the sun glint off the glistening fur of a great bear, and the flash catches his eye:

> In the huge, wide-open, sleeping eye of the mountain
> The bear is the gleam in the pupil
> Ready to awake
> And instantly focus.

Within the cave, like a great eye, the bear's flashing fur seems like the pupil of an eye. The image is telling and evokes a contrast between the enormous inanimate bulk of the mountain and the tiny gleam of life in the 'eye' that is the bear. The same contrast underlies the bear's eye, 'ready to awake' and the dormant, mountainous bulk of a hibernating great bear, its tiny eye lost in the vast depth of black fur. Hughes elaborates two mythic qualities that form the basis for most legends surrounding the bear: its bulk, and its omnivorous devouring hunger. In many cultures the bear is viewed as a mountain god. Sir James Frazer records in *The Golden Bough* that when certain tribesman are asked of their origins they will say 'as for me I am a child of the God of the mountains. I am descended from the divine one who rules in the mountains,'[65] meaning as Frazer adds 'no other than the bear'.[66] They consider themselves to be 'descendents of the bear'.[67] So too the bear's devouring hunger has been the subject of innumerable legends. As for example in the book of Daniel 7:5: 'and behold another beast . . . like to a bear and it raised up itself on one side and it had three ribs in the mouth of it between the teeth of it and they said thus unto it "arise, devour much flesh." '[68] Although the bear Hughes is describing is dormant, in deep hibernation, enormous activity is taking place in his sleep. He is able to hibernate because of the vast layers of fat he has built up from the devoured flesh and bones of animals he has eaten. Thus, Hughes says it is paradoxically through others' deaths that the bear has the ability to outlast the winter season and bridge his life into the next cycle of spring:

> The bear is glueing
> Beginning to end
> With glue from people's bones
> In his sleep.

> The bear is digging
> In his sleep
> Through the wall of the Universe
> With a man's femur.

While we usually think of animal bones being a source of glue Hughes reverses this so that the bear glues its existence together through the continuity of the deaths of those he has eaten. In subsequent stanzas, Hughes conveys the bear's assimilation of everything ('his price is everything') by having each new stanza consist of one less line than the preceeding stanza; the poem is, as it were, being devoured until nothing is left. The encounter with the bear is an integral part of Eskimo initiation rituals of the shaman who is instructed, 'the bear of the lake or the inland glacier will come out, he will devour all your flesh and make you a skeleton and you will die but you will recover your flesh, you will awaken and your clothes will come rushing to you.'[69] The encounter with the bear is a necessary shamanistic element in the 'ecstatic rite of dismemberment of the candidate by demonic spirits'.[70] The shaman's initiation can only be accomplished through a vicarious experience of death and resurrection. The bear is in this context the time honoured animal helper to whom the shaman must acquiesce in order to gain the ability 'to see himself as a skeleton',[71] to be divested of his flesh and blood so that nothing remains but his bones. By seeing himself

freed from the 'perishable and transient flesh and blood he con-
secrates himself'.[72] This explains the enormous importance of
skulls, bones, femurs, etc. for Hughes; he concentrates on
parts of the body which will longest withstand the action of the
sun, wind, and weather after death. For Hughes, as for the
shamans, bones represent 'the final source of life both human
and animal, the source from which the species is reconstituted
at will'.[73] For the Tibetans, for example, 'it is of the utmost
importance that the body should be transformed into a skeleton
as quickly as possible',[74] since these bones are stored in places
awaiting resurrection. Bones, for shamans, have the potential
value of containing, as Eliade observes, 'the inexhaustable
matrix of the life of the species',[75] since shamans believe
bones can become clothed again with flesh. Indeed in some
shaman myths 'the shaman travels to the other world in a
boat made of a chest and uses a shoulder bone as an oar.'[76] It
is significant in terms of the mountain, cave, river imagery that
the descent of the shaman to the 'land of shades'[77] often begins
with 'an ecstatic journey to a mountain,'[78] 'the cosmic mountain'[79] which is often seen as the centre of the world. Thus
bears are often associated with underground regions as for
example in the shamanic rituals of the Vasyugan, who describe
'the bear coming from under the first layer of the earth'.[80]
Hughes compares the bear with a 'ferryman/To dead land', an
allusion to the river Styx, the river over which the dead had to
be ferried. In fact all three associations of the bear,
mountain and river within a cave come together in Robert
Graves's observation in *The White Goddess*, that Callisto, the
bear goddess, had a son, Lycaon, whose wife, Nonacris ('nine
heights'), gave her name to the cliff city from which issued
and flowed 'the water of the Styx'.[81] Two sets of images play
against each other in Hughes's portrayal of the bear; permanence
(in the metaphors of stone, bone, and wall) is balanced against
fluidity (through metaphors of water, stream, and river). These
two ways of perceiving the bear overlap in Hughes's statement,
'the bear sleeps/In a kingdom of walls/In a web of rivers.' In
essence the bear exists both in and beyond time. In a mythic
and historical context extraordinary archeological discoveries
of bear skulls, tooth amulets, and a variety of bear cult objects
have been excavated at Risingham north of Hadrian's Wall (as
reported in *Pagan Celtic Britain*).[82] The elaborate system of
Hadrian's Wall, which stretches across Britain from east to west,
contains innumerable vestiges of bear artifacts. This timeless

quality of the bear, his bottomless capacity for ingestion are part of the mythic substratem Hughes is projecting. At the same time since it is well known that bear cubs are usually born while their mother is in her winter sleep, the imagery of a foetal bear cub developing within the mother's womb, contained by its walls, held in a web of embryonic fluid, transfigures the bear's dead victims into new life.

## SNOW

A number of Hughes's stories are graphic realizations of the radical separation of the initiant from his surrounding environment. It is certainly appropriate that the story Snow[83] appears in the volume of poetry entitled Wodwo since both this story and the poem 'Wodwo' are symbolic parables centering on questions of identity. 'Wodwo' begins with a series of questions ('What am I? What shall I be called? What shape am I?') that begins Hughes's exploration of the conditions under which identity can be established. Snow transforms this theme into a literal exploration of a twilight world in which snow is continuously falling and the speaker finds himself isolated and cut off from the world as he knows it. Each of the metaphors around which the story is constructed are central ideas in Hughes's poetry but seldom stated with such an archetypal clarity that allows their interrelationship to be more directly perceived. The narrator finds himself dropped from the sky into an environment destitute of the most ordinary landmarks by which to comprehend his situation and without memory of his previous existence. Aside from the feverishly working mentality of the narrator struggling to make sense out of his predicament the only other ongoing process is the falling snow, 'filling all the air and rivering along the ground'. The metaphorical relationship between these two processes suggests that the speaker's mind, like the snow, is not just filling in all the 'existential' holes in his environment but paradoxically his mentality is the snow itself. His means of dealing with the environment is what is continuously producing it in the first place. The personality of the speaker is created for us through his assumptions, rationalizations, deliberate self-delusions and mental strategy. Uppermost in importance for him is his ability to 'outlast' his errors. He acknowledges that he is in a hopelessly flawed situation where he must adopt a strategy that will allow him to survive.

Again and again, he wishes he were mindless (like an animal, one might add parenthetically) so that he might arrive at his destination without mental error. The narrator decides as part of his strategy to shield himself from any divergent opinion or relative 'truth' that might make him more vulnerable to destruction. This is the mental situation Hughes's protagonists are often in; as the speaker says, 'I must survive — that's a truth sacred as any, and as the hungry truths devour the sleepy truths I shall digest every other possible truth to the substance and health and energy of my own, and the ones I can't digest I shall spit out, since in this situation my intention to survive is the one mouth, the one digestive tract, so to speak, by which I live.' The underlying metaphor of voraciousness that guarantees one's survival clearly anticipates the apotheosis of this trait later in *Crow*.[84] The image of eating to survive and the need to be a predator simply to live is an inseparable element in a majority of Hughes's poems whose central figures are the hawk, the bear, the wolf, the jaguar, etc. So, too, is the need to be 'mindless', 'My mind is not my friend. My support, my defence, but my enemy too — not perfectly intent on getting me out of this. If I were mindless perhaps there would be no difficulty whatsoever.' The psychological appeal that animals have for Hughes is nowhere more obvious. Governed by instinct, undistracted by thought, eating to survive and above all, without the ability for self-torturing ambiguity they are perfectly created to endure. According to the logic of the situation, the speaker is fully justified, yet one suspects the situation of the story in which the central character is the lone survivor of an aircraft crash has been conveived a priori in order to explore the speaker's mind, his profound sense of precariousness. His need to find a strategy which will give him the 'energy' to endure his predicament ('As long as I have energy I can correct my mistakes, outlast them, outwalk them') is, in a strange way, a restatement of the protagonist's terrible need to re-experience his predicament *until* he understands it.

We see this metaphor again in Hughes's choice of Seneca's rather than Sophocles's version of *Oedipus*[85] and in Crow's 'Song for a Phallus'[86] where Oedipus fails to learn from his tragic fate, experiences no final illumination and must re-experience it all once more. In *Snow* the speaker acknowledges the fact that he's probably travelling in a circle since 'this would

explain the otherwise strange fact that in spite of the vast distance I have covered the terrain is still dead level, exactly as
when I started.' His path through the snow is a vicious circle
from which he will not and cannot escape. If he were to deviate
from his direction by cutting 'out across the wind' he foresees
himself 'falling and groveling' 'staggering round like a man beset
by a mob' in any uncanny foreshadowing of the end that awaits
Hughes's later protagonist, the Reverend Lumb in *Gaudete*. It
is not simply that Hughes's protagonists go to extraordinary
lengths to shield themselves from an unpleasant truth but
that his whole conception of personality is one of unwitting
self-betrayal that can be avoided only insofar as one becomes
like a mindless animal. Ironically the desire to avoid one's
fate circumscribes one in a way that is one's fate, a feature
implicit in the speaker's decision (which he admits may have
been 'a mistake when I first started walking') to make his way
by walking into the wind.

Perhaps taking his cue from *The Tibetan Book of the Dead*[87]
where wind is a metaphor for the irresistible force of karma,
Hughes projects a situation in which his protagonist sets himself against the wind in order to guide himself (even though he
admits the probability of his being led 'to and fro in quite a tight
little maze'). Thus he walks into the wind while acknowledging
that his decision is probably a 'mistake' which costs him precious
energy. The metaphor is striking. The only way the speaker can define his individuality is by setting himself against fate. In effect
the speaker must magnify the rigorousness and difficulty of real
hardships beyond what they would normally be in order to
justify his pre-existent sense of danger and precariousness. This
in turn produces a need for order and compulsion to control
the environment that is in reality largely self-produced. This
however is the last thing the speaker can admit. It would not
only bring disorientation but death itself, 'I would have died
almost immediately, out of sheer bewilderment.' With this in
mind we can understand the significance of the one human
artifact, 'a farmhouse sort of chair', in the context of the
story. This chair is the only other inhabitant of the twilight
world in which the speaker moves. Over and over again he
takes exactly twenty paces into the raging blizzard until the
outlines of the chair blur so that he may re-experience the convulsive joy of finding it again. The existence of the chair pre-
dicates for him an entire pre-existent world inhabited by a
mother, a father and a fiancee named Helen. Yet this world

is, so to speak, a hypothesis entirely supported and sustained by the visible reality of the chair. Finally at the end his fear of losing it is so great that he straps it onto his back with a harness and carries it around with him. Yet, he admits that the world as he dreams it does not contain the harness that attaches him to his chair; as he says 'the harness might well have been invented between that time and the time of my disaster.'

In fact the entire action involves the speaker's re-dreaming of the world he inhabited before his twenty-sixth birthday. The fact that this is the only date of which the speaker is sure suggests its pivotal importance in determining the meaning of *Snow* as something of a profound parable of Hughes's life. The speaker admits that he is able to remember 'nothing at all after my twenty-sixth birthday' and this date and what he refers to as 'the time of my disaster' are linked by more than coincidence. In view of the fact that Hughes's own twenty-sixth birthday saw his marriage to Sylvia Plath, what, we may quite legitimately ask, is the connection between that fact and his statement through the persona in the story that 'for five months I have been living exclusively on will power, without the slightest desire for food.' Has all the paraphernalia of the fictional construct of *Snow* been invented as a symbolic representation of one aspect of Hughes's spiritual life since his twenty-sixth birthday. Certainly, there are similarities between the protagonist's overwhelming need to construct an entirely providential logic arising from his 'excellent pigskin boots, trousers, jacket, gloves, hood' and above all 'chair' and the self-reinforcing, even solipsistic, predator mentality so often evident in Hughes's animal poems. But this is the first time we see Hughes exploring the phenomena of personality dissociation and estrangement from the ordinary world in a urgent manner, using the techniques of shamanism as a way of coming to terms with it.

Both 'Snow' and the following story 'The Harvesting', create a nightmarish world with the quality dreams have of projecting an environment that operates by laws other than those of reality. Both plainly concern a psychological dilemma whose meaning is stated nowhere but everywhere implied. Both protagonists are in limbo, going nowhere and having nowhere to go. The effective block thrown up against any possiblility of objective action turns Hughes's narrators inward, traversing the landscape of their own desolate spiritual state. These stories are half parable, half fantasy and compel us by Hughes's form of presentation to enter the soul of his protagonists at an emotional level. We feel their plight and suffer the ambiguities that torment and threaten to destroy them while strangely giving their lives ultimate meaning, a meaning paradoxically indistinguishable from their continuing struggle.

## THE HARVESTING

The main function of the shaman lies in his ability to 'search for the patient's strayed soul',[88] or what is referred to in modern psychology as a 'withdrawal from the environment . . . attended by a resultant disintegration of the personality'.[89] Thus the shaman's function in archaic societies is intended to recognize and reverse, if possible, disorders in the psychic integrity of both individuals and the community. 'Everything that concerns the soul and its adventure here on earth and in the beyond', observes Eliade, 'is the exclusive province of the shaman. Through his own pre-initiatory and initiatory experiences he knows the drama of the human soul, its instability, its precariousness. In addition he knows the forces that threaten it and the regions to which it can be carried away.'[90] In Hughes's story 'The Harvesting',[91] his protagonist Mr Grooby experiences a mysterious disintegration and flight of his 'soul' while he has come to supervise the last harvest of a wheat field he owns.

The action of the story takes place in the last ten minutes of the harvest in which the remaining wheat will be cut down and whatever hares have been hiding in the wheat will be flushed out. Mr Grooby has brought his gun and intends shooting the hares when they leap from cover. Hughes provides an epigraph to the story: ' "And I shall go into a hare/With sorrow and sighs and mickle care" '[92] taken from a poem quoted by Robert Graves in *The White Goddess*. Its function is to provide a literal description of what actually does happen to Grooby in the story when at the end he has amazingly become a large hare that has just run from the remaining patch of wheat. Grooby hears 'the thin unearthly scream' of a hare, looks up and sees 'the enormous white dog head' looming above him, truly a startling transformation. As Graves describes it, Isabel Gowdie of Auldearne recited the epigraph at her trial as a witch in 1662. In fact, the ritual of pursued and pursuer in the form of 'hare and greyhound' cited by Graves finds its way into the story through the portrayal of the 'big white boney greyhound' that had chased the hare from one side of the field to the other into the remaining patch of wheat. The transformation for which Isabel Gowdie stood accused, which is identical to what Grooby must endure, was hardly unique since the folk customs in every part of Europe, as Frazer relates in *The Golden Bough,* describe in great detail how the last stalk of corn, wheat or rye to be threshed often contains a spirit disguised in animal form. Frazer says that in some countries it is believed that 'the hare sits in the last patch of standing corn and must be chased out by the last reaper'; to cut the last sheaf down is equivalent to 'killing the hare'.[93] Not only is the spirit of the field, the vegetation spirit, often conceived of as an animal (a hare, a fox, etc.) but visitors to the harvest field were subjected to a variety of indignities from which they had to ransom themselves. Frazer sees in this a vestige of more ancient rituals to insure a good crop. As Frazer explains, 'the corn spirit (and by extension the wheat spirit, the rye spirit, etc.) is supposed to lurk as long as he can in the corn, retreating before the reapers, the binders and the threshers at their work. But, when he is forcibly expelled from his refuge . . . he necessarily assumes some other form than that of the corn stalks which had hitherto been his garment or body.'[94] In essence Grooby, as the person who stands nearest to the last sheaf of wheat, experiences a 'flight of soul' in which he and the hare exchange personalities. Throughout the story, Hughes has prepared us for this transformation by equating Grooby's state to that of the hare. Like Grooby, the hare's nerves, as Hughes tells us, have finally 'cracked', a term we normally would only think of in the context of shattered human identity. The hare's state is like that of Grooby's, 'stupified', terrified and exhausted. Hughes's human protagonists, whether Ripley in 'The Wound', the unnamed narrator in 'Snow', the suitor in the story of that name, or most recently, the Reverend Lumb in *Gaudete* are all within a 'hair's breath' of losing control and being terrifyingly close, because of their psychic vulnerability, to destruction. 'This is how it happens', Hughes writes of Grooby, 'his brain was yammering: it can happen, it can happen and its happened. This is how it happens. Everything is going nicely, then one careless touch, one wink of a distraction and your whole body's in the mincer and you're in the middle of it, the worst that can happen forever. You've never dreamed it possible and all your life it's been this fraction of a second away . . . and here it is, here it is.'[95]

'The Harvesting' invites certain immediate comparisons with

another work Hughes wrote titled 'The Wound', which itself was a product of a very strange, yet utterly compelling dream that Hughes had. During this time, Hughes was immersing himself in the shamanic, surrealistic and mysterious work, *The Tibetan Book of the Dead* (the Bardo Thodol). And it is this work which provides a frame of reference for understanding the otherwise puzzling events, characters and imagery of 'The Wound'. In a changed form, a version of this work was broadcast on the BBC February 1, 1962 and later was given its first stage production at the Young Vic on July 17, 1972.[96]

## Chapter Two
## BECOMING THE SHAMAN

### THE WOUND

The title of 'The Wound'[97] literally refers to the head wound Ripley has suffered, yet as a metaphor, we can see that Ripley's perceptions and ability to reason have gone drastically wrong. At the end of the play we learn from a soldier that Ripley's 'animal instincts' have enabled him to make his way, gravely wounded, back to his compatriots over a distance of nine miles. He has returned alive while his companion, the sergeant, has not. He has seen the abyss and returned while the sergeant has died. While the background for the play derives equally from Hughes's boyhood memories of wartime England and Robert Graves's descriptions of his own experiences as a foot soldier in the trenches of World War I, the action in the play has the character of one of Ripley's 'believe it or not' episodes where a soldier miraculously returns to his unit nine miles away although gravely wounded. At the same time, the tearing of the psychological fabric of normality and strange urgency underlying Ripley's self-questioning monologues, recall Rip Van Winkle's first questions, upon awakening out of his own time, as to where he was. The fevered quality of Ripley's questions, the way he breaks off in the middle of thoughts, the elaborate rationalizations of answers to questions that remain purposefully unanswered all suggest a grievously wounded mind desperately trying to shield itself from the knowledge of its true state. Since in reality the sergeant is dead, Ripley's brain supplies the hallucinated memory of the sergeant's invariable terse command 'keep going'.

Hughes's choice of a soldier as his hero is an interesting one since as a symbol for the ego it emphasizes the ability to subsist, endure and survive under conditions of loneliness, deprivation and danger. Dramatically, Ripley is even more heroic because he continues although wounded, although mortality bears in on him — 'Ripley! Pull yourself together — you have nothing but your own parts . . . these have to last you.' Ripley's elemental power of endurance, the simple ability to subsist, is presented as a kind of heroism and reminds one of Crow's self-assessment in 'Examination at the Womb Door' — as Ripley says 'Me. Ripley, in power.' The boundary between this world and the one that Ripley and the sergeant enter has a curious 'Alice through the Looking-Glass' quality (even to Ripley's comment 'I thought you dropped down a hole'). They enter this other realm through water; to Ripley it looks menacingly 'black and deep'. Entering the icy water is like entering death and Ripley's expostulation 'it's icy my feet are going dead' reproduces the physical sensation the body experiences as it nears death (as noted in the Bardo Thodol, *The Tibetan Book of the Dead*).[98]

Most ominous and significant in this realm of the dead are the mysterious women who beckon to the sergeant and Ripley, urging them to cross over. The peculiar ambivalence often seen in Hughes's portrayal of women surfaces fleetingly here as the sergeant says: 'they look like women but there is something funny about them.' Hughes's stage directions tell us: 'As he speaks one of the women laughs, the other laughs . . . silence, a groan, silence.'

The instant they pass over Ripley has a vision of himself from above ('whose this lying here the boot toes are tilted apart and the feet in them don't seem to care'). Underlying Hughes's portrayal of each of Ripley's parts ('where does this arm go off to so purposefully') and scrupulous examination of a neck, a chest, a face, a head, a finger, etc. is a sense of abandonment, dissociation and almost fatal inability to change the condition of mortality by even one iota. Ripley is seen in two different but overlapping ways. In the context of the strewn limbs of the battlefield Ripley is an identityless collection of human parts that arouses Hughes's sense of pathos in the face of such abject and terrifying inconsequentiality. At the same time Ripley is presented as a figure full of cocky pride in the self ('Private Ripley you're a fine figure of a lad . . . you're the memorable Ripley')[99] What we witness here is vehement self-mockery barely held in check by an equally vehement self-assertion. Ripley and the sergeant enter a chateau which, at one and the same time, is gloriously and miraculously intact and yet a complete ruin. Its double existence underscores the reality/fantasy double character of Ripley himself. Incidentally, the scene in the chateau reminds us of the war novels of Erich Maria Remarque (author of *All Quiet on the Western Front*) especially his second novel, *The Road Back* where returning soliders encounter a devastated landscape and a spectral chateau. The fact that the action of 'The Wound' takes place on the 'evening of June 22nd' and the birthdate of Remarque being June 22nd, 1897 (as well as the fact that Remarque wrote the book after his nine-year marriage had ended and Ripley journeys nine miles) are more than coincidental and shows Hughes's impish, if somewhat self-contained sense of humour.[100] On the steps of the chateau, rather ominously, Ripley finds a dead owl, its head gone, and still warm — a condition suggestive of Ripley's own. They knock and in answer they are greeted by a 'Queen' who bids them enter: 'Good evening. You're expected.' She invites them to a banquet and suddenly they hear howling of wolves and squealing of pigs, animals often associated with the enchantress Circe. The threatening implications of their predicament, as prey to a Circe-like Queen who turns men into swine, is not lost on Ripley: 'we're in on an elaborate trap.' The devouring maternal aspect of the Queen is undeniable, for Ripley she is 'Cleopatra the green mummy'.

Taken together the sergeant and Ripley comprise a total human being, apart they are fragmented into man's elemental appetites (the sergeant) and his need to understand (Ripley). Sergeant Massey's name itself tells us of his solid, unreflective elemental nature. The world for him is 'five seconds thick' — the difference between living and dying. He is concerned, as he says, 'chiefly to feed and to be cheerful'; again, he offers 'I am loaded with vegetables and bullocks and my answer is no questions.' He is a rather straightforward, and definitely untragic fellow. Ripley's case of course is quite the opposite.

These two halves, as it were, of one person are greeted by accommodating feminine hostesses who describe themselves. They are dead ('the coroner attended') as a result of the assaults of technocratic science (in a way that anticipates mother earth attacked in the *Crow* poem, 'Revenge Fable'). Again and again in Hughes's poetry the unpardonable sin is expressed in terms of the elemental feminine principle being under attack, abused and injured. This, above all, motivates the revenge of the feminine (as in the Greek play the *Bacchae* where Dionysos's followers are persecuted before they turn upon their male attackers). In all these cases the male intellect, like Blake's Urizen, seeks to dissect life's essential mysteries (to unpick the universe to 'numbers' — in the language of 'Crow's account of St. George'). Ironically, what is sought is the ultimate secret of what happens to man after death. 'And what did they find', asks one woman mockingly, 'the indigestible soles of the feet of all their vanished mysteriously beloved'. Another answers, 'three gallons of marsh gas and a crust of bread' — an answer which provokes shrieks of laughter. What remains of man after death is a fitting subject since, as we later learn, the sergeant has been dead all along, and Ripley is very close to death himself. The action of the play quickly shifts into activity suggested by the Queen, first the banquet, then 'fun and games' and finally, the dance and sleep — all of which provide opportunities for Hughes to explore the sergeant's and Ripley's seduction by the women. Sergeant Massey, as we might expect, is all for it; it follows from his nature. In Ripley, however, we encounter a Hamlet-like revulsion ('lousy old brothel all tarted up that's all it is').

A fascinating aspect of this scene in which Sergeant Massey acquiesces while Ripley resists various seductions is the underlying equation of sex with death. The juxtaposition is startling in that yielding to feminine seduction and even the willingness to admit a capacity for love is symbolically projected as making one vulnerable to death. For the first time the periphery of Ripley's awareness is invaded by his glimmering perception that 'somebody' is hurt: 'this isn't dew on my boots after all'; he is just barely able to shield himself from the realization that his boots are covered with his own blood. To put the point clearly, Ripley's willingness to consider emotional involvement with his hostesses brings him an impinging awareness of the closing reality of his own death. The emotional logic at work here provides a framework for Ripley's intense ambivalence towards being reunited with the archetypal mother earth and his fear of being 'swallowed up' in her. Ripley's abhorrence surpasses human bounds ('just look at these whores maggots

writhing carnivorous pile of garbage ugliest pack of bitches')
and transforms the women into the assimilative properties of
earth itself. Through a parallel logic, Ripley refuses to eat,
while Sergeant Massey accepts all the food offered to him.
Ripley fears the revenge of what he eats; eating fish gives him
cold feet, eating meat gives him nightmares of 'being eaten by
bulls' and eating gherkins gives him 'green skin'. His demeanour
is cautious, and so fearful of danger that he provokes the sergeant to say 'You're not in your mammy's kitchen now.'
Ripley shows a positive disinclination to get involved in the
natural processes. This goes along with his sense of himself
as a soldier on a mission ('Ripley's bitch proof Ripley's dog
poison').

We discover that from the original group of sixty men, Ripley
and the sergeant have survived by turning cannibal and eating
the remains of their fellow soldiers. Sergeant Massey explains
that when you have shot one man into individual bite sized
pieces, anything serves. Sergeant Massey is the pre-eminently
realistic man who is quite willing to admit what he has done
and why he has done it. He describes how his men, and even
he himself, met death. Significantly, at the very moment
Sergeant Massey acknowledges the fact that he is indeed dead,
he is quite literally devoured by an insatiable ('more more
give us more'), frenzied mob of women. Ripley screams, 'Sergeant Massey's been murdered.' A similar fate seems to await
Ripley as a girl takes him aside and begs him 'kiss me love me';
when Ripley refuses she informs him that he might as well
know he has a terrible bullet hole right through his head.
Hughes's stage directions tell us that Ripley 'blunders about
falls over a chair and cries out in pain', saying 'crazy to say
that . . . it's just another nuthouse remark.' Ripley's unwillingness to acknowledge his gravely wounded state is itself responsible for the creation of Massey as a component of his
personality that tells him to 'keep going'. To stop would allow
the realization of his condition to overtake him. Before this
scene he is always one step just ahead of the horror of his state.
His defences fall precisely at the moment when he is told by
the girl that he is shot through the head. Yet even as we expect
this realization to bring the play to a swift close, Hughes does
something that is thoroughly characteristic of the way in which
he portrays suffering in works as apparently diverse as his
translation of Seneca's *Oedipus,* Crow's 'Song of a Phallus',
or the cycle of poems based on Prometheus; he makes his pro-

tagonist, Ripley in this case, re-experience his suffering yet again, as if death itself is too easy, too much of an escape. In response to this need Ripley's mind recreates yet again the dead sergeant (whose death we have seen Ripley witness within the improbable landscape of the story).

As in a diabolical cartoon, parts of bodies are re-assembled, only to be blown apart again, so that the mind may re-experience the reality of suffering. The logic of Ripley's nature demands that his heroism be tested by the larger-than-life suffering he must continually re-experience. Conversely his inability to actually comprehend and absorb the meaning of what he must endure makes it all the more necessary to re-create situations in which suffering must be confronted and re-experienced. Both themes come together in a stream of imagery that describes a face thrown into battle, fighting all the machinery of war thrown against it; the flesh is seared off yet the face continues, the face is demolished yet the skull continues, the skull is shattered yet the stubborn brain continues to fight — the need to continually re-experience suffering in the guise of heroism has become an end in itself.

With the reappearance of Massey the play moves through its predestined phases to the climactic dance scene when Ripley sees a ballroom floor that appears like 'black glass' or a 'black lake'. In an interesting foreshadowing of the split personality of the Reverend Lumb in *Gaudete* Ripley sees his reflection 'perfect but inverted' in the floor/lake. His double looks like a corpse dressed for burial, 'his skin is whiter . . . or made of wax'. He wears a carnation and is described with the significant phrase as 'a dummy estranged from life or the hopes of life'. Members of his company, Moss, Jennings, Baldwin, etc., all of whom he knows to be dead tell him to get in the swing of things ('don't stand round out there like a bloody donkey, folk are dancing'). The strange spectacle of riotous, exuberant life enacted in a place of death is a paradox that looks forward to Hughes's equation of Dionysos with Hades. Ripley finds his temper, his angry rebellious instinct for self-containment, gradually being leached away by the waltz music. He asks one of the girls, 'let's go for a walk outside. Me and you. See the flowers stretching and yawning.' Yet normality, as it is seen here, is but a preliminary signal for destruction to overtake Ripley. This unusual association of normality with a weakness that allows one to be destroyed underlies 'Crowego', in *Crow* as well — Crow devours Ulysses when Ulysses turns homeward, i.e., when he renounces the heroic quest for his simple human desire to return to his home and family. At this point he becomes vulnerable to destruction. Hughes associates music as well with feminine enticement, and sees it as setting one up for a fall. To become human is to become open to death. But as long as one does not admit the fact (and the issue here is not so much being wounded as being human although in truth for Ripley, they are one and the same), one can 'keep going'. This explains the peculiar importance that self-sufficient fragments have in Hughes's work; in the context of his dissociative imagery, fragmentary necks, boots, fingers and faces have consciousness allocated to them and continue to survive.

As Ripley 'gives in' to the offer of the girl to go for a walk, we should not be surprised that he suddenly is aware that fresh blood is pouring from 'somewhere'. Simultaneously, he begins to see the surroundings for what they are, a blackened 'spat out' landscape of war. He fights against it and urges himself 'narrow your mind now Ripley', but to no effect, as the waltz music grows slower and heavier and the dance provokes his mind to recoil in a last, violent convulsive impulse. 'This isn't glass it's mud', he cries, as he realizes that he is not on a dance floor polished like black glass. He, the Sergeant and all of his comrades are being 'devoured' by the malevolent earth, churning mud 'choking their efforts'. A surrealistic scene takes place, 'their women round their necks', 'these women are dragging them all into the ground, it's a massacre.' We sense the overpowering emotion generated by the ambivalence directed towards mother earth. We next see Ripley speaking about himself as if he were two people; he calls, 'Ripley, are you out there, Ripley?' and answers, 'Yes, I'm here, we're not alone, we're with ourself.' (An interesting glimpse into the imagery of *Gaudete* is offered by Ripley's self-adjuration 'let the wind sway you Ripley oak tree Ripley riding the punches'.)

Our last view of Ripley just before the soldiers, at the play's close, find him aimlessly walking about and mumbling to himself, is Ripley's declaration 'marry me' directed to the girl he is with. The metaphor he uses is intriguing: 'I'll put my whole body into your bank and you can let me out to myself on an annuity.' The implications of this climactic moment in the play suggest that Ripley's statement 'marry me' could only come after he has been gravely wounded (he swears his love 'by the two holes in my head') and brought close to a death which he has barely escaped. When the soldiers carry him off for medical treatment we don't really know if he lives or dies but it does seem as if all the events in the play have been constructed to produce the circumstances in which Ripley is able to volunteer his minimal and grudging offer ('marry me') to enter the realm of humanity.

The line in which Ripley describes himself as 'a body abandoned to gravity at 32 feet per second' reminds us that one of Hughes's favourite works, James Joyce's *Ulysses*,[101] contains Leopold Bloom, whose thoughts are constantly filled with the gravitational rate of descent of '32 feet per second per second'; metaphorically speaking, both characters are in freefall. Incidentally, Hughes was thirty-two when 'The Wound' was first published in 1962. The Circe episode which finds Leopold Bloom encountering the enchantress, in modern guise as Bella Cohen, in Dublin's brothel quarter may well have provided Hughes with a scenario and style (Ripley's stream of consciousness interior monologue) for Ripley's hellish, hallucinatory experience with the hostesses/whore-enchantresses.

Despite echoes of novels by Erich Maria Remarque and James Joyce, the most profound shaping force on a mythic level is undoubtedly the schema proved by *The Tibetan Book of the Dead* which portrays, with graphic horror, the kinds of experiences the soul undergoes after death. The tortures which Ripley witnesses, and partially undergoes, correspond to the hellish torment portrayed in the Bardo Thodol: 'the lord of death will cut off thy head', 'thy body is hacked to pieces ... but thou will be incapable of dying.'[102] This is why Sergeant Massey, though dead, miraculously revives. Not only has Eliade described the Book of the Dead as the most ancient shamanic work, but Carl Jung, as well, sees in the chaotic riot of phantasmal forms an initiatory test of the ego at its most profound level.[103] Thus whether literally true as the ancients believe, or profoundly true in a psychological sense, as Jung thinks, what we witness in both 'The Wound' and in the Bardo Thodol is the surrender of the ego's stability to 'karmic illusion'. In Ripley's case fear of self-sacrifice is his most profound trait which defines him to himself and to us. His mental defence mechanisms of rigidity are symbolically extended through the metaphor of his being a soldier. We can see this even in small touches such as the importance placed on his 'boots' as a kind of carapace, or protective covering. As we have seen in *Snow* to be without thought is a kind of defence mechanism. We have seen that women, for Ripley, are feared as agents of destruction. These 'ego' fears predicate an antithetical set of qualities that will hypothetically allow Ripley to save himself from psychic dismemberment. To survive he must act and feel like an animal without self-consciousness or self-awareness, surviving by instinct, and staying alive by eating, sleeping and hunting. Animals do not think consciously about what they are doing and there is less chance of an animal, or a human who aspires to an animal level of existence becoming dissociated from reality. All of these traits are part of Ripley's karma (and let us not forget that he is *Private* Ripley, to underscore the subjective, interior nature of his mental processes). Ripley, as with most of Hughes's protagonists, is in a precarious existential state, so precarious that often only the slightest misjudgment in the 'thirteenth decimal place' is required to tip the balance and plunge his protagonists into the terrifying world of psychic dissociation, an abyss of hellish torments. Since as the Bardo Thodol tells us the thought forms we see after death are evoked by the karma we have created, Ripley's vision of sinister, yet seductive demonic blood-drinking goddesses are actually thought forms called forth by his own nature.[104] The progressively degenerative character of the experience, and its lurid images, are drawn from the Bardo Thodol, as is the very nature of the 'wound' itself from which Ripley is dying. While quite literally a bullet hole in the head, it is one of the nine apertures, according to Hindu belief, through which the 'etheric double' exists at the moment of death.[105] Similarly, Ripley's question, 'what's that great sky-blinking glimmer and the rumble, like the sun trying to rise. I suppose lots of summer thunder goes with all this' and the girl's subsequent answer, 'that's your life, working at the hole in your head' are both drawn from the Bardo Thodol's description of the physical symptoms which precede the disintegrating process called death. The Bardo Thodol tells us: 'Humming, rolling, and crackling noises are heard before and up to fifteen hours after death.'[106] This explains the rather unusual linkage of metaphors, and especially the muffled storm sounds ('Growing sound of storm wind and rain and rumble of thunder of gunfire') that play in and out of Ripley's consciousness.

In 'The Wound', we have seen the rational mind held in abeyance, the normal cause and effect processes of reason suspended, while the unconscious, all that seems illogical, comes to the fore. In fact what we are witnessing is nothing less than a sacrifice of the personal ego to the universal, if inscrutable, will of God. The form of sacrifice, albeit with changed characters, continues in Hughes's 'Song of a Rat' where the sacrificial imagery implicit in 'The Wound' becomes an explicit crucifixion. This challenges Hughes's totem animal protagonist to adapt and redefine himself once the traditional meanings of his world have been shattered.

## SONG OF A RAT

In 'Song of a Rat'[107] Hughes presents, with shattering intensity, the mechanism of death and rebirth that is such an integral part of the process of becoming a shaman. 'The potential shaman',[108] observes Andreas Lommel, 'senses how the spirits kill, dismember and consume him. During his cure he feels the various parts of his body join together again and his personality become restored', [109] although one must add, not at all as it once was. To a great extent becoming a shaman is a 'self-healing process which the totential shaman had to undergo'.[110] Each stage of the shaman's symbolic death and resurrection is reflected in the 'Song of a Rat'. Hughes's totem animal, the rat, undergoes a mystical experience in which it becomes aware of vital factors of which it was previously ignorant and thus gains admittance into a new sphere of being. The structure of 'Song of a Rat' follows the stages of a typical shamanic mystical experience: purgation ('The Rat's Dance'), illumination ('The Rat's Vision'), and transcendence ('The Rat's Flight'). In 'Song of a Rat' these three steps provide a basis for the poems's division into three sections.

The process of purgation described involves the physical death of the rat. Moreover, the physical mutilation, agony and death the rat suffers serve to prepare it for its transfiguration. Lines 1, 8—9, 13, 19 of the first section present the basic situation of the poem. The rat struggles to escape from a trap in which it has been caught: ('The rat is in the trap, it is in the trap'), but the trap kills the rat by breaking its backbone ('Iron jaws, strong as the whole earth/Are stealing its backbone'). Hughes's major concern is with the rat's attitude towards this situation. Initially, the rat reacts with belligerence and ferocity. It refuses to submit to its inevitable death through the agency of this inexplicable instrument. Instead, the rat directs its screams of defiance ('attacking heaven and earth with a mouthful of screeches like torn tin') at the universe that has betrayed it to this agony. Unlike man who has recourse to theology or philosophy when confronted by existential mysteries, the rat finds its situation totally incomprehensible:

When it stops screeching, it pants
And cannot think
'This has no face, it must be God' or
'No answer is also an answer.'

                                                                    (I,4—7)

The rat reacts like the irrational animal it is by voicing its instinctive objection to extermination with its interminable screeching. Finding escape impossible the rat still refuses to accept its fate until its experience reveals new dimensions to its predicament:

A rat that goes on screeching,
Trying to uproot itself into each escaping screech,
But its long fangs bar that exit —
The incisors bared to the night spaces, threatening the
    constellations,
The glitterers in the black, to keep off,
Keep their distance,
While it works this out.
The rat understands suddenly. It bows and is still
With a little beseeching of blood on its nose-end.

                                                                    (I,12—20)

Within this first section, Hughes sets up a tension between the human world and the natural world. As a representative of the animal world, the rat shares the irrational, instinctual qualities of any animal. But Hughes relies on the specific emotions the image of a rat will arouse in the reader to establish the rat's supremacy as a symbol of the non-human world. Because of its association with filth and disease (as a carrier of typhus and bubonic plague), the rat is seen by man as a threatening, repulsive beast. The rat represents a mode of being completely alien to man. With his choice of pronouns Hughes maintains the distinction between the rat's and man's world. Instead of personifying the rat Hughes places it in the category of objects by referring to the rat (in phrases such as 'it is in the trap', 'it pants', and 'its long fangs') as 'it' and emphasizes its separation from man by repeating this pronoun eleven times in these first twenty lines. At the same time, the rat exhibits its force-fulness in its determined efforts to escape ('trying to uproot itself'), in its aggressive attitude towards the heavens ('attack-ing heaven and earth'), and in its savage use of its fangs ('the incisors bared to the night spaces, threatening the constella-tions').

Although there are no human characters in 'Song of a Rat' there are a number of human artifacts (including 'the farm', 'the old barbed wire' and 'the cracked trough by the gate') which serve as representatives of the human world. Principal among these is the trap which Hughes presents as having cer-tain unique properties. The jaws of the trap are as 'strong as the whole earth'. In killing the rat, the trap causes a collapse of the universe and replaces intellect with irrationality, ('For a crump-ling of the Universe with screechings,/For supplanting every human brain inside its skull with a rat-body that knots and unknots'). In the rat's world the trap initially seems to serve the function man's conception of God does (' "This has no face, it must be God" '). At least it appears as an inscrutable force superior to the rat. The stanzaic form Hughes employs in this first section underscores the nature of the trap. Fifteen end-stopped lines and the couplet form impose restrictions on the poet's freedom in much the same way as the trap confines the rat.

As the representative of man in the poem the trap's proper-ties serve as a grim comment on human nature. The trap exhibits none of man's more humane qualities. Instead it embodies man's negative characteristics. As Hughes presents it the trap and by extension, man, has no redeeming qualities. In his manu-facture and in his use of this mechanical device, man has em-ployed his intellect in the service of destruction. In the trap's forcible restraint, gagging and torture of the rat, Hughes pre-sents man's indifference to suffering and ferocity in bringing that which opposes him under brutal domination. The trap, in effect, symbolizes both man's drive towards dehumanization and his regression into bestiality.

Before the rat dies, it must understand what is happening to it. Literally, the rat's vision (described in section II) which supplies it with the necessary insight occurs between line 18 ('While it works this out') and lines 19–20 ('The rat under-stands suddenly. It bows and is still,/With a little beseeching of blood on its nose-end'). It is not so much death that the rat objects to as the trap itself. As long as the rat sees the trap as

an intrusive object in its world, the rat feels betrayed and continues to struggle. By the end of section II however, the rat
is able to reconcile itself to this mean of execution because it
realizes how the trap itself embodies the intent of the universe (the 'godhead').

During its vision, the rat communes with the wind, the stars,
and some objects on a neglected farm:

> The rat hears the wind saying something in the straw
> And the night-fields that have come up to the fence,
>     leaning their silence,
> The widowed land
> With its trees that know how to cry
> The rat sees the farm bulk of beam and stone
> Wobbling like reflection on water.
>
> (II, 1—6)

Like the rat the farm has suffered at the hands of man.
Its structures have fallen into disrepair, and the land lies barren.
Unlike the rat these inanimate objects can do little but bemoan
their fate. Although most of the objects in this scene are personified, the wind is the most active principle and it initiates
the rat's vision:

> The wind is pushing from the gulf
> Through the old barbed wire, in through the trenched
>     gateway, past the gates of the ear, deep into the worked
>     design of days,
> Breathes onto the solitary snow crystal
> The rat screeches
>
> (II, 7—10)

The images of breath and abyss that are here associated with the
wind suggest that the wind is an emissary of some dark, primal
force capable of undermining time itself. The alternate existence and non-existence of the stone buildings in a dream-like
vision ('The rat sees the farm bulk of beam and stone/Wobbling
like reflection on water') also testifies to man's vulnerability.
Upon seeing these things the rat screeches in anguish and fear
as it begins to get an intimation of its new role.

Although the rat is in its death throes the dandelions, cinders
and trough beg the rat to remain with them, and the stars
command it to stay:

And 'Do not go' cry the dandelions, from their heads
    of folly
And 'Do not go' cry the yard cinders, who have no
    future, only their infernal aftermath


And 'Do not go' cries the cracked trough by the gate,
    fatalist of starlight and zero
'Stay' says the arrangement of stars
Forcing the rat's head down into godhead.

                               (II, 11–15)

Because of man's neglect, the weeds, cinders and trough have
become objects incapable of changing their condition. The
dandelions are too foolish. The cinders have been reduced
to ashes and are incapable of further burning. The trough
has resigned itself to its fate. However, their condition is not
entirely hopeless for the rat's active rebellion against the trap
is evidence of a power capable of avenging what has been done
to them. They implore the rat to remain as a power in the
universe. In this entreaty, Hughes's unorthodox use of messianic Christian imagery becomes apparent. These objects need a
divine saviour to deliver them from the humiliation and ruin
they suffer in bondage to man. They find their redeemer in the
rat. The concurrence of the stars with this view (' "Stay"
says the arrangement of stars/Forcing the rat's head down
into godhead') further implies that the rat's godlike role has
been ordained by a cosmic power that is hostile to the human
world.

The rat's vision reveals a common bond between the rat,
nature ('the wind', 'the night-field', 'the widowed land') and
human artifacts ('the farm', 'yard cinders', 'cracked trough').
All have suffered because of man's murderous disregard for the
consequences of his actions. All are non-human by nature
not by choice. Ironically, by allowing the bestial side of his
nature to gain supremacy man has reduced himself to the
level of an object in the world and is, therefore, subject to
the transcendent cosmic power that manifests itself in the
rat. By relying on imagery traditionally associated with the
Apocalypse (in the Book of Revelation 6:12–14, 8:5) and by
applying it to the rat Hughes describes in section III 'The
Rat's Flight', the cosmic changes brought about by man's
renunciation of his humanity:

The heaven shudders, a flame unrolled like a whip,
And the stars jolt in their sockets.
And the sleep-souls of eggs
Wince under the shot of shadow —

That was the Shadow of the Rat
Crossing into power
Never to be buried
The horned Shadow of the Rat
Casting here by the door
A bloody gift for the dogs
While it supplants Hell.

                                            (III, 1—11)

By pandering to the primitive elements of his nature man has
admitted an influx of evil into the world and abrogated his
place of supremacy in the universe. Amidst thunder and lightning
the spirit of the rat heralded by the biblical signs of glory and
power (vide 'there were voices, and thunderings and lightning
and earthquakes' Revelation 8:5) assumes domination over the
universe. The dark, irrational bestial forces freed by man's
brutality and represented here in the character of the rat
become a permanent presence and an active principle of evil
in the world. As a result, the rat's spirit 'supplants hell' by
taking over Satan's task of making evil predominate. For Hughes
then, the new order brought about by the rat is a universe of
implacable metaphysical evil arising from man's inhumanity
and characterized by terror, violence and death.

It should be noted that this poem, along with 'The Howling
of Wolves', was written within two weeks after Sylvia Plath's
suicide.[111] Thereafter, Hughes wrote no poetry for three
years. With this in mind we can understand why the techniques of shamanism have historically and traditionally been
resorted to in an attempt to resolve a life-crisis. As Lommel
describes shamanic initiation in Siberia, 'the Tungus say of their
shamans: "Before a man becomes a shaman he is sick for a long
time. His understanding becomes confused. The shamanistic
ancestors of his clan come, hack him to bits, tear him apart,
cut his flesh in pieces . . . and only when these [shamanic an-
cestors] have cut up his body and examined his bones can he
begin to shamanize." '[112]

The trap in which the rat is caught, the earth that 'creaks'
and the 'steel traps' in 'The Howling of Wolves' tell us that

Hughes now sees his predators caught and suddenly vulnerable, as less powerful creatures often are. Ironically while Hughes portrays both rat and wolf as vulnerable he will elevate defence-less, assailable creatures like the skylark and gnat to the level of apotheosized deities whose very destructibility is the pre-condition for their unexpected transcendence.

## SKYLARKS

The myth underlying Hughes's choice of the skylark or 'crest-ed lark' as the creature with whom he most closely identifies Sylvia is related in the *Ornithes* of Aristophanes. According to Aristophanes, 'the lark was not only the first of animals but it existed before the earth and before the gods Zeus and Kronos and the Titans. Hence, when the lark's father died, there was no earth to bury him in; then the lark buried its father in its own head (or in its pyramidal crest).'[113] The extent to which Sylvia Plath incorporated the memory of her dead father, Otto, as a central image in many of her poems (e.g., 'Daddy') is well established.[114] As the metaphor has it she, like the skylark, did indeed bury her father in her own head and carried his grave continually with her, as the lark bears its crest. Inter-woven and supporting this theme, Hughes has drawn into the poem a number of references to poems by Hopkins, Keats and Shelley which portray birds as tutelary spirits capable of pro-viding poets with guidance, solace and inspiration. In stark contrast to Hopkins, Keats and Shelley, Hughes projects into the skylark's condition the central predicament of Sylvia's life and poetry — the terrifying ambivalence of a personality so open to the powers of creation that it brings on its own self-destruction. For this reason, Hughes portrays the attri-butes of the skylark in a way totally alien to the skylark in Shelley's poem who is a 'blithe spirit' exempt from the force of gravity, released from the desires and pull of mortality. Hughes's skylark is an all too human bird whose glory for him consists, paradoxically, in its willingness to pay the price and seek transcendence at the cost of its own life. He has recourse to the dynamics of the shamanic technique of trans-ference to vicariously possess himself of qualities he feels he lacks ('My idleness curdles seeing the lark labour near its cloud').[115]

We must remember that this was one of the first poems

Hughes wrote after three years of inactivity following Sylvia's death. With enormous skill, he carefully creates the exacting conditions that circumscribe the lark's existence. Hughes radically transforms the model he found in Hopkins's 'Windhover' where the kestrel hawk threw out both the challenge and rebuff to Hopkins to transcend his human limitations and follow the example of Christ towards greater self-sacrifice. Not self-sacrifice but self-immolation is the theme as Hughes draws into the poem traits of Sylvia's nature and poetry. In Hughes's portrayal the skylark's song is not effortless but rather a product of violent stabbing impressions of pain, its resistance to gravity and its own inner need. Its song tells of its own destiny, a destiny that commands it, fulfills it and endangers its life. We know very well that poetry for Sylvia Plath was an agonizing process. From the turbulent interior, her poetry is a series of screams, contortions, recriminations, a symbolic drama with her self as suffering victim, daring and beseeching others to save her.[116] Her poetry rises from incredible self-torment. She is a victim of her talent, a talent which has shaped her with as devastating sureness, as Hughes implies, as the evolution of the skylark has shaped it ('barrel-chested . . . like an Indian') for climbing in an atmosphere too rarified for normal flight. The skylark has 'a whippet head, barbed like a hunting arrow', formed by nature to hunt, shaped to wound and to turn those wounds into poetry, the barbed notes of inspired song. The shape, the form and the legends surrounding the skylark become Sylvia's emblem. Her incredible suffering defines itself against 'the earth's centre' as the protagonist in *Snow* defines his destiny by facing into the wind of karma and as the gnats in 'Gnat Psalm' are described as 'fighting' against the 'centre'.

To define one's fate by struggling against one's fate implies an openness to destruction and vulnerability quite different from the various forms of release from the flesh projected by Keats and Shelley. Hughes's own work is so completely involved with the theme of self-preservation and the penalties concommittant with accepting existential risks that a nature like Sylvia's where everything is put on the line, nothing is held back without reserves to draw on, is a spectacle of the most profound fear and admiration. 'Skylarks' is an attempt at one and the same time, to embrace and exorcise the fascination he experiences in the presence of a nature constructed on a wholly different and antithetical basis from his own. Two con-

flicting visions are struggling for dominance here: his extraordinarily deep-rooted shamanistic identification, which is
practically an instinct, with powerful predators like the hawk
and wolf and, at the same time, the fearful valour the skylarks
embody. He tries to push the vision off, to dissociate himself
from it — 'heads flung back . . . wings almost torn off . . . like
sacrifices'. Two very different roads are opening up for his life
and poetry — either continued identification with the predators or a new realignment with the victim. One has the
clear impression of someone trying to fend off, through various
strategems, a crushing fate that is gradually settling down-
wards. In effect, his own ambivalence tears him this way and
that and compels him to project onto the skylarks his own inner
dilemma. Working at a second level within the poem is Hughes's
reconstruction of some of the central poems within the English
poetic tradition. His reconstruction is not merely a continuation
but a reply. The phrase 'plume here buckle' in Hopkins's 'The
Windhover' is transformed to 'buckling like razors' to bring
into sharper focus a selfless sacrifice paid at the gravest cost
that provokes Hughes to a mixture of envy and respect and
takes it out of the Christian context of Hopkins's poem. The
movement of the skylark until it is lost to sight, which Shelley
relates as 'thou art unseen', Hughes reworks as 'my hearing
floats back', pinning our attention on the still heard song.
So, too, Shelley's phrase 'keen as are the arrows' supplies
the hunting arrow metaphor; Shelley's image of the race just
begun is transformed into the skylark's struggle against the
centre and Shelley's comparison of the skylark to a high-born
maiden in a palace tower becomes, in Hughes's poem, the
'towered bird'. Despite the similarities, Hughes radically re-
structures the implication of the skylark's flight. For Shelley,
the skylark's song suggests 'ignorance of pain' whereas for
Hughes the skylark sings because of a pain which is indistinguishable (to those listening) from its song. Hughes transfigures
Keats's phrase in the 'Ode to a Nightingale' from 'leaden eyed
despairs' to the much more literal, telling and appropriate 'lead-
en with muscle'. So, too, Hughes transfigures the fire imagery
in Hopkins's 'The Windhover' — particularly the description
of how burning embers spew up a last dying spark of life before
they are extinguished — into the metaphor in stanza six: 'those
flailing flames/That lift from the fling of a bonfire'. The allitera-
tion is characteristic of Hopkins as well.

While these sources are available to every poet what is remarkable is the use to which Hughes puts them. The fierce upward struggle of the skylarks is conveyed in bursts of short lines one and two words long that simulate a fearful upward climb achieved only in painful stages. Correspondingly, as the skylarks swing back to earth, Hughes's language conveys the glide and release experienced by the skylarks. Underlying his description of their flight is a good deal of self-recrimination. Although 'leaden with muscle' at the outset, the skylarks make their 'plummeting dead drop/With long cutting screams buckling like razors' and pull up at the last moment out of what appears to be a suicide dive. At the end, they 'land on a wall-top, crest up,/Weightless,/Paid-up,/Alert,/Conscience perfect'. The para- dox, for Hughes, is that the skylarks are saved because their willingness to go through the painful struggle purges them and makes them weightless. Their willingness to sacrifice them- selves saves them. They become weightless signifying that in the process of being 'burned out' and 'sucked empty' they have complied with the command which determines their existence. Hughes's self image, through his persona projec- tions, aspires towards the solid, the mountainous, that which is able to outlast, endure, and be powerful. Yet he is drawn with admiration towards things as incredibly destructible as skylarks and gnats. The implication is clear. For him, Sylvia, like the skylarks, has fulfilled the instinct within her. She is 'paid-up'. And Hughes at the time of writing this poem is not.

In both 'Skylarks' and 'Gnat Psalm' the importance of Hughes's protagonists lies in inverse proportion to their dimi- nutive size. The paradox of a fateful destiny accompanying a destructible skylark or gnat is the central theme of both these poems. The existence of a heroic capacity for survival at the level of what we would normally perceive as the unnoticed and insignificant clearly forecasts the emergence of Crow as pre- dator-victim. At the same time, giving a skylark, a crow, or a gnat human sufferings has the effect of making that suffering, however horrible and unbearable it may be, seem strangely alien and inacessible to our empathy. Hughes obviously has to walk a very fine line indeed in presenting human suffering from an insect's point of view.

## GNAT-PSALM

Along with 'Skylarks' 'Gnat-Psalm'[117] was one of the first

poems written by Hughes after the three-year hiatus in writing
poetry that followed Sylvia's death. Both poems explore, in
different contexts, what it means to be drawn up into a more
than human destiny in terms of the woeful suffering and endurance of injury entailed. In this poem as in 'Skylarks', 'Howling
of Wolves', and 'Song of a Rat' Hughes continues to examine
the condition of creatures that are in the exact opposite condition to the enormously powerful jaguars, bears and wolves in
his earlier poetry. The title, 'Gnat-Psalm', suggests that this
poem is to be a song of praise honouring the least enduring,
most inconsequential creatures still visible to the eye. The proverb with which the poem opens ' "The Gnat is of more ancient
lineage than man" ' announces this theme; although infinitesi-
mal and incredibly vulnerable, the species is durable, perhaps
more so than man. Hughes's description of the movement of the
gnats when they first appear at night creates an impression of
rapid and constant motion. As they constantly reshape themselves into what Hughes calls a 'crazy lexicon' or 'dumb Cabala'
their rapid motion makes them seem to be 'scribbling on the
air'. What they write is not just mysteriously incomprehensible; Hughes's reference to the occult Hebraic work, the
Cabala, alerts us to the religious metaphor underlying the poem.
The gnats are described 'sparring sparely' and 'shuffling' which
transforms them into a fighter shadow-boxing with an opponent whom we discover is 'the sun'. Only when the sun is going
down can they come out using leaves to protect their delicate
eyes and fragile bodies against the light and heat of the sun.
The situation of the gnats is clearly precarious. They only
exist in the shadow regions of established society. And bearing
in mind the religious level of metaphor underlying the poem we
begin to understand the dimensions of the myth Hughes is
creating. They are the religious martyrs in any age, the early
Christians against the Romans, they are Jews in the death
camps of Nazi Germany. Hughes describes their utter passivity
('everybody else's yoyo') while at the same time alerting us to
their incredible destiny. As individuals they are no more than
iron filings aligning themselves around a centre of fateful
magnetic force; in groups they look like 'immense magnets
fighting around the centre'. Their destiny defines and expresses
itself through their song which embodies their fate. Many verbs
in the first four stanzas end in 'ing' to further strengthen
our impression of rapid motion.

Beginning with the fifth stanza, however, Hughes shifts

his attention from the gnats and their movements to the surrounding landscape. To underscore their stability, para-doxically in the midst of flux, everything but the gnats is described as being in motion while they alone provide the one stable element in an otherwise chaotic world. The wind, the cities, all is in aimless motion while the gnats are 'the nails/In the dancing hands and feet of the gnat-god'. These wretched yet superior beings communicate to Hughes a sustaining order, destiny and guidance that is outside the boundaries of conventional religion. Their son 'is of all the suns' not merely the one which is 'too near'. In effect their song does not limit them to one god, 'one sun', it is of all suns. Like all religious minorities they are oppressed by the power of the official state religion; it 'blasts their song'. They only exist in the shadow recesses, fearful of the centurion 'broad thrusts' of established power. They wor-ship in catacombs and other secret places and only really emerge when the existing empire is passing from supremacy into decline — an impression Hughes conveys in the image of 'the dusty stabs of the late sun'. They blur distinctions between one divinity and another as their wings are described 'blurring the blaze'. The whirring sound produced by innumerable wings compose their song — a sound that mysteriously merges with 'the wind bowing with long cat-gut cries', the long sorrowful mourning sounds of those who are about to die enclosed by their own mortality. Hughes speaks of 'the wind's dance, the death dance,/Plunging into marshes and undergrowth/And cities like cow droppings huddling to dust'. These are the same towns 'camped by their graveyards'. The imagery is complex and evocative. For the people in these towns there's nothing be-yond death. The imagery suggests not only the plague-ridden Middle Ages, carrying the death spore of bubonic plague but the mass deaths and burials in German concentration camps. This is an inevitable idea in view of Hughes's description of the gnats as 'little Hasids' with their 'little bearded faces'. While indivi-duals may die the gnats as a whole are able to remain just one step beyond extinction, hanging 'a little above the claws of the grass' (an image which invokes Isaiah's comparison 'all flesh is grass'). While their belief dooms them, 'giving their bodies to be burned', it allows them, as a species, a transcendence denied to the inhabitants of the towns whose suffering lamentations fill the air.

The capacity of the gnats to adapt, and their faith which

requires sacrifice, compel Hughes's admiration: 'you are the greatest of all the galaxies!/My hands fly in the air, they are follies/My tongue hangs up in the leaves/My thoughts have crept into crannies.' Throughout, Hughes's relation to the gnats is that of a shaman undertaking an ecstatic journey, replete with drumming, singing and dancing. Here, he attempts a shamanistic identification as his hands fly up and he addresses them as does the shaman among the Yenisei tribe who cries, 'Oh my little fly, rise still higher I want to see farther!'[118] When the mongol shaman 'dons his costume' and puts 'wings' on his shoulders he feels he is changed into a flying creature which will carry him beyond his human state.

Although insignificant, the persecution and death the gnats willingly embrace tell Hughes of the existence of a superior power in whose name they willingly die. Ultimately, Hughes realizes he cannot share their experience. Their destiny is their own. Their faces weave through the air and their feet dangle 'like the feet of victims' of an execution. He calls them 'the angels of the only heaven'. As a species they are tied to a belief that will survive when all the surrounding towns and cities will have long ago returned to the earth from which they came. In short their suffering has meaning, a meaning and destiny from which Hughes is excluded. He is still himself with useless hands ('my hands fly in the air, they are follies') and a tongue that has become inarticulate ('my tongue hangs up in the leaves'). But significantly this poem confirms Hughes's shift from his previous identification with predatory animals to victims whose participation in destiny allows them to 'outleap' the threshold of their suffering. This poem along with 'Skylarks', Snow, 'Song of a Rat' and of course, 'Wodwo' all have in common a radical reorientation towards that which suffers instead of that which inflicts suffering. Clearly an emotional shift of some magnitude has taken place and the volume Wodwo both defines and explores the implications of this metamorphosis.

The diminutive, the destructible, the hidden, the view from the underside of things — these qualities signify a transformation in Hughes's vision. The conditions are being created for the appearance of first 'wodwo', a small, obsolete, quirkish creature, ever aware of life's anomalies, and then, with startling vividness, Crow. Unobtrusively, Hughes is moving toward fantasy, then satire and the grotesquely comic world of Crow.

## WODWO

Hughes, in an Author's Note that prefaces the volume *Wodwo*, observes that: 'The stories and the play in this book may be read as notes, appendix and unversified episodes of the events behind the poems or as chapters of a single adventure to which the poems are commentary and amplification.'[119] The nature of this 'single adventure' can be divined from the poem, 'Wodwo',[120] which Hughes took for the title of the volume. The situation 'wodwo' finds itself in is much like the predicament of the narrator in 'Snow', dropped 'out of nothing casually'.[121] Here, too, we have Hughes exploring the dilemma that nothing the unknown creature is able to do seems to give it any definite clue as to what it really is, where it has come from, or what it should be trying to do. Thus, by extension, all of *Wodwo* comprises stages within an overall questioning exploration as to what one's identity is and should be, what tentative implications can be drawn from the results of one's actions, skills and inclinations. The underlying unspoken question which peers out, so to speak, from this poem, is a curious but vaguely sorrowful inquiring search for a proper basis on which to reorient oneself. Throughout, the lack of end-stopped lines, an absence of internal punctuation, the rhythmic pulsing, hesitating movement superbly mimics a wary animal tentatively and rather gingerly moving about in an unknown territory:

> What am I? Nosing here, turning leaves over
> Following a faint stain on the air to the river's edge
> I enter water. What am I to split
> The glassy grain of water looking upward I see the bed
> Of the river above me upside down very clear
> What am I doing here in mid-air? Why do I find
> this frog so interesting as I inspect its most secret
> interior and make it my own? Do these weeds
> know me and name me to each other have they
> seen me before, do I fit in their world? I seem
> separate from the ground and not rooted but dropped
> out of nothing casually I've no threads
> fastening me to anything I can go anywhere
> I seem to have been given the freedom
> of this place what am I then?

Wodwo's perceptions are very much those we might expect of

an animal; when it moves, it perceives the world moving towards itself in a totally naive way. If it stands still it perceives everything stopping to watch it. It applies everything outside of itself to itself; hearing the rustling of weeds it wonders, 'do these weeds know me.' Although capable of entering into the secrets of nature ('why do I find this frog so interesting as I inspect its most secret interior and make it my own'), its own inner workings remain clouded in mystery. While an embodiment of the play of pure perception, wodwo's unwillingness to ask more questions is experienced as a limit 'that's touching one wall of me.' Amphibious, it can move in air or water, and while lying quietly underwater and looking upward into the mirror-like surface of the water seen from underneath it only sees 'the bed of the river above me upside down very clear'. Significantly, it does not see itself reflected in the mirrored surface, a fact which implies its lack of self-awareness. The dilemma projected through its questions, 'have I an owner', reveals to us the creature's need for attachment, yet, at the same time, it claims to have 'no threads fastening me to anything'. It possesses freedom — but freedom to what purpose? Its state is rather unhappy, 'picking bits of bark off this rotten stump gives me no pleasure and it's no use'. Thus nothing the creature does is capable of bringing about a relationship between itself and the environment. It exercises its peculiar, and considerable, skills of inspection in a vacuum, as it were; nothing it can do can bring it to a stage of greater self-actualization.

In the context of Hughes's work this poem states a theme that is to be unusually important in his poetry from this point onwards. It is, in fact, a premonition of the dissociative split between soul and body, self and world, that is such a persistent theme in Hughes's writing, whether in the detached observer Crow or in the literal split of the Reverend Lumb from himself in *Gaudete*. As Hughes says in 'Wodwo', 'me and doing' have 'coincided very queerly'. What one is and what one is able to do are out of synchronization with each other and have produced a radical split in the self. At the end of the poem, the 'wodwo' says, rather resignedly, 'I suppose I am the exact centre/but there's all this what is it roots/roots roots roots and here's the water/again/very queer but I'll go on looking.' Somehow his consciousness has got outside of himself and beyond him in a way that he cannot quite grasp. While he believes that his very acute consciousness should provide the centre on the basis of which he can create an identity, in reality it has not worked out this way at all. And so the poem ends rather sadly with the 'wodwo', a creature who by this time we have grown quite fond of, looking for an answer that will unite him to himself; this is why the word 'roots' is repeated so often. He has fallen, theologically and existentially and is trying to get back to the condition he was in before he fell — to the identity he had before this strange split of self and world occurred.

With Crow, Hughes departs from the rather sad, somewhat lugubrious quietism of 'wodwo' and erupts into violent, comic nihilism, often stylized, that clearly places him among the foremost poets and, indeed, fictional artists of our age. Older than humanity itself yet mysteriously just born, Crow transforms our century through his Trickster's vision. Crow's vision is of such frightening intensity, incredulity, vulgarity and pathos that to share it, even for a moment while we read *Crow*, is so deeply intolerable that, indescribably, we wish there were ten more books of Crow poems to read.

# Part II    Trickster

'It takes a very long time to learn to be a proper crow.' In Carlos Castaneda, *The Teachings of Don Juan: A Yaqui Way of Knowledge* (New York: Pocket Books, 1974), p. 176.

## Chapter Three
## CROW'S EYE VIEW

Ted Hughes produced, in his 1971 volume of poems, *CROW: From the Life and Songs of the Crow,* a new mythology.[1] Singly and together the Crow poems comprise a sequence akin to a folk epic where a series of inventive and often surrealistic narratives reverse the Biblical account of the Creation, the Fall of man, the crucifixion of Christ, the Apocalypse and a number of Classical myths. Within these poems Crow emerges as a creature from a primeval world who functions on a number of levels: as an elemental force in the universe, as a projection of man's instinctual nature scavenging on the dead constructs of his intellect and as an ancient symbol out of legends and folk mythology. The Crow's songs are often mocking versions of well-known myths presented in a relentless, grim and matter-of-fact tone that suggests a persona who is hoaxproof. To Crow's perception all of man's myths are but make-shift attempts to explain man's precarious relationship with God and the natural world.

The precarious, lonely yet resilient figure of Crow owes its genesis to the portrayal of the Raven as Trickster in the myths of the North American Indians, particularly those of the Haida and the Tlingit on the North-west Coast. Paul Radin, the most prominent authority on North American Trickster legends, observes:

The overwhelming majority of all so-called trickster myths in North America give an account of the creation of the earth, or at least the transforming of the world, and have a hero who is always wandering, who is always hungry, who is not guided by normal conceptions of good or evil, who is either playing tricks on people or having them played on him and who is highly sexed.[2]

The cycles associated with the Raven as Trickster portray 'the creation of the world' and 'natural phenomena' and relate how through 'Raven's insatiable hunger' he obtains all he wants.[3] Throughout his adventures which are often grotesquely humorous, his 'voracious appetite, his wandering and his unbridled sexuality' lead him to suffer insult and injury.[4] Side by side with his role as arch-Trickster is the rather surprising portrayal of Raven as a 'typical culture hero' whose self-education from 'immaturity to maturity' parallels his attempts 'to make the earth habitable for man'. Yet the benefits he brings as 'divine culture-hero' are but incidental to the Trickster's desire for self-expression.[5]

'Two Legends', our first introduction to CROW, initiates us into the element of blackness we find throughout the book. The form of 'Two Legends' is modelled on the creation myth and is literally a legend of the creation of Crow. Crow is a flying negative, a bubble of anti-matter, a hole in the universe. This is how we first see him, barely aloft, an emblem of precarious existence, always about to be reclaimed by the realm of negatives from which he has been hatched. Hughes emphasizes Crow's apartness from the usual life-forces of the universe. He is like the rock blocking the flow of water. He is like the gall, acrid and bitter, separate and apart from the 'bed of blood'. The circumstances from which Crow is born provide a clue to his nature, realm and meaning. The obscure, the hidden, the spaces between things, the photographic negative image of the positive are part of Crow's meaning. As Jung reminds us 'the Trickster is a collective shadow figure, and epitome of all the inferior traits of character in individuals' and since 'the individual shadow is never absent as a component of personality the collective figure [of Trickster] can construct itself out of it continually.'[6]

The first part of 'Two Legends' deals with Crow's pre-natal, even pre-foetal, existence. The inner lightless world of lungs, liver, bowels, brain, the inchoate unexpressed 'tombed vision' together create an overwhelming awareness of how little of life is actually given over to the light and how much is claimed by the underside of existence, the night-side of the day world. Hughes shows us Crow's own growing sense of his coming birth, his awareness of the body he will inhabit in this life. This first poem is like a saga, weaving together the appearance of the foetus in the womb with Hughes's insight into the void at the heart of life, mingling the history of crows with that of Crow himself. Hughes had not merely created a character but an environment, a realm of emptiness whose symbol is 'a crow, a black rainbow/Bent in emptiness/over emptiness/but flying'. The rainbow, as covenant between God and man, is twisted in meaning to connect with a truer reality which outbulks the daytime world of groundless optimism. It is typical of Hughes's poetry that we move from immediate perceptions grounded in the most common biological images to vivid spontaneous insights of the most elemental kind.

'Lineage' projects a cosmogony whose driving force is the hunger and helplessness of the newly hatched Crow, 'In the beginning was Scream/Who begat Blood/Who begat Eye/Who begat Fear/Who begat Wing/Who begat Bone . . . Who begat Adam . . . Who begat God . . . Who begat Nothing . . . Who begat Crow.' Significantly, one feature of the Raven cycle gives him a 'divine pedigree'.[7] The theological first cause of Crow's universe is a 'Scream'. Crow's scream for blood develops the 'Eye'. The faculty of sight breeds 'Fear'. The desire to escape the source of Fear produces 'Wings' which in turn evolve 'Bone' and finally Crow as a scavenger; 'Screaming for Blood/Grubs, crusts/Anything/Trembling featherless elbows in the nest's filth'. The long series of negations that extend from the most elemental instincts of self-preservation to exalted concepts of Divinity not only produce Crow but make God a relatively late arrival on the evolutionary scene. 'Lineage', in effect, is an existential reversal of the creation myth as related in Genesis I: 1–31. The same inverted logic prevails in the Tlingit Trickster Myth where Raven is begotten from a man named Kit-kaositiyi-qa and then proceeds to 'make the world'.[8] The cycle of life is portrayed as a never-ending struggle; the force behind life is a bottomless hunger, voracious and insatiable, a devouring urge whose ultimate expression is Crow. Hughes, in effect, turns the normal order of things on its head. By presenting Crow as an isolated creature, generated differently from the rest of creation, Hughes associates Crow with the Indian conception of Trickster as an elemental force in the universe who antedates the civilized conception of God. Crow is begotten by nothing and remains a creature whose survival hinges on his own primal hunger.

In the next poem, 'Examination at the Womb-Door', an un-born foetus is being examined by death. The poem is a series of leading questions used in the examination of baptismal applicants to Christianity. The irony, of course, is the difference in the final answer, since Christianity is based on the hope of a Saviour who is stronger than death, and baptism is a rite of renunciation of death and an affirmation of an eternal life through Christ. The primitiveness of Crow stems from the des-cription of him in the previous poem 'in the nest's filth'. Death is presented as a harsh and ruthless inquisitor and the questions to which Crow is subjected are belittling and derogatory. The poem projects an indifferent universe; the foetus is a meagre, unsupported creature whose whole life is but a moment. The questions taunt life with its own futility. Yet, the paradox is that as long as something lives death is powerless. Hughes acknowledges that death owns all things, is stronger than hope, will, love and live and yet, in some mysterious way Crow is proclaimed as 'stronger than death'. In folklore, myth and legend, Crow is a scavenger who derives his strength and nourish-ment from assimilating what death is incapable of ingesting, what death leaves behind. Thus, Crow is stronger than death since he feeds off death itself. The conclusion is both para-doxical and inescapable; for Crow the only secure basis on which to build a life is not hope, will or love, but death.

The image of the 'womb-door' derives from the command inscribed in the *Tibetan Book of the Dead*; 'Thereby thou wilt obtain liberation without having to enter the door of the womb.'[9] Significantly, Hughes describes the unborn foetus in terms that could, with equal appropriateness, be applied to someone who is dying. The choice of adjectives ('scrawny', 'bristly', 'unspeakable', 'questionable', 'messy', 'occasional', etc.) emphasize the fragility of life and magnify the vulnera-bility of Crow to destruction. The poem is a confrontation of existence and non-existence on the most elemental level. Each attribute of Crow is undercut by an extraordinary self-scrutiny. Crow's face is 'scorched', shrivelled up. His lungs are 'still-working' to remind us they are destined to stop. His guts are 'unspeakable'; they cannot speak and they aren't worth speak-ing about. His brains are 'questionable' and thus call into ques-tion the validity of all judgments arrived at by brains such as these. As the interrogation of life by death proceeds, Hughes quickens the pace by omitting the phrase 'who owns' in the last four lines of the first stanza. This brings the answer 'Death' home more forcefully.

Life, in effect, is a time of pending trial where the ultimate outcome is never in doubt. The composite of life's attributes, feet, face, lungs, muscles, guts, brains, are all merely loaned and ultimately belong to death. The image of a 'utility coat of muscles' reduces musculature to the level of clothes, a mere layer. The total effect is to further degrade the unborn foetus in graphic terms. The earth itself is a rainy and 'stony' sphere devoid of physical and metaphysical comfort. Consciousness is described as 'this occasional wakefulness' — an image of power and pathos to underscore the brief trivial time within which life exists, and the death-watch or 'wake' that death keeps.

Hughes creates the emotion of intense expectancy as if waiting for a jury's verdict. When it finally comes, it is so startling that it unexpectedly catches us off guard: 'but who is stronger than death?/Me evidently/Pass, Crow.' The passing nature of all life, passing an examination and a temporary pass given to Crow to pursue his life are all implicit in this poignant phrase. It is as though Crow, by ruthlessly stripping away self-deception, wins the right to live as a mobile expressive, breathing, functioning, living being. Yet there is no victory, only a temporary concession — 'Pass, Crow.'

'A Kill' is based on the premise that every incarnation into life is perceived as death by the spirit. To an entity capable of infinite movement having legs would be experienced as being 'flogged lame'. By the same logic, having ribs would nail one down, and being born with eyes capable of only a single angle of vision would feel like being blinded. Thus the account of Crow's birth entails the worst torture imaginable. Yet since Crow is an embodied negative, the imagery of birth as death is appropriate. Even as he falls from eternity into the flesh, so Crow sees 'a dream flash as he drowned in his own blood' as dying men are supposed to see their lives flashing before them. Hughes reverses the usual image of blood sustaining life into blood in which Crow is drowned. As a spirit he had been free, now he is bound by a body, tied to the earth and all its miseries. As Crow is born, he hears the faint and far-off cry 'It's a boy', then everything goes black. Although a victim of what would normally be construed as unspeakable torture and persecution, the place of violence in creating life is something for Crow to endure. Crow comes to earth, sliding out, falling to the ground and smashing into 'the rubbish' — a marvellous touch for the scavenger Crow's beginning. So, on the occasion of life's most vibrant moment, Crow is flogged, shot, nailed, strangled, clubbed and smashed.

In numerous Trickster cycles, including those of the Winnebago Indians, Trickster's birth always entails the death of the mother.[10] And in 'Crow and Mama' Crow's first sign of impending independence is viewed as disastrous: 'When he laughed she wept.' Crow's independence as a living entity costs his mother pain. This is a parable about dependency where the child wants to break away from Mama. As the story unfolds it is clear that wherever Crow goes he is under the influence of the inescapable mother. Yet escape from one womb necessarily entails incubation within a womb at the next level. Hughes chooses a typical adolescent milestone, getting the car keys, to symbolize Crow's desire to get free of Mama, but she retains control. He takes a plane, 'But her body was jammed in the jet—/There was a great row, the flight was cancelled.' Crow always exists within a womb, constrained within each environment, emerging from the mother's womb, to the womb of the family, to the womb of society, and ultimately beyond the womb of mother-earth herself. Interestingly, the vehicles of escape suggest the phallic self-sufficiency that comes with adolescent puberty, since Crow gets clear of the earth's gravity in a rocket ship that 'Drilled clean through her heart'. Throughout the poem, technology, in the form of cars, planes, and rockets is the masculine attempt to escape from feminine mother nature. The ultimate mother, for Hughes, is mother-earth. Hughes explores the pull of maternal possession using both the force of gravity and the umbilical 'towrope' which holds Crow's car tethered, and thus foils his escape. The urge to escape the womb, be it the womb of childhood, adolescence, or the gravity womb of earth leads at each stage to an illusion of independence that quickly gives way to a realization of dependency in the larger environment. Ironically, Crow, to his dismay, discovers that just at the moment of breaking free from the earth's atmosphere (in a phallic rocket that connects Crow's independence with his emerging sexuality) he is still under 'his mother's buttocks'.

Like Satan flying from sun to sun to find the earth, so Crow 'flying from sun to sun' finds his new home. The transition from the previous poem 'Crow and Mama' has Crow searching for a new environment in which to use his power in much the same way as Satan, exiled from Heaven, travels the abyss searching for earth. In the first stanzas the reader is presented with a graphic image of a solid earthy wall ('The world's earthen wall') in which plants and earth creatures are described, using the idiom of a somewhat pedantic tourist guide, as living and growing. Crow alights through a doorway (that he has seen 'opening and opening' in the previous poem) in this wall. It's appropriate that Crow entered the world through 'a black doorway' — through the underside of reality; this black doorway is also the 'eye's pupil'. Since the eye traditionally stands as the window of the soul and the earth is described as a human being, Crow has both stepped into the world and flown into the mind of its creator. Appropriately, other doorways are mentioned in the poem, 'the flowerless navel', 'the mouth', and the 'eye'. These are three channels through which life force enters at various levels. In both this poem and the one following, 'A Childish Prank', Crow is clearly identified with Satan.

As one might expect, in 'A Childish Prank', Hughes inverts the Garden of Eden myth by presenting human sexuality bequeathed to Adam and Eve by a Satanic Crow for his own amusement while God lethargically dozes. Like the Winnebago Trickster, Crow is mentally a child for whom 'no ethical values exist'.[11] And as a Trickster he is oblivious to the consequences of his actions. Crow, not God, gives man the sexual impulse without giving man a soul. Like the Norse god Loki, Crow as Trickster first surfaces here as a mischievous prankster and crude mischief maker. Crow takes God's creation of man and woman and revises it to his own advantage. In effect Crow becomes creator and the 'Worm, God's only son', becomes the archetypal victim. Crow is blissfully oblivious to all the suffering he has caused, much as the Trickster is shown often 'laughing at the discomfiture of those on whom he has played a trick'.[12] By infusing man with sexuality instead of a soul, Crow plays a trick on God who is not only presented as indecisive and sleepy but incompetent as well, since the problem of infusing a soul was so great 'It dragged him asleep.' This is clearly a parody of Genesis Chapter 2, Verse 7, where Adam is formed from the earth's dust and has an immortal soul breathed into him. By contrast, Crow playfully and maliciously infuses man with an animal lust which bewilders and torments him. Crow's identification with Satan, as in 'The Door', consists in the fact that Satan alights on earth and like Crow is responsible (as a serpent) both for mortal sin and sexual awareness. We know, of course, that the serpent or 'Worm' is a phallic emblem in many folk myths. In one South American

Indian Myth,[13] when God created man and woman, men had no sexual organs and in turn the women were satisfied sexually by a mile-long blue serpent. Finally, one of the men got tired of this situation and cut off the worm's head. The women were very angry and demanded another serpent right away. It was at this time that God gave man his sexual anatomy by cutting up and grafting little pieces of the dead serpent onto the men. Now the men could satisfy their wives themselves. The idea that the 'Worm' is 'God's only son' is not as bizarre as it might first appear since in many areas of the Americas and in India the serpent is associated with eternal life. God in 'A Childish Prank' is portrayed as he will be in most of the Crow poems, and indeed, as he is seen in a majority of the Trickster legends, as a naive bumpkin, erring and unaware. Crow plays with God by meddling with God's first human creation, much as Satan (as Milton portrayed him in *Paradise Lost*) had intended to do. Significantly, this is the first poem in which Hughes introduces Crow's 'laughter' as a theme. Crow is not aware that he can do serious damage, or that there is such a thing as evil. Childlike, he simply laughs at the confusion he causes and plays jokes without understanding the consequences. After playing his first prank by creating an intensely painful conflict between the sexes Crow is ready for school in 'Crow's First Lesson'.

God attempts to instruct Crow and civilize him, especially in view of his irresponsible behaviour in the previous poem. Yet try as he may, Crow just cannot learn something that goes against his nature. Each of Crow's attempts to say 'love' produces evil, first in the form of 'the white shark', then 'a blue fly, a tsetse, a mosquito' — disease carrying insects, and finally an agonized and urgent sexual drive. Despite God's attempts to teach Crow to speak the word 'love', what results is destruction, disease, and desire. Love is something that Crow quite literally can't swallow: 'Crow convulsed, gaped, retched.' While Crow is incapable of love, as is the Trickster, it's interesting that Crow doesn't laugh as he did in the preceding poem. Crow feels guilt and his guilt ('Crow flew guiltily off') reflects Adam's guilt after the fall (Genesis Chapter 3, Verse 8) where man hides himself from God. Crow seems to be becoming aware of his ability to create both good and evil; this marks another step in his development. Although an unwilling student who translates God's word 'love' into Crow's equivalent — instinctive physical sex — Crow feels guilty that he has failed to learn this lesson and so flies off, only to land in the next poem 'Crow Alights'. Crow's ability to botch up God's work, plague him with mischievous actions, and enrage him, is entirely consistent with incidents in the Trickster cycle. But Hughes stresses above all that Crow can't be made to go against his nature. Although now, for the first time, elements of guilt, suspicion, pain and death enter man's world, significantly, they enter through Crow.

'Crow Alights' initiates Crow's very personal encounter with death that extends through the next three poems. The detachment Crow maintains in the face of human suffering gives way to his horrified realization that the world in which he is placed is alien to him. Worse, the reality of death makes its first impression on Crow and he realizes that he cannot leave; he is here to stay for the duration. Crow is frightened that he will have to exist in a strange environment, a world tainted with 'the virus of God', and so he shivers, feeling the 'horror of Creation'. The poetry has suddenly become quite serious. Images in this poem and the next ('That Moment') deal with the same person, the same face, smoking the same cigarette, held by the same hand, and describe the anguish that might be expected upon witnessing a probable suicide. Hughes takes in the panorama and then zooms in for a close-up. The images of the sea coiled around the earth like a snake, massive mountain ranges, and interstellar spaces give way to human artifacts ('this shoe, with no sole, rain-sodden,/Lying on a moor') that collectively testify to the bottomless despair of creation for Crow. The situation is significant; Crow is not part of it: 'He blinked. Nothing faded./He stared at the evidence', yet he is compelled to deal with it. While creation is described, it seems as though all things have ended; it is dusk, the end of day. The 'waste of puddles' fills Crow with an apocalyptic sense of horror and emptiness. Crow is looking at the blacker aspects of reality and particularly at a fateful scene which simply will not go away. 'Nothing escaped him. (Nothing could escape).' The mountain of circumstantial 'evidence' underscores an existential vision that suggests what Crow's role is to be — a helpless observer of Fate.

Crow's function is to give perspective — in fact a 'Crow's Eye View' — to that which is too terrible to deal with directly. 'That Moment' gives us an intimation of the therapeutic benefit available to Hughes through such a unique vantage point. Crow's fate is grimly trapping him. The aura of playful innocence traditionally associated with Trickster

dramatically lapses before a sense of impending doom. It is
certainly more than chance that the image of suicide coin-
cides with the precise moment when Crow feels the oppres-
siveness of a world without further possibilities closing in on
him. From this undeniably central episode (variations of which
appear throughout Hughes's work) we can generalize Hughes's
sense of powerlessness to alter a fate that is perceived as en-
trapping him. This scene continues the image of the rat caught
in a trap (in 'Song of a Rat'). This feeling of futility is balanced
against Crow's need to 'start searching for something to eat'
i.e., to function on the most basic, instinctive level of self-
preservation. This dramatic part of the poem is a central theme
in Hughes's poetry. Food, for Hughes, is a symbol of nourish-
ment for the soul. When Hughes says that nothing fills Crow up,
that Crow is everlastingly voracious (a trait drawn directly
from Trickster) and that no food Crow eats ever permanently
fills the open craving maw of the void he is expressing his own
dissatisfaction with the lack of a lasting and nourishing truth.
Thus his search for a truth that will permanently satisfy him
is reflected by Crow's continuing search for 'something to
eat'. This poem describes a central moment in the 'Crow poems'
and it is probable that all of them were intuitively written to
give perspective to this moment. Crow's spiritual hunger, expressed paradoxically through the instinctive reflex of the need
for 'something to eat', is precipitated by the disappearance for
all time of that for which Crow will forever search. The phrase
'And the only face left in the world/Lay broken/Between
hands that relaxed, being too late' has a crushing finality about
it that might seem to make Crow's enigmatic response appear
to be callous. In truth his reaction has been displaced and projected into the previous poem where he shivered at the 'horror
of Creation'. At first Crow seemingly has no relation to the
death he has witnessed; yet suicide of the person one most
loves ('And the only face left in the world/Lay broken') empties the world of humanity. We should not be deceived by the
air of casualness with which Hughes makes the suicide look
like an everyday happening, 'like a cigarette lifted from an
ashtray'. Crow's meaning here is that he derives his existence
from being a scavenger, from feeding on corpses and the meaning of death itself. Hughes's inability to assimilate the meaning
of death in a personal context is reflected in Crow's continual
need to search for food. In the Trickster cycle Crow has now
passed through the childhood stage; while he is slowly becoming

aware of the earth he inhabits and its blacker aspects he does not yet know that this somehow relates back to him. In fact his intention to 'measure it all and own it all' forms the basis of the next poem 'Crow Hears Fate Knock on the Door'. The emotional logic behind Crow demands that in this most personal of all poems Crow must look with a sense of detachment on what most would consider a source of anguish. The speaker in the poem does not even conceive of himself as possessing a face since 'the only face left in the world lay broken'. This same image of the faceless narrator devoid of identity reappears in much the same circumstances later in *Gaudete*.[14] Underlying this poem is an anguished sense of great loss and pathos as well as the implication that in this case at least, all human effort is insufficient. This poem brings to a close the first section of CROW where Crow has been merely a passive agent to whom everything has happened and ushers in a sequence of poems where Crow assumes control of his own destiny.

In myth and folklore crows are commonly perceived as birds of prophecy, a fact which underlies 'Crow Hears Fate Knock on the Door'. Crow's relationship to his as yet unknown destiny is metaphorically equated to a steel spring that, when ingested, uncoils tearing the insides of the animal that has been unfortunate enough to swallow it. What Crow has attempted to ingest, that now tears his insides, is the intimation of the diabolical nature of the universe that he first suspected in 'That Moment'. The universe for Crow is an infernal machine and it is significant that Crow investigates things that are themselves dead ('a stone', 'a dead mole', 'the spaces between the stars') to find the meaning of his existence. The analogy between the world he is in and the prison cell of 'cold quarantine' provokes Crow's response; 'I WILL MEASURE IT ALL AND OWN IT ALL/AND I WILL BE INSIDE IT/AS INSIDE MY OWN LAUGHTER.' While Crow has clear associations with the fallen Satan — a cursed being doomed to a realm of death and darkness — Crow's method of 'getting inside it' is the Trickster's characteristic mode of ingesting, consuming and digesting the world. The previous poem, we recall, established the relationship between eating and the assimilation of suffering. A creature of blackness, Crow listens to 'the translucent starry spaces' for a clue as to what his fate will be. His method is the Trickster's one of laughter which penetrates to the heart of things, although the pain it causes him makes him grimace. In fact this peculiar blend of pain and laughter ultimately becomes an important iconographic element (that of the grin) within *CROW* and Hughes's later poetry as well. Crow's awareness in this poem is twofold. First he begins to realize how intricate the world is just at the point where he falls victim to his own feeling of insignificance. In that second before he falls to join the masses of grass, stones and dead moles, the prophecy latent inside of him unwinds and he knows that someday he is to be the master. While he sees the universe as deterministic he responds with individuality, with laughter and with ironic detachment.

'Crow Tyrannosaurus' explores Crow's attempt to answer the question as to how we deal with suffering. He becomes aware that life itself exists through the cannibalism of animals eating each other and thereby he discovers the reality of evil and suffering. He is powerless, however, to alter his own instinctive participation in the process. The Tyrannosaurus Rex was the most destructive flesh-eater ever to live on earth and Hughes plays on the theme of ingestion as a metaphor of the assimilation of the meaning of suffering. Ironically, the closer one gets to the human condition the more deaf, dumb and blind man becomes to the agony accompanying the death of those upon whom he feeds.

A death processional goes past, a cortege of insects, a cat, dog and man. The farther up the evolutionary ladder the less sorrow is felt. Whereas animals, according to Hughes, feel the anguish of the victims they have eaten, man kills abstractly. Although it is beyond Crow's power to stop eating, for a moment at least, he becomes fully conscious of the suffering his need to eat has caused. As each order of life destroys others in succession, the experience of the victim's pain is deadened and less emotion at death is displayed. While the swift 'pulsates' with the anguish of the insects it has eaten, the cat only 'feels' sorrow. At the next level of indifference, the dog 'hears' (but does not feel) 'screeching finales'. Man alone 'incinerates' the outcry; it never even reaches his ears. In man alone we have the 'ear's deafness' to suffering, an indifference which reaches its peak in the ability to overlook the incinerators at Auschwitz: 'even man . . . was a walking abattoir . . . his brain incinerating their outcry'. Man is the only animal, as Camus noted in *The Rebel,* that kills for abstractions of dogma and ideology while repressing his awareness of the pain and sorrow of his victims.[15] The poem ends with the phrase: 'Thus came the eye's roundness/the ear's/deafness.' The eye's roundness tells us of the false naivete by which 'higher orders of life' make themselves less sensitive to the agonies of those they must kill to live. We see Crow eating, killing and weeping. His weeping becomes indistinguishable from the weeping of the insects he has killed. Crow is truly discovering the laws by which he must live; his need to live by eating is stronger than his desire to avoid killing. But for a moment he must assimilate the meaning of the deaths of the animals he must consume without filtering out his capacity to feel. This poem sets the stage for 'Crow's Account of the Battle' where the same lack of concern and awareness of others' pain is extended throughout the globe in a graphic presentation of the archetypal battle that has been waged through eternity. At this point Crow's compassion is strongly at odds with his previous indifference.

While all Trickster cycles include strong elements of 'satire on human stupidity and foibles',[16] Hughes has developed this feature of the Raven legend to a degree that is almost unimaginable, given the original myth. 'Crow's Account of the Battle' contains Crow's testimony to the horrors of wars past, present or future, beginning with the mythological battle of the Titans and extending to the war to end all wars. Unlike Milton's account in *Paradise Lost* of the war of the angels in Heaven, Hughes uses simple diction and straightforward narration to deflate war of all its heroics, its self-rationalization and insensitivity. For this reason war is spoken of as an immensely 'educational experience'; prayers don't help and mutilated men on the battlefield know that 'even on the sun's surface/ They could not be learning more or more to the point.' The battle is un-named; it could be any battle. Crow witnesses how easily war develops on the least difference of ideology. He learns how ordinary and how perfectly acceptable war is, how the unconcern for other's pain seen in the previous poem explains why everything 'happened too easily with too like no consequences'. The end of civilization can be achieved with startlingly alarming ease. The ability to repress feelings that might arise at the death of others means that man can kill through science, dissociate himself from the act of murder and in the process transform war into a merely haphazard concommitant of existence ('sudden traps of calculus,/Theorems wrenched men in two'). The blood of innumerable victims drains into the spaces between the stars. What Crow describes in a very straightforward and realistic way seems to be the last battle of all, a war without internal checks where it is simply easier to keep on killing. Hughes's technique is superb; the superfluidity of cascading lines mimic the lack of internal restraints. Wars become easier to start and life has less value. The lack of anything within human nature to stop, slow or even check the onset of mass killing of the species is as intolerable a thought to Crow as it is for most people and so Crow decides to search in 'The Black Beast' for the creature responsible.

The absence of any inner controlling principle implies for Crow the presence of an active force of evil personified as 'The Black Beast'. Not surprisingly Crow searches everywhere to discover the source of evil except within himself. In other days the black beast has been called the dragon, Satan, Lucifer or the bloody beast prophesied in Revelation Chapter 13 who would supposedly appear in the earth's last days. The strength of the black beast rests on the fact that he is unseen, hence unknown. Crow tells 'loud lies against the black beast' goading him to come out into the open. Ironically, of course, Crow can never find him although he 'flailed immensely through the vacuum' and 'screeched after the disappearing stars/Where is it? Where is the Black Beast?' Crow's frantic search threads its way through references to Cain and Abel ('Crow killed his brother and turned him inside out'), occult investigation ('Crow split his enemy's skull to the pineal gland') and modern science ('Crow crucified a frog under a microscope'). As is usual the search for the source of evil engenders more evil than had originally existed. Through the violence of his quest Crow transforms the universe into a Manichean struggle between the forces of good and evil. This begins a series of poems that take up questions of philosophy and theology. The anthropomorphic projection of the black beast as death in life leads to the poem 'A Grin' where the grin of the skull lies beneath the surface of the face. The narrative of 'The Black Beast' is reminiscent of a story told by Chaucer of three men who set out to kill death. To everyone they meet they ask: 'Tell us, where is the same death that killed our friends?' They bully an old man and he directs them to an oak tree where they discover a large cache of gold, immediately forget their quest for death, and wind up killing each other. And indeed, Chaucer concludes: 'They did find death.'[17] Seen in this light, the black beast refers not to death itself but to Crow's quest for a figure to blame for his own fear of death. Above all, what Crow does not know is that he is the black beast.

'A Grin' is a metaphor for the fixity of death reaching into the flow of life. Its proper home is in the skull but it tries to install itself into the musculature of the face. It appears in human beings at the most extreme moments of their existence: a woman in the agony of childbirth, a man in a car-crash, a steeple-jack the instant before he hits the pavement. It appears in the ecstacy of lovers and the contorted face of grief, in transcendent happiness and murderous madness. When human strength fails, in pain or in the extremity of death, the face, says Hughes, instinctively shapes itself in a flickering premonition of the grin of the skull. 'A Grin' is certainly a hideous poem that intertwines motifs of death with those of the laugh and smile. We recall that the devil in Hughes's play for children, *Sean, the Fool, the Devil and the Cats*, kills with demonic laughter.[18] The pressure of the search for that which cannot be found within 'The Black Beast' has, in effect, brought the grin to the fore; it floats up in Crow's consciousness. In essence the grin of the skull reaches into life and tries to exist beyond its proper realm. The minute it touches anything human and alive the face writhes in contortions of agony and subsides. The grin, of course, finds 'a permanent home' in the skull; finally discouraged, the grin 'temporarily non-plussed' must sink back into the skull and out of the picture. Hughes's attraction to the grin is that it emerges only when all pretenses are dropped, when all knowledge has been forgotten and when everything exists on a purely elemental level. This is another poem in a series that has to do with the nature of evil. In 'The Black Beast' the search was begun; here death reaches into life. In the poem following, 'Crow Communes', Crow takes literally the injunction in John 8:32, 'And ye shall know the truth and the truth shall set you free' and seeks divine help to understand the nature of evil. Finally, in 'Crow's Account of St George' the search for evil is projected outward as an archetypal quest. What Crow does not realize of course, is that like the grin, he too is homeless, brings death and sorrow and has to keep moving. As Crow comes from nothingness and finds no permanent place in the world so the grin comes from death and to death must ultimately return. Both share qualities of the exile, the outcast. The grin cannot exist for more than a few seconds within life since it ultimately belongs to the skull; Crow is the death bird, harbinger of sorrow and not fated to ever truly belong in life.

In 'Crow Communes' Crow is the 'hierophant', a novice to be initiated in the divine mysteries. One day Crow decides to have

a chat with God but finds God too tired to even talk. He takes
a bite of God's shoulder to become an interpreter of sacred
mysteries but hardly has taken it when he becomes speechless
and gapes 'appalled'. Crow discovers that the more of God he
ingests the less he understands. Phrases in the poem parody
the language of communion and Crow transforms the 'the
peace that passeth understanding' quite concretely into a piece
of God. God is described as a snoring mountain and it's hardly
surprising that Crow should become less illumined through the
ingestion of such a bovine divinity. The underlying reference
is to the illumination of the apostle Paul. Crow attempts to
commune with God by literally partaking of his body and blood,
as in John 6:35, 'For my flesh is the true food and my blood
is the true drink. Everyone who eats my flesh and drinks my
blood is in me and I in him.' Crow approaches God, who is
depicted in his customary half-witted condition and demands
answers to questions that have plagued man since the beginning
of time. Quite characteristically Crow tries to assimilate God
literally. But the joke is on Crow ('That was the first jest').
He becomes denser for the effort. Instead of greater sublimity
the opposite occurs. He suffers a diminishment of his understanding and becomes 'appalled' — death-like (a play on pall-
bearer). The poem is filled with an abundance of puns. 'God
lay, agape' reminds us that *Agape* in Greek means divine love.
Crow's search for the ultimate answer within this poem foreshadows St George's quest (and indeed all quests for ultimate
truths) in 'Crow's Account of St George'.

'Crow's Account of St. George' presents a modern hero, very
coldly assured and direct in his quest for the absolute number —
an apt symbol of the twentieth century obsession with passionless facts and statistics. In works of medieval hagiography (such
as the St George of Raphael) St George is a patron saint of
knighthood who is depicted as a warrior holding a lance poised
and ready to slay the evil serpent or dragon (whose nature is
described in Daniel 14: 22, 27; Revelation 12: 3, 7; and Isaiah
43:20). In addition to Biblical and Gnostic sources, Hughes may
be drawing on the legend of Lambert of Aschaffenburg where a
pilgrim sees in a dream a horrid crow which caws and flies
round Cologne and which is hunted away by a splendid horseman; the pilgrim explains that the crow is the devil and the
horseman St George.[19] In contrast, Hughes's hero proceeds,
contradictingly, as 'He makes a silence . . . refrigerates an
emptiness . . . Then unpicks numbers' in order to get to the

root of the Ultimate Number, that is, the ultimate knowledge. The hero first surgically dissects the life-giving and mysterious 'gluey heart' of reality which then becomes commonplace. As he probes the hero hears something and catches a brief glimpse of a monster 'grinning in the doorway' which is steeped in dung. It vanishes and he's 'confused/Shaken' but still 'aims his attention—/Finding the core of the heart is a nest of numbers'. In effect the closer he gets to his goals the more hideous the demon becomes — as if it hinges on and is inseparable from his degree of knowledge. Thus, the Crow's account of St George is a reversal of the archetype of the conquering hero who vanquishes chaos, evil and temptations after having conquered elements of weakness within himself. Consistent with this pattern of a hero-quest myth the opposing forces he confronts can be seen as manifestations of his own deepest fears. Apparently defeating the first threat, he's now attacked by 'A bellyball of hair, with crab-legs, eyeless' which 'Jabs its pincers' into his face. It takes the 'ceremonial Japanese decapitator' to hack and scatter the lopped segments of the demon before 'the opposition collapses'. Seemingly victorious he 'Steps out of the blood-wallow' and looks back to the bloody scene to discover that 'his wife and children lie in their blood'. What he has killed in his unwavering, scientific search into the heart's depth, in his pursuit of scientific truth, is ironically the depths of feeling in his own heart and his ability to love. Crow's version extends to inhuman extremes traits of ascetic denial inherent in the figure of the questing Knight so that the subjugated adversary is his own family. His wife and children, those most dependent upon his love are consequently slaughtered unwittingly in his technocratic quest for the Ultimate Knowledge.

This is the first time in *CROW* that Hughes presents a description of a man who unwittingly destroys his family, just as legends say Hercules killed his wife Megara and their children in a fit of madness. This poem projects a tale where the search for truth destroys what one loves best. It falls into the same category as 'Crow Communes' except that Hughes parallels Crow's search for the answer through religion with the modern scientist's quest 'in a track of numbers'. Our grail is the almighty scientific knowledge which demands what we love and our innocence as well in payment for its revelations. This poem is therefore a bizarre, twisted account of the twentieth century's conception of the hero. The modern scientist is for Crow a grotesque parody of a knight of old who first kills his own emotions before undertaking his quest for facts and figures. It is interesting that Hughes condemns a trait which is strongly in evidence as a defence mechanism in his own poems and stories, i.e. the tendency to totally analyze a phenomenon in order to defeat it. Here, the scientist's method of discovering the truth through detachment (in contrast to truth-seeking through spiritual communion dramatized in the previous poem) unleashes demons that demand a compensatory sacrifice from a scientist who wants to have no emotional ties with what he is studying. As Jung reminds us, 'In the Christian legend of St George slaying the dragon, the primeval rite of sacrificial slaughter again appears.'[20] While 'Crow's Account of St George' projects the story of an individual's destructive search for truth 'A Disaster' illustrates what happens on a global scale when cultures become infused with messianic fervour in the quest for truth.

'There came news of a word./Crow saw it killing men. He ate well.' So begins a poem where Crow, true to his nature, arrives at the scene of a 'disaster' feasts upon the carrion and flies to a vantage point where he observes the holocaust in safety. The 'word' that produces such massive destruction can be identified with almost any religious or political ideology or even the ideology of technological progress itself which kills men and as it grows destroys cities and chars entire lands. Beginning as 'news of a word' (a play on 'gospel' i.e. good news), all the revelations says Crow become devouring monsters capable of producing thermonuclear 'collapsing mushrooms' and when the smoke clears nothing has been accomplished except that millions of people have been destroyed in the interests of a particular 'truth'. Wartime is especially good for scavengers and so Crow 'ate well'. The initial effect of the word is its explosive annihilation of life; to satisfy its voraciousness the word begins to nourish itself with the milk of human life and it is described as a great parasitic 'lamprey'. To underscore the comparison of the word to a lamprey, a grotesque slimy monster akin to a leech, Hughes employs images of 'drinking', 'digesting', 'lips', etc. In turn, the earless, eyeless mouth makes a superb metaphor for the insensitivity of ideology in general and technology in particular. Scenes of burning 'breath' and 'excreta poisoning seas' are devastating images of the air and water pollution that technology brings in its frenzy after bulldozing 'whole cities to rubble'. Crow alone resists being ingested and remains outside the fold of ideological conversion. The word sweeps the earth like a scourge and in the face of such destruction Crow displays not fear but curiosity and a sense of wonder. Crow flies 'clear' and remains uninvolved while whole populations are eliminated. He is the essence of objective detachment and does not even lose his appetite in the face of death. The poem draws on a number of literary and legendary sources including Matthew Arnold's depiction of the shrinking sea of faith in 'Dover Beach', and Shelley's image of the vast desert in 'Ozymandias', where 'nothing beside remains' (Hughes transforms this to 'all that remained'). Most prominent, of course, is the imagery of a great flood which destroys cities and gradually passes away as the water dries up to a puddle, an image that links this poem with the legend of the raven's departure from Noah's ark after the Great Flood. In this century, the metaphor of 'poisoned seas' and 'burning lands' might well refer to thermonuclear radiation which is 'eyeless' and 'earless', makes no sound and can invisibly destroy and digest all animate life leaving a landscape emptied of human inhabitants. Ideologies come and go, each one taking its toll in death and destruction but Crow stays 'clear' and observes it all. He is beyond the power of mere words; words however are not willing to let Crow go free and in 'The Battle of Osfrontalis' they assault him.

'Osfrontalis' is the section of the head which is the site of the higher thought processes. Since logic and the power of words originates within the osfrontalis the battle takes place here. With the experience of St George (the scientist) and 'A Disaster' behind him Crow is watchful of words. What they offer are ideas empty in themselves but which so often have stirred people into the destructive furies dramatized so effectively in 'The Battle of Osfrontalis'. Words try to seduce Crow; they appeal to his greed, sensuality and fear of death (through the promise of redemption). Crow refuses to be drawn into the trap. He is a creature of pure immanance and remains unharmed because he does not yield to their persuasion, force or seduction. Each time he thwarts their attack on a pragmatic level: dead men cannot take out insurance policies, madmen are not conscripted by the Army and so on through all the blandishments of sex, alcohol and linguistic enticement. The phrase 'the skull of a dead jester' refers to Yoric, in *Hamlet*, a master of word play and 'infinite jest'. The image brings into focus the confrontation which Crow re-enacts between the philosophic mind of Hamlet and the mocking spectre of death's empty silence. Hughes saves this enticement to the last since the final stronghold of words is the need to conceptualize a life after death. But Crow knows better; 'he had picked that skull empty' long ago. The indirect reference to Hamlet explains Crow's use of pretended madness as a ruse to remain propaganda-proof. He is not fooled into thinking of salvation after death as an answer. What is dead is dead. Crow's reaction throughout remains ingenuous yet disdainful and blasé, a perfect answer to the super-cerebral bombardment of words. He watches objectively, never taken in, always in control and never fooled one bit.

'Crow's Theology' is a poem about the control of the world. It is clear from the context that Crow perceives the universe as an arena where two Gods struggle for control. One God 'loves his enemies'. Yet, Crow intuitively acknowledges the presence of a God who 'loved the stones and spoke stone' i.e. the part of nature that is usually considered not eligible to be saved since it is beyond the bounds of 'salvation'. Crow's anger that the God which the Western world so piously regards as the only God falls short of what Crow expects in a deity provokes him to an attack of brash presumptuousness in the next poem 'Crow's Fall' where he dares match his power against that of the sun. The underlying theme is that the universe is not governed by divine love but by power and one God is bigger and has 'all the weapons'. 'Crow's Theology' points out an underlying paradox of creation. Crow defers to a God who loves him and 'speaks Crow' (an amusing play on 'to eat crow'). Yet, which God loves the 'shot-pellets' by which crows are killed. Paradoxically, even though Crow is sustained by the God of love (an indirect reference to the sparrow fallen by God's edict in *Hamlet*) he feels more at home with the God of stone, silence and shot-pellets. Crow is rather resentful of the God who not only loves his enemies but has 'all the weapons'. In context with the previous poem Crow is being tested — this time with the sin of pride which might understandably overtake someone who believed that 'God loved him' and moreover, 'spoke Crow'. Western theology of necessity entails the sin of pride, particularly in view of the dogma that states God created man in his own image. Yet Crow's outrage over the fact that the God of love is in control leads him to challenge the status quo in 'Crow's Fall'.

## Chapter Four
## PLUCKED CROW

The warning implicit in Crow's recognition that the God in charge has all the weapons is ignored by Crow and pride inflates him with a false feeling of power. Consequently Crow begins overreaching himself which leads to 'Crow's Fall'. In this poem Hughes draws on a central episode in the Winnebago Trickster Cycle where Trickster's 'Buttocks got thoroughly scorched and sore for what he had trapped was the sun'.[21] While calling to mind the egocentrism described by the Greek idea of hubris, the Christian concept of pride (the Original Sin according to St Augustine) and the self-centredness denounced by Camus in the non-Christian context of *The Fall*, Hughes's 'Crow's Fall' draws upon two Hellenic myths. Both involve Apollo the god of the sun whose spiritual significance in mythology is identified with light which displaces darkness. In one story, during the war against the giants, Apollo transforms himself into a white crow. A second tale presents the crow as being originally white; Apollo, however, became angry at the bird for bearing news of the adultery committed by Princess Koronis and turned Crow black.[22] Besides being the god of the sun Apollo is often referred to as the god of truth. Thus Crow, by bringing Apollo the story of the falsehood of his Princess, is in effect making Apollo aware of his own limitations. And since the Crow was originally Apollo's favourite bird he acts on what the Crow has told him and kills his wife with one of his death darts. Too late Apollo repents of his rashness but he punishes the Crow for its untimely disclosure by changing its feathers from pure white to intense black. Moreover he forbids the crow to fly any longer with the other birds, an incident that provides the basis for the next poem, 'Crow and the Birds'. We also recall that Apollo was coerced into permitting his son Phaeton to drive the chariot of the sun. Phaeton came too close to the earth, scorching it and forced Jupiter to shoot down the chariot, killing Phaeton. A parallel Greek myth concerning Daedelus and Icarus ended similarly with the death of Icarus when he flew too close to the sun.[23] Viewed in the context of the entire book's development, 'Crow's Fall' marks Crow's first ebb of strength. He is seen refusing to accept his own limits as he challenges the sun, a force far superior to a white crow. He attacks this disconcerting power for being 'too white'. In his vanity he gets 'his strength flush and in full glitter' and fluffs 'his rage up'. He attacks but returns from the battle 'charred black' and then denies his obvious defeat. 'Up there, he managed,/Where white is black and black is white, I won.' Rationalizing his defeat in a way that suggests pathos, humour and self-deprecating irony he deludes himself and denies his limitations. Just as the first disobedience of man brings sin and death into the world (Genesis: Chapter 3) and as Lucifer was cast down for his presumption, so the next poem 'Crow and the Birds' presents an image of Crow ostracized to his proper realm — garbage.

Despite Crow's sardonic attitude 'Crow and the Birds' finds him forbidden to fly with the eagle 'through a dawn distilling of emerald'. His rationalization of his defeat in the previous poem recalls Satan's involved self-justifications after being cast out of heaven in *Paradise Lost*. Here we find Crow the way Dante pictured Satan in *The Divine Comedy,* buried up to his neck in ice. While other birds are singing and flying Crow is found 'spraddled head-down in the beach-garbage, guzzling a dropped ice-cream', in what might be an indirect reference to 'let be the finale of seem' (the end of all self-delusion) in Wallace Steven's poem 'The Emperor of Ice Cream'.[24] All the other birds steer clear of man and his products; 'the Woodpecker drummed clear of the rotovator and the rose-farm/ And the peewit tumbled clear of the laundromat.' Only Crow guzzles garbage and true to his scavenging nature eats the leftovers. The Trickster, we recall, is as often a victim as a perpetrator of trickery and punishment is the theme of both this and the next poem 'Criminal Ballad'.

This poem is Crow's song of a man stained with death at the moment of his birth. He grows through childhood and with his every step someone dies. When the time comes for him to aid his own wife and children, he refuses. He has the blood of two generations on his hands: those who died giving him life and those he allowed to die by refusing his responsibility to them in life. The title of 'Criminal Ballad' probably refers to the ballad Francois Villon wrote in the fifteenth century titled 'Ballad of the Hanged Man'.[25] At the time, Villon was a convicted criminal awaiting his own hanging and wrote the poem in prison. Like the main character in this poem Villon refuses to take the responsibility for his crimes; the rain, he says, has washed hanged men clean and he defends himself by pleading to God for absolution (all the while crows come to pluck out the eyes of hung men). This is a poem about paying the piper. For every birth ('When he was born') and for every life ('When he sucked') there must be a death ('An old lady's head sank sideways'). This is the law of Karma, yet the man will not pay the price. He laughs in selfish glee at both the suffering caused by his indifference and at his ability to avoid the consequences. Trickster, we recall, always prided himself on his ingenuity in being almost always able to escape the punishment due him for his frauds and deceits. The connection is obvious. The man is a criminal since he always has others pay the price for him. When he has sex a woman has to bear his child. When he was born a woman died. Ironically, by not paying all along, he ultimately must relinquish his wife and children — a sacrifice which drives him to a laughter indistinguishable from an insane detachment, 'And under the leaves he sat weeping/Till he began to laugh.' The reference to 'the sparrowfall natural economy' and the 'woman of complete pain . . . calling to him all the time/From the empty goldfish pond' suggest one of the earliest acknowledgments of having 'assailed the daughter of God', as Hughes later expresses it in *Gaudete*.[26] The reference to the sparrow's fall in *Hamlet* is a recurrent metaphor in Hughes's poetry. For everything man receives he must contribute something; the natural economy is one for one. But this criminal lets women, men and his own children pay the price for him. His crime is getting something for nothing. The imagery suggests a parasitic vampire that connects with Crow's voracious hunger. The criminal greedily sucks in and stores all the life around him and his mind, like a clogged waterpipe, shatters driving him mad, much like the story of Admetus who has his children die for him. One cannot break universal laws and be exempt from suffering. Consequently, the next poem 'Crow on the Beach' continues the exploration of what is meant by 'Crow's Fall' and illustrates the eternal suffering that grows out of the avoidance of punishment.

In the Blackfoot cycle of Trickster each episode marks a stage in Trickster's education. While the first tales deal with 'the creation of the earth, the origin of languages', and the 'origin of death', at the end Trickster has evolved and becomes 'a more differentiated individual . . . conversant with nature . . . good and evil'.[27] Thus while a specific crime was responsible in 'Criminal Ballad' for one man's suffering, 'Crow on the Beach' is shaped around existential suffering and the sea is used as a generalized symbol for that which is beyond man's

limited awareness. Crow watches the actions of the sea and
ponders without being able to understand. Crow, lonely and
naked, 'knew he grasped/Something fleeting'. His suffering
arises from the realization that nature does not depend on
Crow. Crow grasps the absolute indifference of the universe
to his existence; 'He knew he was the wrong listener unwanted/
To understand or help.' While he confronts eternity, looking at
the sea in awe, he understands there is a larger meaning to life
but, tragically, he knows it is unavailable to him. He stands in
much the same position as the narrator in Matthew Arnold's
poem 'Dover Beach'.[28] 'The turbid ebb and flow' of human
misery that Arnold sensed so poignantly in the context of a
lost faith, symbolized by the ebb-tide of humanity, becomes in
'Crow on the Beach': 'the sea's ogreish outcry and convul-
sion'. The difference is that while Arnold knows that his suffering stems from the ebbing away of the religious faith which
once linked Western man together, Crow, the beast, cannot
divine the source of his pain and cannot understand 'what
could be hurting so much'. In fact, the unavailability of Christ
and his suffering leads Crow to contemplate Christ as 'The
Contender'.

In 'The Contender' Hughes alters aspects of the Christian
redemption myth so that instead of a self-sacrificing Christ
we have a self-assertive, obstinate and self-centred protagonist:
'There was this man and he was the strongest/Of the strong.'
Although an obvious Christ-figure, embodying the mightiest
powers and forces of the earth as he 'gritted his teeth like a
cliff', his purpose in Crow's account in coming into the world
was not, despite Old Testament literature, to move mountains and free the Jewish people. This poem instead presents
Christ as an adamant, self-contained entity who ignores the very
people who considered him their saviour. Rather than comforting those women who, according to the Biblical account
(vide Matthew 27: 55—56 'and many women were there which
followed Jesus from Galilee, ministering unto him: among
whom was Mary Magdelene and Mary the Mother of James')
came to salve his wounds as he lay on the cross, this Christ
offers no solace to them or himself as 'their tears salted his
nail-holes/Only adding their embitterment/To his effort'.
Unlike the Biblical story where Christ leaves the imprint of his
visage on Veronica's cloth, Hughes's figure merely 'abandoned
his grin to them' — the rictus of concentrated self-involvement.
'His sandals', which in the Gospels are mentioned in the con-

text of going out and spreading the news of salvation (as in Acts 12:8 and Mark 6:9) 'could not move him . . . All the men in the world could not move him' with their arguments. Instead of gathering little children around him and telling them theirs is the kingdom of Heaven (as in Mark 10: 14–16) he leads them to despair: 'And they lost their courage for life.' All of these futile efforts further emphasize the fact that his coming had nothing to do with man's redemption but rather with his own ego. He is seen enduring and outlasting the most moving forces this world offers: mountains rose and fell and the pleas and tears of women, the arguments of men and the appeals of little children seem powerless to alter his impassive nature. Although eons pass and the oak forests and mountains disappear 'with the hawks wing', the Contender still 'lay crucified with all his strength/On the earth', still struggling. As he grins 'toward the whole paraphernalia of the heavens' Hughes gives the impression that Christ disdains that vast universe created by God his father and thinks it all rather superfluous. He continues grinning 'Into the ringing nothing' ultimately proclaiming the non-existence of anything beyond the obvious paraphernalia of the stars.

While all religions utilize the theme of the test of the would-be saviour (e.g., the Buddha-to-be is tested by Maya, the lord of illusion under the bo tree), Hughes's 'contenders' (for the title of saviour) suffer out of self-centred not magnanimous and self-sacrificing, endurance. In this version, Christ refuses to die and lives on and on. In doing so he forfeits for man the salvation which is contingent on his death and successful resurrection. This, after all, is the purpose for which he was sent. His pride is related to his unwillingness to accept fate; his suffering benefits no one although his state of torment might have been brought to an end at any time. Christ, like Oedipus, Prometheus and several other of Hughes's larger-than-life protagonists, seems incapable of death. He nails himself to the cross voluntarily, not as an act of salvation but as a 'trial of strength' that is admitted to be senseless. Yet strangely, throughout his trial Christ is grinning. There is no mention of his death or resurrection; he just extends his death into life and life into death. This self-centred figure is not only a key to poems in CROW (e.g. 'Oedipus Crow' and 'Crow's Vanity') which pivot on the theme of pride but 'The Contender' clearly anticipates Hughes's later choice of Prometheus (the immortal Titan chained for centuries in intolerable torment upon a high crag in punishment for giving man the gift of fire) as a central character in a series of poems, *Prometheus on His Crag*.[29] The difference is that whereas Oedipus and Christ suffer, no positive benefit proceeds from their anguish. Prometheus suffers because he refuses to repent of what he has done and Hughes clearly believes a positive benefit comes from his suffering. In effect Hughes sees suffering in a new light, especially as it relates to the self-sacrificing aspects of the scapegoat.

'Oedipus Crow' is a cautionary tale which alerts Crow to the tendency within himself from which Oedipus suffered: pride. Oedipus was lamed as a mark of his swollen ego and Crow also is pictured dangling 'from his one claw-corrected'. The story of Oedipus is one of the most literal portrayals of the inescapable nature of one's origins. Crow too suffers from the same arrogance and over-confidence that destroyed Oedipus. First, Crow tries to free himself from his mother ('Mummies stormed his torn insides/With their bandages and embalming honey'). Crow fears being turned into a corpse by the sickening sweetness of a mother who binds him to her with the force of death. Unable to tolerate her binding sweetness, Crow 'vomited empty' — losing his tortured insides and the benefits (as well as liabilities) of a mothering influence. Next, the force of tradition oppresses him and he uproots himself by biting his foot, as animals sometimes do to escape a trap, 'through the bone'. But this too leaves him bereft of equilibrium. Polybus had named the foundling Oedipus precisely because of his maimed foot. In both cases the physical malady is symbolic of psychic self-mutilation. Love too he perceives as entangling his brains 'with primroses, dogroses' and he next forfeits his capacity to love to rid himself of the threat. One after another he rejects the forces which guide his life as soon as he perceives them to be threatening to his freedom. But all anyone has, as Crow is reminded, is the earth, a mother, the chance to love and death itself, so that to flee from these elements is to mutilate oneself. Having rejected and consequently been rejected by the sources of life and continuity, Crow at the end is only 'just alive', the 'One-legged, gutless and brainless . . . rag of himself'. For the first time in CROW we observe a central element common to several variants of the Winnebago Trickster cycle: Crow feels fear and this indicates 'an awakening consciousness and sense of reality, indeed, the beginning of a conscience'.[30]

The element of self-delusion present in 'Oedipus Crow' underlies 'Crow's Vanity' as well. Everything in the material world, states Ecclesiastes 5: 10—17, is a potential source of vanity. Every monument man constructs is meant to conceal the grinning face of what is waiting behind the mirror — the reality of death. Crow's breath 'in the evil mirror' forms visions of civilizations as he tries to look beyond the world (here symbolized by brief glimpses of some of the seven ancient wonders) to the ultimate reality. But the tangible hides the intangible from his sight. The towers, the hanging gardens of Babylon and burning furnaces appear (as in Daniel 3: 13—25). Crow is caught in a web of ceaseless reasoning, a spinning out of images for which Hughes finds the metaphor of 'breathing too heavy and too hot'. In his breath that fogs the mirror Crow sees all the things of which man is proud. Again and again he wipes the mirror in a vain attempt to see 'the usual grinning face'. The irresistible force of illusion which Hughes equates with self-deluding vanity keeps projecting new images, making self-knowledge impossible. The ceaselessly generated wonders of the material world keep arising, coming between Crow and his 'grin', his real self. Ultimately a belief in the reality of what are after all but vain monuments built from pride prepares the way for 'A Horrible Religious Error'.

The fall from grace is closely related to the sin of pride and self-deluding vanity. Lucifer, as a serpent, used the appeal to vanity inherent in his offer of immortal life and God-like awareness as the chief argument in favour of the forbidden fruit (in Genesis, Chapter 4). The promise of immortality is conveyed by the serpent's 'double flameflicker tongue'. When 'man's and woman's knees melted' and their brows bumped the ground Hughes indirectly refers to the punishment visited on the serpent for his part in betraying man to his own weakness. Crow's attitute throughout the poem is quite nonchalant; while man and woman collapse, whispering 'Your will is our peace!' Crow 'beat hell' out of the serpent and ate it. The serpent is described as 'the sphynx of the final fact', a reference to its role in throwing out a riddle to perplex human reasoning. The devil appears wrapped in alibis ('its alibi self'), riddles and deceit. The special twist here is that Crow is able to deal with evil far more ably than a virtually impotent God. This points up the function of Crow as a saviour/trickster, an idea present in almost every version of the Trickster cycle. As Jung comments, the Trickster is 'a forerunner of the saviour . . . he is both sub-human and super-human, a bestial and divine being'.[31] Hughes combines this feature of Trickster mythology with Spenser's description of the combat between the forces of truth, personified as the Red Cross Knight, with religious error as a dragonlike serpent in Book One of his philosophical allegory *The Faery Queene*.[32] According to one of the original shaman myths of the Winnebago Indians, Trickster was created to protect human beings from being molested by evil spirits. From beyond memory this is one purpose they believe Trickster has always had and it certainly explains Crow's eagerness to dispose of an evil serpent before whom God is impotent and man and woman are utterly submissive. In view of Hughes's later attraction to the Prometheus legend this dramatization of Crow beating and eating 'the serpent' plainly shows Crow's kinship as a younger immature version of Prometheus — both figures have elements of the saviour in their makeup.

In 'Crow Tries the Media' Hughes plays with the fable of the Rook Among the Muses, which is about a crow who wishes to sing as sweetly as a nightingale.[33] This cannot be and instead of the nightingale's lightly trilled notes all that comes out of crow is a raspy caw as though 'a tank had been parked on his voice'. Nightingales were often kept, according to legend, to sing in captivity for Roman Emperors, a point referred to by Crow when his 'throttle was nipped between the Roman Emperor's finger and thumb'. Crow wants to sing clearly, simply and to the point; he is not, however, that kind of bird. He cannot leave himself behind. Even as he tries to express himself like the nightingale, the very syllables he produces are debased by his crowness, a fact he can not go beyond. The inappropriateness of his attempt produces the guilt which weighs him down 'like the slow millstone of London'. He tries to express his sense of the ethereal beauty of worlds beyond his own but his crow nature produces a twisted parody which causes him to lose sight ('her shape dimmed') of what he wants to express. Crow does not want to use the bastardized language of the detergent commercials or the ostentatious and romantic comparisons of the Cavalier poets. Interestingly, we remember that Hughes himself tried the media as a script reader for the J. Arthur Rank Studios in London, a fact implicit in the image of the movie 'Tycoons' in conference 'in a fog of cigar smoke'. Finally, Crow has to relinquish his delusion that he can reject being a crow in the interest of a more sublime vocation. Not to do so would ultimately torture him with the inescapable nature of his crowness, a situation dramatized in the next poem 'Crow's Nerve Fails'.

Forsaking his aspirations to be a nightingale Crow becomes more and more oppressed by who and what he is. In rejecting his nature he becomes a prisoner of it. He cannot come to terms with his past and he cannot be forgiven, so 'heavily he flies' burdened with his self-engendered guilt. He has eaten so much of the earth's crime and misery as a scavenger that he discovers in 'his every feather a fossil of a murder'. Crow, we remember, is alive because he has lived on the deaths of others; death is necessary for his life. His victims compose an integral part of his body. He is literally black ('visibly black') because each feather is the living result of a murder. Together, his feathers imprison him in the black garb of the prisoner: 'clothed in his conviction,/Trying to remember his crimes'. He flies 'heavily' because as he considers, conjures and reflects his burden of consciousness and suffering weigh him down. In essence, Crow is all too aware of the consequences of his guilt. The exact opposite situation prevails in the next poem, 'In Laughter'.

'In Laughter' explores our ability to laugh at other's tragedies with detachment. Laughter itself is a deliberate obliviousness to the destructive consequences of violent action. 'In Laughter' is an extraordinary slapstick view of birth, sex and death: three agony/ecstacies examined in light of the havoc they create. We visualize a cartoon in which scenes are happening that are so awful that we must laugh. 'The haggard mask on the bed' of the dying person, the 'wails' of the newborn and bones jumping from 'the torment flesh has to stay for' and finally sexual surfeit are the three archetypal events that transpire in a superimposition of centipede legs on a bed where cavorting, spasmodic agonies fuse together in a triple image of death, birth and sex. Aristotle was the first to observe that people laugh when there is violence without consequences.[34] In the imagery of the poem 'cars collide and erupt luggage and babies/ In laughter'. The most colossal joke played on humanity is sex. After human genitalia have had 'enough' man has to stay and pay the price. Sex and laughter are both described as scampering on 'centipede boots'. At the heart of the episodes described in the poem is violence. What we find funny is that towards which we are at least partly sadistic. Even though we know it's terrible to find such violence funny it is 'only human' to laugh and ultimately even violence becomes tiring and provokes our indifference. Our ability to be amused arises from our ability to detach ourselves from potentially tragic events by turning them into comedy through an emphasis on the kinetic qualities of cars colliding, aircraft crashing, a steamer upending or a meteorite smashing 'with extraordinarily ill luck on the pram'. In 'Crow's Nerve Fails' Crow felt imprisoned in a situation from which he could not escape — the condition of guilt itself, from the feeling that he was unable to be forgiven. The opposite situation prevails in 'In Laughter' where nothing carries a price tag and no situation is irrevocably serious. Finally, we reach a point where we have had 'enough' and then comedy becomes tragedy and the smile of the laughing mask becomes inverted in the following poem 'Crow Frowns'.

Crow's strength is prophesied in 'Crow Frowns'; from this point on we see him using that upon which he is fed to create, to produce and to play God's game. This poem marks the halfway point for Crow. While fully aware that he is made 'of nothing', he senses his destiny drawing near, 'he is the long waiting for something/To use him'. He begins to make the transition from Crow eating to Crow creating. The tragic frown after the comic laugh signals his longing for the fulfillment of the prophecy made in 'Crow Hears Fate Knock on the Door'. Each set of questions asked in the first stanza ('Is he his own strength?/What is its signature?/Or is he a key') is answered exactly within the second stanza: 'He is a prayer-wheel, his heart hums/ His eating is the wind.' The imagery is complex and beautiful: a key not only opens locks but is a musical notation which ties in with the prayer-wheel that accompanies a mantra chanted while the wheel turns. At one stroke Hughes combines the image of a musical 'signature' or key with Eastern mysticism and the ancient medieval concept of one's own individuality being a mirror of the cosmic signature. Crow defines himself as the 'long waiting', his 'footprints assail infinity' as the crow's track often appears as an inverted cross. From this point onward Crow tries his hand at creation but in 'Magical Dangers' the results are the opposite of what he expects.

Each time Crow thinks of something the tables are turned so that Crow is subjected to his creations run rampant. This poem is Hughes's variation on the theme underlying both Pygmalion and the story of Frankenstein: the creator overwhelmed by his creation. Crow creates thoughts which should bring him freedom but everything he creates whether 'a place', 'a fast car', 'the wind's freedom', 'a wage'. 'the soft and warm', 'intelligence' etc. turns on the creator through a quality of excess inherent in the original thought. Women he invents, as

Faust (after Christopher Marlowe's play) bodied forth Helen of Troy, 'gangplanked' Crow into a volcano. Intelligence jails him and everything he makes is his undoing. The image of the 'wage' that is 'cut unspoiled' from Crow's stomach not only refers to salt, the first wage paid and its role in preventing the spoilage of food, but the whole story of King Midas. Bacchus granted King Midas his wish when Midas asked to have everything he touched changed into gold. At first, he was overjoyed to have his wish granted (much as Crow is overjoyed to discover he can create what he wishes). Then Midas found to his dismay that whenever he touched bread it hardened in his hand. He now hated the gift he had coveted. Finally in answer to his prayer Bacchus delivered him from his problem by withdrawing the gift.[35] Although King Midas had a golden touch he nearly starved (as Crow says 'It choked him') before he could get rid of it. Hughes's ambivalence towards the dangers inherent in limitless creativity find expression here. Each of the references within the poem is a famous example of a wish that, once granted, undoes him who desired the wish. Thus the 'fast car' alludes to the myth of proud Bellerophon who, because of his pride and aspiration to be God-like, was thrown from Pegasus and was condemned to wander to earth for the rest of his life alone, friendless, no longer a proud warrior i.e. spineless ('It plucked his spine out'). So too Crow's wish for a palace fabricated from nothing, whose 'lintel' crashed on him, refers to Camelot and the legend of Merlin the Magician's role in its creation and destruction. At the end Crow is left immobile and his intellectual creations symbolized as 'a row of his black children' fly off on their own leaving him nothing. Hughes's choice of an unrhymed couplet to heighten the movement from wish to disastrous conclusion underscores the thesis/antithesis that one's mind makes a good servant but a poor master. The picture of motionless crows grouped in trees in communal roosting patterns emphasizes the intellectual sterility of Crow's endeavour. It is appropriate too that Hughes should show crows gathering in groups as they often do in Autumn and Winter since the following poem 'Robin Song' explores the yearly re-emergence of the natural forces of creation after a Winter lull.

Pliny tells the story of an argument between a robin who boasts that its plumage is beautiful in the Spring and a crow who answers that he is always equally beautiful.[36] 'Robin Song' is connected both with the previous poem and the poem

following, 'Conjuring in Heaven', through the idea of creation.
Here it is the yearly re-creation of the world each Spring which
is equated in the following poem with a magician's trick of
pulling something out of a hat of nothing. Just as the creator
was pursued by his creations in 'Magical Dangers' so here the
robin is hunted and crushed by Winter. 'I am the maker/Of the
world/That rolls to crush/And silence my knowledge.' 'Robin
Song' develops an aspect of Trickster that illuminates Crow's
position as a King in hiding. The Trickster is always presented
as a fool to stress that he is a king in exile, dwelling in the lower
worlds that he may bring forth the potential of himself and become a spiritual master.

'Conjuring in Heaven' takes the form of a magic act which
begins with a conspicuous show that Hughes has nothing
up his sleeve; 'So finally there was nothing./It was put inside
nothing.' After an elaborate display in which 'nothing' is
squashed, chopped up, shaken, turned inside out and finally
dropped to the ground, 'There lay Crow, cataleptic', in the same
state in which he was last seen at the end of 'Magical Dangers'
('Crow never again moved'). There is, of course, 'prolonged
applause in Heaven' at the ultimate rabbit out of the hat trick.
Crow, we realize, has simply been hibernating and is now again
ready to try his hand at creation in the next poem 'Crow Goes
Hunting.'

'Crow Goes Hunting' continues Crow's attempt to create,
this time using words. As with all of Crow's creations things
start well, go through various transformations and end up as
nothing. Crow hunts for the right words but he sees them
change form and lead him in a circle. Always too late to catch
them Crow remains 'speechless with admiration'. The poem is
circular. The bounding hare Crow seeks to describe becomes,
in quick succession, a concrete bunker, a flock of starlings, a
cloudburst, an earthquake and finally again a hare which eats
Crow's words. Crow's words are always one step behind the
hare that eludes his clumsy attempt to capture reality. The
sterility of intellectual constructs becomes, in turn, the theme
explored in 'Owl's Song'. The circular semantic game that
puts words into the position of limping behind the reality
they seek to describe is Hughes's acknowledgement, as a master
of language, that defining reality with words is intrinsically
doomed to failure. Interestingly other versions of the Trickster
legends portray Trickster as a Hare, always escaping his pursuers and mocking them by his speed. In one scene, Hare is

chased but easily eludes his pursuer; ' " Ooh, Hare, you will die for this.' " exlaimed the other and ran in pursuit of him. Whenever he was about to overtake him Hare would jump aside and thus escape.'[37] Hare is presented as a more sophisticated and more self-aware version of the Trickster and the underlying parable of Crow chasing Hare tells us that Crow is seeking to become, although unsuccessfully here, his higher self.

'Owl's Song' and 'Crow's Undersong' balance each other. In 'Owl's Song': 'He sang/How everything had nothing more to lose', a message of nihilistic despair. In 'Crow's Undersong' a mysterious 'she' communicates a message of hope. This poem is included to allow Hughes to distinguish Crow's message (which, on first hearing, might seem to bespeak anarchy and nothingness) from a true Nietzcheanism − symbolized by the Owl. As Coleridge once wrote: 'Forth from his dark and lonely hiding place . . . the owlet Atheism sailing on obscene winds to thwart the moon drops his blue-fringed lids and holds them close, and hooting at the glorious sun in Heaven, cries out "Where is it?" '[38] Whereas Crow perceives the world, stark and clear, as it is, the Owl thinks the world worse than it is. Since the Owl kills crows by night it appears as Crow's antagonist in a variety of legends.[39] The Owl's cry is especially feared since it is taken as a sign that death is near and although the Owl is traditionally associated with wisdom his 'wisdom' merely states that things will always get worse. Just as the previous poem explored the limitations of intellectual reasoning in truly capturing reality so the Owl's 'song' is a parody, ultimately self-defeating, of masculine logic. The Owl makes a pretence of casting off all hope. To show that he alone among all animals exists without sentimentality he deromanticizes the swan, symbol of courtly love (which makes the swan grow white with fear 'blanched forever!'). Next the Owl sings 'how the wolf threw away its telltale heart/And the stars dropped their pretence/The air gave up appearances/. . . The rock surrendered its last hope.' Although known for its courage in combat, the wolf becomes cowardly (with an aside to Edgar Allen Poe's story 'The Telltale Heart'); stars are no longer something to wish on − they 'drop their pretence'. Just as the 'air of hope' relinquishes its 'hopeful air' so the rock, symbolic centre of the Rock of Ages, centre of faith, surrenders 'its last hope'. Ironically the Owl's message of Sartre-like existentialism provides no comfort but terrifies him instead. When the Owl

stops and hears that all the rest of creation has been silenced
by his song he at last hears his own song; since it now applies
to him, with its message of hopelessness, he is frightened
out of his wits. The now totally inanimate universe seems to
be attacking him in the form of a giant owl and he 'sat still
with fear/Seeing the clawtrack of star/Hearing the wingbeat of
rock/And his own singing'.

'Crow's Undersong' is the antithesis of 'Owl's Song'; it begins
as a statement of the limits of the female principle in nature,
yet concludes with an affirmation of that upon which everything else is ultimately shown to depend. Woman, sings Crow,
emerges at birth a sheer animal and can only handle herself:
'She cannot manage an instrument'. Yet because of her all
pain is suffered and all mankind is built. She is identifiable with
the most elemental nurturing force and clearly foreshadows
the importance of the White Goddess in Hughes's later poetry.
Thus, Crow's answer to Owl begins as a comment on the short-
comings of women but concludes with the devastating observation that without her there would only be sterile intellect,
'no city' i.e. no civilization and no Nietzchean Owl prophets
who decry the possibility of hope: 'If there had been no hope
she would not have come/And there would have been no crying in the city/There would have been no city'. With her
nature is secure and the poem's title is an 'undersong' since
Crow sings about the underlying principle on which everything is constructed. In the next poem 'Crow's Elephant Totem
Song' the hyena and elephant replay the conflict between intellect and instinct within the larger cyclic unity of nature
that encompasses both forces.

Totem comes from the Ojibwa word 'Ototeman' which
means 'he is a relative of mine.'[40] A totem is a sympathetic
identification with an animal and usually only the Shaman is
privileged to unite with the animal symbol that stands for a god
in the totem ceremony. The purpose of the totem symbol is
to allow Crow to complement his nature and transcend himself
by uniting with the particular quality of the Elephant as animal
spirit. The Hyenas are crow-like with their 'blackened faces'.
They envy the self-sufficiency of the Elephant. They exist
in constant agony and self-torture whereas the Elephant seems
grand and placid. Beneath their compliments ('The Hyenas
sang in the scrub. You are beautiful') they desperately need the
Elephant to redeem their wretchedness. They blame him for
being unwilling to teach them the secret of his peace, to lead

them from their time-wracked existence, 'In hourly battle with a death the size of the earth'. Underlying the poem is the parable of the Pharisees' antagonism to Christ and a hatred that stems from their rage at being unable to partake of the qualities they see him possessing: they kill him not so much to destroy him as to try to tear out his entrails and assimilate his meaning. This drama underlies the poem's expression of all men's hope for something beyond immediate reality. The Hyenas, by contrast, sing: 'Beautiful is the putrid mouth of the leopard/And the graves of fever/Because it is all we have.' Crow-like with their grinning expressions the Hyenas are forced to slink about, eaters of carrion, sickening on their own laughter. They avenge themselves on the Elephant, because he cannot save them, by tearing his entrails. Although they can eat the Elephant they cannot assimilate his tranquility and must then deceive themselves and make the dismal best out of their position. The Elephant, resurrected like Christ, is now immune to destruction and with his 'ageless eyes of innocence and kindliness' inhabits a realm of 'deathless and painless peace'. He becomes a 'deathless star' taking his place in the Heaven that the Indian Vedas traditionally assign him.[41] He has travelled beyond time, space and death to find the light, the same realm towards which Crow aspires to move.

'Dawn's Rose' balances the imagery of new life (beginning 'A cry/Wordless/As a newborn baby's grieving') with the grief of old age, parting and death. Crow is newborn, yet ageless like time itself. The poem's scenic elements replay the death by gunshot seen previously in 'Crow Alights'. In that poem Crow was seen as Lucifer falling toward earth and this poem explores the connection between the 'star of blood' (which traditionally has been associated with Venus appearing red in the sky at dawn) and Lucifer, the fallen angel (whose name is a compound of red fiery light). The end of the life by gunshot is balanced against a baby's cry. The redness of dawn signifying the day's beginning merges with the redness of the 'star of blood', representing death. Underlying this poem and 'Crow's Playmates' as well is the loneliness and desolation of Crow, the aloneness of coming into the world and leaving it. The isolation Crow feels makes him attempt to create 'playmates'.

'Crow's Playmates' projects insights into why the gods were originally created — to humanize the universe, to offset loneliness and principally to project outward against the backdrop of the sky controlling forces in a universe desolate of meaning. The underlying myth has Crow (a pun on Chronos, the father of the gods) creating Zeus the mountain god, ('Lonely Crow created the gods for playmates — /But the mountain god tore free') whose home was on Mount Olympus and Poseidon, the river god: 'The river-god subtracted the rivers/From his living liquids'. Just as Zeus attacked his father Chronos and usurped the rulership of the universe, so all of Crow's creations reject their maker. What Crow creates is not his to possess. Crow's attempt to emulate God by creating the gods as playmates carries its own penalty as 'each tore from him/Its lodging place and its power.' Now more desolate than he was in 'Dawn's Rose', as each of his creations desert him we find Crow reduced to his essential self: 'So the least, least-living object extant/Wandered over his deathless greatness/Lonelier than ever.' Both this poem and the next 'Crowego' define the relationship of Crow to the god-heroes of mythology.

In 'Crowego', Crow's grinning visage is nourished by feeding off man's ego projections as they manifest themselves in the heroic legends surrounding Ulysses, Hercules and Beowulf. Whereas 'Crow's Playmates' explored the impulse behind the creation of god-playmates to populate the outer world, now Crow turns inward to create an 'ego' based on the heroes he has digested. Myths of different cultures are often quite similar; these myths generally are created around heroes with whom people can identify. Heroes, moreover, have both super-human powers and all-too-human weaknesses that destroy them. Crow steps in and scavenger that he is catches the heroes and devours them after they have failed to answer the culture's demands which they were created to satisfy (e.g. Ulysses was the last hero from the heroic age of Greece; Beowulf was the last pre-Christian culture hero). Heroes represent the collective ego of mankind and man will always need these heroic projections. Crow will always be supplied with the food of heroic images after they have been discarded and anticipates gorging himself, 'like a leopard into a fat land'. The three myths within the poem show Crow assimilating heroes at the point where they are no longer heroic. As an infant Hercules strangled two serpents sent to kill him but he himself was later unwittingly killed by Dejanira, his wife. In the poem, Crow 'strangled in error Dejanira' and gets the best part of the dying Hercules 'the gold melted out of Hercules' ashes' when Hercules cremated himself on Mount Aetna. Wrapping oneself in buffalo hides and wearing the horns and mane of the buffalo as a head-dress is a usual practice of chiefs, medicine men and Shamans in order to gain the animal's immense strength. Crow does the same with Beowulf's hide and 'Drinking Beowulf's blood' gains the strength to succeed where Grendel failed in his combat with Beowulf. The case of Ulysses is more subtle; 'Crow followed Ulysses till he turned/As a worm, which Crow ate.' In Crow's view when Ulysses, after Troy has been conquered, turns to go back home to resume a normal non-heroic existence (i.e., he fails to remain a hero) Crow eats him. Thus, appropriately, the great Ulysses is compared to a worm (e.g., the worm turns) which appropriately enough, Crow, a bird after all, then eats. Whereas the libraries of the world are filled with innumerable pages of books describing the exploits of every variety of hero Crow is portrayed as a completely inked black page whose wings are book covers; 'His wings are the stiff back of his only book./Himself the only page — of solid ink'. Like Spenser's 'deformed monster, foul and black as ink', Crow is never other than himself and is not compelled to dream up heroes to vicariously live out unreal wishes. Man may need heroes to measure himself against but Crow is his own measure and needs no other heroic projections on which to model himself.

'The Smile' begins a group of poems that join together the twin themes of tragedy and laughter. Like 'the grin' the smile comes at the most awful times and discloses the intrusion of death into life. The smile brings with it death in the form of a crucifixion and transfiguration; when nature smiles the earth cracks open revealing a chasm beneath man's superficial reality. The smile is portrayed as an earthquake that opens underfoot, splitting the 'skin of the earth', 'tossing the willows, and swelling the elm-tops/Looking for its occasion.' When it hits, steel screeches open, the pavement jumps and the poem focuses on 'the unlucky person's eye/Pinned under its brow', as the grin of ultimate reality lights for one instant on the face of the 'unlucky person'. The smile seems to occupy a special position in Hughes's mythology. It swings the direction of Hughes's poetry toward a pictorial form of expression — the poetry of gesture — associated with the Trickster. Hughes sees Crow as the arch-Trickster whose smile underlies the acid smiles of deceitful Machiavellian villains, the 'visor' smiles people use to mask reality and the aggressive smiles that 'went off with a mouthful of blood' or 'left poison in a numb place'. The poems in which the grin, the laugh and the smile are featured display profound annihilistic tendencies behind these gestures, an apocalytic intent which looks forward to the self-castigation and self-mockery implicit in Hughes's portrayal of an unnamed man in the next five poems.[42] The insulting and derisive representation of this un-named 'victim' begins here with the description of 'the crowd, shoving to get a glimpse of a man's soul/Stripped to its last shame'. Hughes's purpose in portraying the faults and exaggerated weaknesses of the 'unlucky person' in a series of poems which intertwine the smile with the grimace of caricature is to reveal the true man behind the mask of pretence. We note the absence of any trace of playfulness in this sequence which depicts the pathetic inadequacy, psychic ugliness and spiritual deformity of the subject-victim. Bearing in mind that Crow is a gallows bird, we understand these poems to be a form of hanging-in-effigy, a self-degradation, designed to give vent to both aggressive and regressive impulses.

In 'Crow Improvises' Crow takes to himself the prerogatives of godlike creation. The results suggest more of Frankenstein than Michelangelo's depiction of the Creation on the ceiling of the Sistine Chapel. Crow's improvisation consists in taking everything he has learned and trying to piece life itself together. Every attempt at creation produces destruction instead. In fact, the terrible destruction wrought on the man in the poem, as he loses his time sense, his name, his laugh, his 'weeper', his 'wordage', and his gonads, throws light on the punishment often visited, in myth, on the artist who violates the unspoken taboo of competing with the Creator. The 'spark' jumps between all the polarities of past and present, life and death in an obvious reference to the role played by the lightning spark, in the story of Frankenstein, which was intended to animate a body composed entirely of remnants. Since creation is held to be a prerogative of the divine it first looks as if the man is being destroyed as an expiation of the guilt incurred by competing with God for the title of creator. Looking closer we remember that we see this scene through the eyes of Crow. This is not a god-man who has been punished for attempting to transcend limits imposed by nature, but a victim, a grotesque monstrosity, the butt of caricature to be laughed at, grinned and mocked at by Crow. He is in the condition depicted by Jonathan Edwards in his sermon on the interminable agony of the sinner in Hell, like a spider suspended over the flames: 'So in one hand he held a sham-dead spider,/With the other he reached for the Bible'. While the impulse behind Crow's improvisation may have been to create a new man the result is a Frankenstein-like monster, an experiment that did not take. In the following poem, 'Crow's Battle Fury', Crow tries to re-assemble, after a fashion, this shattered hulk: 'His tattered guts stitched back into position/His shattered brains covered with a steel cowl'.

Just as a battle focuses aggressive instincts, so Crow's grinning laughter is not only an expression of his 'battle fury', but a defence against the anxiety experienced in the presence of the suffering creature he has created. It is impossible to say whether Crow is the tormented victim. He seems ready to both laugh and cry at the same time. Pandemonium breaks loose as Crow sounds his 'battle cry'. The imagery suggests the sordid side of night life in the city fused surrealistically with the painted masks of the dead lying in coffins after being made up by morticians. Crow's laughter at this spectacle appears as a contorted grimace, an expression of anger, fear and sobbing. Laughter is seen as a mask that forces aside expressions of grief and pain, a facial distortion that, in this poem, literally tears the face apart in a sudden upheaval of emotion. Crow suffers 'an attack of laughter' and is convulsed by it. At the same time, to laugh is to be beyond pain, to be superior, powerful and strong so that each appearance of laughter alerts us to a dreadful anxiety close at hand. 'Crow's Battle Fury' contains the imagery of a man going insane, becoming a casualty in the battle of life. When Crow attempts to rescue the man and put his torn body back together, Crow's re-creation is flawed when compared with the original. Crippled, blind, mentally incapacitated, the reconstructed man takes step by painful step. For Crow, the therapeutic importance of his laughter is that it allows him to fulfill the prophecy outlined in 'Crow Hears Fate Knock on the Door': 'I will be inside it as inside my own laughter' and although the man is beyond help Crow can still laugh himself away from humanity and its death. Laughter is a way of staying clear of the lurid images of pain experienced by the 'patient'. At the end the re-assembled 'patient' comes forward 'a step,/and a step,/and a step' (the shape of the words actually resemble stairs) but Crow is clearly laughing at the disaster his improvisation (in 'Crow Improvises') has caused.

The maimed figure at the centre of the series of poems beginning with 'Crow Improvises' and extending through 'Crow's Battle Fury', 'Crow Blacker Than Ever', 'Revenge Fable', and 'A Bedtime Story' is drawn from the archetype of the mutilated king (as portrayed in innumerable legends, including Osiris, Attis, Parzival, etc.) waiting to be healed. Significantly, this figure looks forward to Hughes's later choice of Prometheus chained to a mountainside, a vulture tearing perpetually at his liver. This one scene is a central episode in Hughes's poetry. It is presented and redisguised again and again, although certain distinguishing signs allow us to identify it wherever it occurs. In 'Crow Improvises' man's personality is shattered by an awareness beyond his capacity to endure. When he returns he is not as he was. Instead of being reborn stronger, happier and more in harmony with a universe whose energies he freely brings into productive harmony with himself, this man is in dire need of being healed from the experience of being blasted away from the realm of normality. Watching this scene is the figure of Crow, a grinning gargoyle, a comic devil looking down on the suffering picture which, in some mysterious way, he has been responsible for creating. The hatred Crow exhibits for the man, a hatred verging on tears, is the hatred of one part of the self that watches the other part of the self that has been mutilated. The man exists, as it were, under the evil eye of his own scrutiny — projected as the object of Crow's constant inspection. In essence, this scene is a metaphor of self-loathing. The dynamics of such an archetypal situation seem to demand that a sense of inner impoverishment expressed in images of desolation, worthlessness, emptiness, impotence, coldness, deadness and dryness must be answered by the voraciousness of Crow always hungry, feeding constantly. Hughes's poetry forever alternates between these two extremes. While his earlier poetry concentrates on predatory animals who draw others' lifeblood for their necessary survival, his most recent poetry in *Gaudete* renounces such isolated self-sufficiency and drawing on the myth of the Scapegoat manifests an underlying wish for complete absorption and merger into the eternal feminine. The person in the sequence of Crow poems no longer has a sense of his own identity. He feels himself to be unreal and disconnected. The imagery that describes him suggests a dead object, an automaton, a Frankenstein robot. Not only has he become an object, a thing without subjectivity but his personality appears as a parody of selfhood, an actor's impersonation of what it feels like to have a self. Knowing this we understand why Crow looks on his detached, disembodied, mutilated yet rebuilt true self with a mixture of helplessness, amusement and hatred. The split between the self that suffers and the self that watches is, paradoxically, a manoeuvre to preserve an identity that fears being devoured. The fear of being devoured is projected into Crow as that which does in fact devour life. What is most feared is the engulfment of the ego, here projected as the devouring force embodied in Crow. These two extremes, total isolation with its accompanying fragmented and emptied personality on one hand or complete engulfment where one is swallowed up on the other, comprise the extremes of a basic dilemma repeated over and over again in Hughes's poetry. To strip onself of the capacity to be devoured, to be lonely, isolated — that is, safe — determines the choice of self-depersonalization where one becomes an object. A universe in which there are only two possible extremes, detached self-sufficiency supported by perpetual stoicism or a complete merging and overthrow of identity through attachment to another, suggests the reason the split has occurred. The 'patient' has turned himself into a piece of machinery, ironically enough, to undercut the possibility that this will happen to him through a relationship with another person. What he most fears is engulfment so he takes away his capacity to act autonomously before a relationship with another person deprives him of his autonomy as a matter of course. In effect, fear of dependency produces an utter dependency.

'Crow Blacker Than Ever' projects onto the universe the dissociation of body and soul from which the fragmented man is obviously suffering. Crow takes God's place (and turns the idea of Christian redemption upside down) in fostering an unsuccessful attempt to 'nail heaven and earth together' without Christ. In 'A Childish Prank' Crow amused himself by playing a joke on God, man and woman but his attempt here is qualitatively different. We sense the urgency of his need to order the universe in his own image. Hughes's account of Crow's radical deviation from the usual account of Christian redemption centres around two qualities — God's discontent and man's dissatisfaction. The Bible shows a God who is sympathetic towards man and his plight after the fall and so he promises a Son who would reopen the possibility of spiritual grace to man. In this version, 'God, disgusted with man,/Turned towards heaven' deserting his creatures. And man instead of repenting and offering prayers and sacrifices is 'disgusted with God' and 'turned towards Eve'. Things were truly 'falling apart'. Now, deviating from the original story, Crow comes along and 'nailed them together,/Nailing heaven and earth together'.

Crow displaces Jesus as the instigator of resurrection, just as God, through Christ, provided man with a taste of what it is like to be God and God a chance to partake of human existence. Hughes draws on Dostoevsky's belief, expressed through his Grand Inquisitor, that Christ's arrival put man in the untenable position of being torn, on the one hand, by the prospect of an unreachable salvation through Christ while being tortured by the human condition which now appeared to man as entirely bestial. Neither man nor God could return to their initial state. Man could not give in to unqualified lust for Eve while being tormented by the possibility of spiritual fulfillment he had not known existed and God could not claim it was entirely man's fault since the situation had grown worse precisely because he had entered it ('Man could not be man nor God God'). In the usual view Christ's crucifixion was a victory over death but Crow's creation is the epitome of misery, death and decay. It is a patchwork job that does not work, a graft that simply will not take; 'then heaven and earth creaked at the joint/ Which became gangrenous and stank.' Like the Frankenstein creature in the previous poems whose psychological bonding is forced and thus begins to rot, creation itself is split into body and soul ('heaven and earth') and the attempt to rejoin them is doomed to failure. Gangrene develops when tissues are cut off from oxygen and creation itself, like the un-named man in the previous poems, is split from itself and not being able to live begins to die and dying begins to stink. Yet, it is precisely this image of body and soul joined by a 'gangrenous' crucifixion that constitutes the territory over which Crow sets the 'black flag of himself' — the skull and crossbone with which he stakes out his realm. The following poem 'Revenge Fable' takes this double vision of radical dissociation between body and soul into an examination of a man who so despises his connection with the earth that he steadily undercuts his own position until 'His head fell off like a leaf'.

Modelled on Aesop's Fables in which animals teach man lessons, 'Revenge Fable' expresses a moral about the probable results if man should succeed at his attempt to defeat nature. A man first determines the laws by which nature governs herself and then invents 'numbers and equations and laws' which direct nature's laws against nature herself. In the process of exploiting the earth for her material wealth and beating her into submission man has undermined and poisoned his own existence. Unwittingly, he has cut his own throat ('His head fell off like a leaf'). Although projected in the context of ecological despoliation this poem extends the theme of 'Crow and Mama' and 'Crow's Undersong' that the feminine principle of the earth-as-mother is the chief source of strength from which one cannot be severed without peril. The process of self-impoverishment by 'a person' who 'Could not get rid of his mother' is presented as an aggressive assault by civilization against mother earth, 'Obliterating her with disgusts/Bulldozers and detergents/Requisitions and central heating/Rifles and whiskey and bored sleep.' But, of course, mother-earth's revenge is that when she goes, man goes with her. The fear of engulfment that we saw projected in 'Crow and Mama' produces a reaction of such depersonalization that ironically, 'the person' destroys what he thought he was defending. As a way of underscoring the point, Hughes mentions Tolstoy who became a raving moralist 'Forbidding, screaming and condemning' at the cost of his own enormous gifts; the prolific novelist became the arid philosopher. After examining how and what it means in fable form to deny one's own nature and abjure nature itself through fear of having one's identity devoured, 'A Bedtime Story' depicts the emotional condition of 'a person' whose head has just fallen off.

It is plain that the person Hughes describes does not experience himself or his relation to other people in the ordinary way. This poem is an interior view of the fragmented person patched together in 'Crow Improvises'. Not being a total person he merely sees the surface of things with the 'camera' of his eyes. The real essence of things forever eludes him. We have the impression that he has just stumbled on the fact that he has been pretending for years to be real. In fact, he feels unreal as if he were becoming a thing: 'His arms had become just bits of stick.' He can no longer fool himself. Feelings of awe, amazement, heartfelt reactions are beyond him and in fact are something he fears. Just at moments when he begins to start to have real feelings his hands become 'funny hooves just at the crucial moment' as the bestial element intervenes. He lives through the eye of the camera and sees himself as a dead, sticky, tar-baby — half of a personality from which the most vital half has been cut. He does not need to see things with his eyes because all that matters to him is the surface of things. In fact references to scenes of the Grand Canyon and various natural disasters suggest an ironic portrait of a typical tourist. The metaphor of the camera suggests an essentially passive personality, someone

capable of precise description of what he has seen but incapable
of either initiating actions or sharing in the substance and weight
of relationships with others. Indeed his frenetic efforts at ob-
serving reality with his camera are violent simulations to con-
vince himself that he is real after all. Each time the person is in
danger of being overwhelmed he withdraws still further into a
state of quiescence. He turns himself as a matter of strategy into
something that's dead as a means of preserving an identity he
feels is under attack — plainly a vicious circle since each voluntary decrease in one's sense of self generates even more anxiety
and this sense of augmented helplessness has to be even more
desperately defended by a further reduction in lifelike qualities.
In desperation, he 'sat down to write his autobiography', that
is, to create a self through writing, an act of presumption for
such an unreal person. The possibility of coherent self-compre-
hension is beyond him and the attempt flounders. ' "I give up",
he said. He gave up./Creation had failed again.' Not surprisingly
Crow takes each obstacle that defeats man in this poem and
turns it into a triumphant celebration of himself in 'Crow's
Song of Himself'.

While modelled on Whitman's 'Song of Myself' in *Leaves
of Grass,* (even to the incantory pattern), 'Crow's Song of
Himself' is a grotesque parody where each attempt God makes
to get rid of Crow produces some additional evil. Whitman's
pantheistic, rampant egotism (Whitman is in everything and
everything is in Whitman) translates itself into Crow's extraordinary megalomania in claiming to be responsible for gold,
diamond, alcohol, money and all the tangible instruments
traditionally associated with man's greed, moral weaknesses,
etc. This poem is Crow's way of saying that he is integral to
creation and nothing can exist without him. The brutal
attempts by God to destroy Crow — he is hammered,
roasted, crushed, torn, blown-up, hung, buried and chopped
into two — each fail in a different way and contribute to
Crow's sense of omnipotence. Yet it is precisely this overweaning pride that sets up Crow for a tragic fall, through
*hybris* in 'Crow Sickened'.

Several interesting clues help us to define the nature of
the illness plaguing Crow. Crow's eyes are 'sealed up with
shock, refusing to see'. What he refuses to acknowledge (by
literally shutting his eyes to it) is not only his divorce from
an aspect of himself but a desperately maintained act of defence as well. What terrifies Crow most is meeting himself.

The fear that Crow meets is his own fear projected outward and re-experienced as if it were originating from a separate entity. We have the spectre of the self persecuted by its own fear. Crow's condition of separation from himself is, in essence, what is destroying him. One side of Crow 'Dived . . . journeyed, challenging', while viciously attacking the side of Crow that is mute, defensive and most importantly subject to attack. At one moment he is this self and at another the tremendously fearsome predator, Crow, the destroyer, who is capable of going through anything to feed on what he wishes to consume — who justifiably inspires dread. The imagery of the poem is divided between a portrayal of Crow's fear of being consumed, an inside view so to speak and the destructive attributes of Crow breaking in from the outside. Crow is not only estranged and in conflict with himself but, paradoxically, the more one aspect of Crow gathers power, other selves within Crow feel subject to invasion. This terror before the mercilessness of an aspect of oneself has a peculiar edge to it that stems from the need to conceal from oneself the realization that one no longer has an integral identity. This explains the fearful, yet plaintive, question: 'Where is this somebody who has me under?' Who, Crow asks, is making me incapable of participating creatively in the world? Who causes me to feel powerless, null, dead and void? The imagery suggests being held under water until one is engulfed, or a wrestler who has clamped one's extremities to the mat. The horrifying realization that Crow is his own worst enemy betrays a tragic self-ignorance that accounts for Crow's ambivalence and dread: 'With all his strength he struck. He felt the blow./Horrified, he fell.' This poem not only sets the stage for Hughes's examination of the tragic self-ignorance of Oedipus in 'Song for a Phallus', but it places Crow squarely in the context of the Trickster who is 'forever running into pain and injury' and not only plays malicious jokes but falls victim in turn. Crow creates evil, violence and destruction from which he himself is not exempt. Literally this is what happens in 'Crow Sickened' as Crow decides to ambush death and kill it. The instant he strikes, he discovers to his horror that every movement he directs towards finding his illness leads him back to himself. Finally, with supreme effort, he closes his eyes, strikes and discovers he has ambushed himself. His condition is like the Winnebago Trickster, as Paul Radin says, 'whose right hand fights with his left, who burns his anus and eats his own intestines, who endows the parts of his body with independent existence and who does not realize their proper functions, where everything takes place of its own accord, without his volition'.[43] With Crow, as with the Trickster, 'it's impossible to tell where his cunning ends and his stupidity begins and which of the two qualities is the primary one.'[44]

A number of Crow poems, such as 'Oedipus Crow' and 'Song for a Phallus', are variations on the Oedipus myth.[45] In 'Song for a Phallus' Hughes starts, as did Sophocles, with the child Oedipus who was told by the oracle at Delphi that he was destined to slay his father and commit incest with his mother. In this poem the father is apparently aware of the prophecy as he cries to the child yet in the womb: 'You stay in there . . . Because a Dickybird/Has told the world when you get born/You'll treat me like a turd.' And in an unwitting fore-warning of the second part of that dread prophecy his mother shouts, as her husband prepares to castrate the boy (and avoid the inevitable): 'O do not chop his winkle off/His Mammy cried with horror/Think of the joy will come of it/Tomorrer and tomorrer.'

The original story where Laius, Oedipus' father, knew the gods did not decree empty prophecies and so had the child abandoned to die on a lonely mountain (Mt Cithaeron) with its feet pierced and tied together, forms the background for Hughes's, 'Daddy had the word from God/He took that howling brat/He tied its legs in crooked knots/And threw it to the cat/Mamma Mamma.' Besides being a grotesque and excrutiatingly funny parody that pokes fun at the myth of Oedipus, Hughes reworks the ballad form so that the refrain 'Mamma, Mamma,' is transformed both into a mock chorus and captures the sound a doll makes when it is squeezed.

As legend tells us Oedipus was rescued from the ordeal by a shepherd and raised as the son of Polybus and Merope in Corinth. In Crow's account, Oedipus 'had the luck/For when he hit the ground/He bounced up like a jackinbox/And knocked his Daddy down.' Moreover the first half of the prophecy is un-knowingly fulfilled as 'Stone dead his Daddy fell'. In Greek mythology Thebes was then ravaged by a frightful monster shaped like a winged lion with the breasts and face of a woman, the Sphinx. Seated on a rock she put a riddle to every Theban that passed by and whoever was unable to solve it was killed by her. The riddle asked the identity of 'A being with 4 feet which has 2 feet and 3 feet and only 1 voice; but its feet vary and when it has most it is weakest.' In the dramatization of

Sophocles Oedipus answers the riddle posed by the Sphinx
(man as an infant, in his prime and finally in old age supported by a stick) after which the Sphinx inexplicably kills herself. In Hughes's version, 'The Sphinx began to bawl/Four legs
three legs two legs one leg/Who goes on them all', but instead
of his classic intelligent answer resulting in the Sphinx's death,
'Oedipus took an axe and split/The Sphinx from top to bottom/
The answers aren't in me he cried/Maybe your guts have got
em.' So this first major deviation from the original story presents Oedipus not as an intelligent, rational man but rather
as a homicidal maniac.

What the Sphinx held was far from favourable, as 'Out there
came ten thousand ghosts/All in their rotten bodies', mirror-
ing perhaps, the devastating drought and sickness which plagued
Thebes in consequence of the incestuous marriage of Oedipus
and Jocasta. In a fulfillment of the second part of the prophecy
Oedipus 'stabs his Mammy in the guts/And smiles into her
face'. But his mother bemoans the fact that 'What you [Oedipus]
can't understand . . . You sleep on it or sing to it.' In the original
story Jocasta hangs herself out of shame and grief upon learning
the truth. Here Jocasta tells Oedipus that he can only relate
to what he does not understand through sexual aggression or
aesthetic enticement. In effect Oedipus reacts to what he
cannot comprehend with his emotions rather than with his
intellect. Blinded, as in the original tale when he tore out his
eyes that he might not see the misery which he had wrought
but here figuratively by his irrationality, 'Oedipus raised his
axe again/The world is dark, he cried/The world is dark one
inch ahead/What's on the other side?' Oedipus' unwillingness
to acknowledge his own ignorance not only provides him with
a justification for his irrational acts but dramatically projects
his own blindness onto the world. He asks the question underlying all other questions: What lies beyond the grave? To find
the answer he probes not with his mind but with his axe and
'Split his Mammy like a melon'. What he finds is 'Himself
curled up inside/As if he had never been born'. Violence is so
much a part of Oedipus' nature that to find out about the
afterlife he splits Jocasta open and discovers himself as a foetus
in the womb. At the end Oedipus is back where he started.
The imagery is clear; he's never progressed at all. His frantic
violence, his murderousness have been directed not to discover truth but to try to cheat fate and escape the burden of
understanding himself. Because of his blind irrationality and

primitive reactions he is no further in his quest for truth than when he started (unlike the long-suffering but wiser Oedipus in Sophocles' *Oedipus at Colonus*) and is thus fated to re-experience the vicious cycle of his own life forever. This poem and the next, 'Apple Tragedy', provide comic relief while telling us that Crow's limitations are those of man as well since time began.

'Apple Tragedy' is an explicit and bizarre reversal of the Fall in the Garden of Eden. God is assigned the role of corruptor and accordingly introduces the apple to Eve saying, 'You see this apple?/I squeeze it and look — cider.' This is a prank such as might be played by Trickster. Crow here has a freer hand than he did in the earlier Eden poem 'Childish Prank', but the problem is that Crow has his characters mixed up. Although using Eden as portrayed in Genesis as the basis Crow inverts things so that the serpent not God is shown resting 'on the seventh day' after creating the universe (as in Genesis, Chapter 2: Verse 2). God, strangely enough, is cast in the role of tempter but apple cider not the apple is the catalyst (in contrast to Genesis, Chapter 3: Verses 1–19). Traditionally the blame for corrupting mankind is put on the serpent. Here God is assigned that role albeit inadvertently. He is depicted as doltish, senile and utterly without foresight as to the results of introducing fermented liquor into Eden. God appears as little more than a glorified bartender who is pleased with the new concoction he has dreamed up. Fermented cider gives Eve a sex drive and the serpent accommodates her. Adam is told and tries to commit suicide by hanging 'himself in the orchard', an indirect reference to the suicide of Judas incurred by his guilt over betraying Christ. Here God betrays man by introducing sin into the world. Eve stamps on the serpent's head (screeching 'Rape! Rape!'). This is an ironic reference to the many medieval depictions of the Virgin stamping on the head of Satan. God, rather inappropriately, says 'I am well pleased' in an obvious reversal of God's approval of the Biblical Creation. One fascinating detail is Hughes's picture of the serpent 'curled up into a questionmark' after having a 'good drink'. The questionmark is an apt symbol for man's curiosity about the knowledge of good and evil which a bite from the apple plucked from the forbidden tree of knowledge was supposed to bring. In 'A Childish Prank' Crow, not God, had given Adam and Eve their souls and here it is through God's intervention that the sexual instinct comes into the world in the most destructive way. God's appearance results in chaos, not order; the serpent is seen as the creator and God is the tempter. At this point the ideal paradise of Eden is transformed into a scene of irreconcilable discord between man and woman and man and God as Eden mysteriously provides a 'chair' with which Adam smashes the snake. The serpent tries to explain 'But drink was splitting his syllable'; his message becomes unintelligible because of his forked tongue. Throughout CROW God has been seen as an inactive dolt, or a foolish, childish and naive interloper. Here, for the first time, he exerts himself on man's behalf and what results is apple cider, a sex-crazed Eve and everything gone to Hell. The starkly etched black comedy of 'Apple Tragedy' arises from Crow's detached viewpoint and his objective, if somewhat confused look at cherished human beliefs. Crow is, after all, the Trickster and understandably his versions of familiar Biblical stories, human situations and character traits tend to be sardonic caricatures and often grotesquely funny parodies of Christian (as well as Classical) myths.

The underlying metaphor of 'Crow Paints Himself into a Chinese Mural' is 'becoming incognito' by literally painting oneself and blending into a landscape. The central figure in this poem is a great general, now a ghost, forever silent at a chess game fingering one piece and deciding which move to make out of all the innumerable possibilities. The chess piece he's considering moving would, most probably, be the castle or rook (since both Crow and the 'blackbird' mentioned in the poem belong to the same species). The chess metaphor continues through the following poem 'Crow's Last Stand' where we see an embattled Crow withdrawn to the tower of a 'scorched fort' (i.e. of a castle). Placing Crow in a Chinese mural is Hughes's way of emphasizing his immortality in the context of the work of art, in much the same way as scenes depicted on the Grecian urn immortalized by Keats (as well as Wallace Steven's 'Thirteen Ways of Looking at a Blackbird'). Yet even as Crow blends into the environment and becomes part of the scenery his disappearance into invisibility as a principle in nature that will always exist is compensated for by the repeated cry of earth itself 'trying to speak' in order to raise itself back into life. The poem dramatizes the appeal of ceasing to exist along with the fear that one may disappear altogether in a way that may prevent regaining a foothold in life. A ghost may quite legitimately be described as an entity whose existence is that of death in life. Like the ghost, the Chinese mural is two dimensional and accurately mirrors the entombed state of the speaker. Despite the reference to the ghost as 'a great general' his situation suggests utter impotence coupled with a compulsion to make contact with the real world. A mood of futility pervades the poem. The cause of the detachment and estrangement from reality endured by the ghost is clearly connected with the image of a wedding photo 'scorched black edged in wet ashes', an image of penance for the dead. It is not accidental that the photo is blackedged like a death announcement since the world in which the ghost exists, in the mural, is in limbo. Why does the ghost hesitate for one million years motionless to make his move and why do the dusk, the spears and the banners all wait for his decision. He's perpetually about to act: he waits in a state of empty omnipotence in which the possibility of moving a chess piece is a delusion, a phantom creativity that barely disguises a profound powerlessness. In fact, the powerlessness of the speaker in the guise of endless possibilities is the driving theme of the poem. The ghost's elaborate, yet futile preparations as to which move to make suggest that as long as nothing is done, everything is possible. The ghost wishes to remain perpetually uncommitted, to forever withhold itself from making a choice. Thus the law governing Crow's ascension to power demands a lessening of the speaker as a human being. The purpose of this poem and indeed the next five is to set Crow up as a principle in the universe. First the sun, then the sea and stone are seen in relationship to Crow. These are three of the four basic elements (fire, water, and earth). Crow himself, of course, represents the fourth (air).

'Crow's Last Stand' projects an image of the sun's burning expanse raging and charring against Crow whose precarious strength is reduced to a scorched 'eye-pupil'. Crow, evidently, cannot be finally extinguished although burned to his very essence and rendered as one renders metal; he endures every effort to destroy him and survives. Throughout *CROW* he has been hammered, beaten, roasted and subjected to fiercely destructive onslaught, yet his essence cannot be destroyed: the 'Crow's eye-pupil' that first peeped through the black doorway of the wall in 'The Door'. His condition is equated with Custer's last stand and here the 'glaring' sun is his enemy. This image suggests that Crow has been subjected to the gaze of an extraordinary penetrating power that glares at him with such scrutiny that everything aside from his power of observation has been withered; he is being incinerated by the look of 'the other'. What endures in Crow are his perceptions. The imagery of the furnace in the previous poem ('the sulphur blast . . . the fright glare') becomes here the burning sun which has rendered Crow back to his original state. In a reflexive way, Crow is being subjected to his own scrutiny projected outward and experienced as if it were an evil eye 'glaring' at him. This poem is intimately related with the theme of the disappearance into the landscape of 'Crow Paints Himself into a Chinese Mural'. Crow's existence at this point in the Crow cycle is presented as a defensive, embattled isolation; Crow is one to whom everything has happened. Crow is a victim of his own evil eye, magnified to such an extent that its glaring gaze is experienced as the scorching, withering power of inspection. Pitting Crow against the scorching flames of the sun is a way for Hughes to bring Crow into the arena of natural forces. Since the Trickster, as Radin observes, is 'admittedly the oldest of all figures in American Indian Mythology . . . probably in all mythologies . . . he is frequently connected with the oldest of all natural phenomena, rock and sun'.[46]

'Crow and the Sea' provides an opportunity for Crow to come to terms with an all-embracing power. The sea is 'bigger than death, just as it was bigger than life'. At first Crow tries to ignore the sea but its size makes it impossible to shut out of his life. He tries talking to the sea; he tries sympathy then hate. All his attempts to communicate with the sea fail. The sea simply refuses to acknowledge Crow's existence. Hughes focuses on Crow's reactions: 'His brain shuttered', 'his eyes winced', he feels 'shouldered', wretched, insignificant, shallow and finally crucified by his own immobility. Why this should be so is obvious. Crow by definition exists apart from nature and is incapable of establishing a relationship with anything outside of himself. The metaphor underlying the poem is clear. Crow is a creature who cannot make contact with the flux of life, the flow of existence. He appears crucified and motionless in an existential tableaux in which his nature forms the context for his own punishment — a mirror reflection of Crow as the negation of life. Cut off from the continuity of things each frantic attempt by Crow to escape from the prison of himself, to return to a metaphor in an earlier poem, makes the walls of the prison thicker and the light that comes in through the bars dimmer. Crow finds himself in an indifferent universe at the mercy of a vast sea with which he can not communicate. This epic encounter defines Crow to himself and brings him one step closer to the ultimate self-knowledge in 'Truth Kills Everybody'.

Proteus was a sea deity who had the gift of prophecy as well as the power to assume different shapes. In 'Truth Kills Everybody' Crow grapples with several metamorphoses of Proteus to learn the ultimate truth, 'Crow pounced and buried his talons'. Like Menelaus in the *Odyssey*, he grabs the everchanging Proteus and tries to hang on. While Proteus as the son of Poseidon knew the past present and future he would desperately avoid being questioned on his knowledge and only would tell the truth if someone could outlast and endure the various guises he assumed. The series of changes Proteus takes Crow through present aspects of great violence, horror and ugliness — yet Crow hangs on. Proteus becomes 'the famous bulging Achilles', mythical son of the sea-goddess Thetis, but Crow 'held him'. Next Proteus becomes 'the oesophagus of a staring shark', 'a naked powerline, 2000 volts', yet Crow won't let go. The pattern of the struggle suggests its meaning for Crow. What was a drawback in 'Crow and the Sea', Crow's inability to attach himself, becomes a positive force in Crow's quest for self-knowledge. As he watches disguise after disguise of reality appear and disappear before him he discards each one, wishing to find the truth beneath the little relative truths that satisfy others. None of the answers which have satisfied men down through the ages satisfy Crow. He wrestles with the 'rising, fiery angel' like Jacob in the Bible; it will not suffice. Not even 'Christ's hot pounding heart' holds the answer for Crow. As the relative truths of mythology, the Bible, technology and divinity itself metamorphosize into each other, Crow hangs on. Ironically, the ultimate truth he meets is the 'nothingness' which spawned him in 'Lineage'; the ruthless discarding of self-deception, the stripping away of illusion after illusion is Crow's ultimate meaning. He remains outside of all relative human truth.

'Crow and Stone' is one of two poems that associate Crow with the elements of earth and stone (the second is 'Fragment of an Ancient Tablet') and weave him into the eternal fabric of things as a permanent, infinitely enduring principle of nature. The Trickster, as legends tell us, 'apparently has always existed'. [47] 'Crow and Stone' is framed in terms of the archetypal warfare between 'stone, champion of the globe', representing the earth, and Crow. Throughout their encounter stone 'battered itself featureless' until it becomes pulverized and just a speck in Crow's eye — a speck that is the earth itself ('the very globe'). Crow's devastating gaze, 'his mere eyeblink', holds the earth itself in terror and Crow prevails. Although the globe that began as earth is now a speck of dust in Crow's eye, Crow has only been 'just born'. The battle has raged for billions of years, yet Crow has not aged one day. The poem graphically shows that Crow's existence is not dependent on the earth. He exists eternally, a timeless principle that is more permanent than any that can be discovered in the world. The earth for him has simply been a temporary home through which he has moved after flying 'from sun to sun' (in 'The Door'). The paradox of the poem centres around Crow as both invincible, ageless, deathless, unafraid and monstrous while being as completely helpless as a newborn infant. Yet Crow triumphs, never ages and never dies because in one sense he has never entered life. He is the embodiment of the strategy of defeating death by never having lived. He has never entered time, hence, he is timeless. His triumph, however, is presented as a terrifying fact ('Crow has become a monster') whose self-destructive implications set the stage for Crow as the 'King of Carrion'.

The 'Fragment of an Ancient Tablet' referred to in the title is the emerald tablet of Hermes Trismegistus which, in the Hermetic tradition, embodied the antithesis of macrocosm and microcosm, heaven and earth, above and below and the eternally balanced opposites of Yin and Yang.[48] Within the poem Hughes explores this duality by examining a series of correspondences implicit in woman. Hughes contrasts the upper half of woman's body to the lower half and suggests a division in creation akin to the division of heaven and earth in Genesis. Diametrically opposite and yet dependent upon each other the romantic and chivalric ideas woman has inspired have their basis in earthy sexual images. The sacred and the bestial mirror each other in both spiritual idealization and carnal conceptions. Both stem from Eve, temptress and guide. Hughes begins the poem by depicting the separation of heaven and earth, light and darkness, soul and body. But soon a profound ambivalence toward the feminine principle starts to appear in a series of frightening images. She becomes 'the ticking bomb of the future' and the woman's 'perfect teeth' ominously acquire 'the hint of a fang at the corner'. The image of 'the face, shaped like a perfect heart' is brought into contrast with 'the heart's torn face' in order to compare the ideal with the reality. Bearing in mind the Hermetic, gnostic and alchemical associations of the title this poem has a unique, if esoteric, place in the book of Crow. This poem transforms Crow's encounter with the stone in 'Crow and Stone' into the legendary meeting with the 'philosopher's stone' which played a key role in alchemical transformation. The alchemist's quest for gold was, as Jung has well established, both a material and psychological quest through a tortuous process of self-purgation. The most crucial stage of the 'dark night of the soul', through which the alchemist had to pass in his quest for the philosopher stone, was often called 'crow's head'. The putrefaction (spiritual, moral, and material) represented by the stage of alchemical transformation known as 'crow's head' implied a necessary stage through which the alchemist had to pass, in order for the transmutation into gold to take place.

The re-creation of the earth is one of the most essential exploits performed by the Trickster and in 'Notes for a Little Play' the whole world is apparently destroyed except for two creatures: ('Two survivors, moving in the flames blindly'). The destruction is violent and sudden 'without a goodbye'. The opening is similar to the Biblical creation myth except that here the earth is first destroyed and human survival is out of the question ('the demolition is total'). What survive are a nuclear Adam and Eve, products of a demolished earth and the sun's final flare. The finality of this nuclear apocalypse is underscored by frequent end-stopped lines. The most significant aspect of the poem is that two mutations survive and mate to start the cycle over again while existing in absolute suffering, without God, or the possibility of redemption. The lovers seem to be devouring each other helplessly: 'they do not know what else to do'. Their marriage is unillumined, celebrated 'in the darkness of the sun,/Without guest or God'. We understand why Crow is finally described as a 'King of Carrion' continuing to rule over a world that has destroyed itself. The next poem 'Snake Hymn' explores the nature of the force that joins the survivors together — a force which goes beyond mere lust in its possessive destructiveness. Their expression of mutal love is then the basis for 'Lovesong', and the fruit of their union is 'The Lovepet'.

Our tradition decrees that after Eden was created a snake enters bringing the knowledge of sexuality that, in 'Snake Hymn', 'adam swore was love'. Yet this Adam and Eve are compelled by an instinct which causes them to create and then simply sluffs them off, as a snake sheds his skin. The sexual force is described as a twisted love 'that cannot die'; it drives them to reproduce and uses them for its purpose, which is to survive. 'The million faces/And skin of agony' of age after age of endless births and deaths are as meaningless as 'an empty husk'. Amidst the grimaces of death in the faces of people spawned by this force, it continues oblivious to the suffering it has caused without suffering itself. While men are born to die the devouring 'love' described here is deathless.

'Lovesong' explores the possessive nature of love implied in the portrayal of the sex drive in 'Snake Hymn'. This poem gives the suffering associated with love a human face. The lovers in 'Lovesong' devour each other. They are portrayed as enemies battling for supremacy. The male's will to dominate and the female's desire to possess totally is shown in all its horror. Their union entails the negation of the individuality of each. They become so close that they lose their own identity and find it in each other's face, a bizarre echo of Plato's Symposium where man and woman seek to become the 'one head with two faces' they were before being separated. The pure intention of love is corrupted and love becomes a force to be feared. Woman's smiles become 'spider bites' and she nails down man's hands and traps him with her sexuality. The poem is a picture of possession so complete that each assimilates the other. The lovers are vampiric and gluttonous, bent on such absolute possession that it transcends lust. The portrayal of a love-hate relationship between the female who fights to possess while the male fights to dominate piles blackness upon blackness until their fiercely consuming mutual love has become a ravaging predator.

As an extension of the force consuming all the masks of love in 'Lovesong', the 'Lovepet' appears as a monstrous reproduction of Crow who is, at the same time, an ungrateful child taking all from his parents. Lovepet immediately begins eating; it starts 'softly . . . with sugarlump smiles . . . and kisses' but soon 'ate the colour of the sun . . . it waited for them.' As love personified the 'Lovepet' is carefully cultivated but soon becomes an all-consuming monster: 'it bit at their numb bodies they did not resist/It bit into their blank brains they hardly knew', devouring their lives from the inside. How addicted the couple are is proved by their desire to call it back; 'they wept they called it back it could have everything', despite all the pain it causes. Eventually, having 'stripped out their nerves', it deserts them destroying their world and leaving them alone; 'Only their tears moved.'

After this last 'Glimpse' at Crow, Crow takes refuge in silence. While Crow cannot die or be destroyed he is literally cut off, as the metaphor of the poem tells us, from participation with nature: ' "O leaves", Crow sang trembling, "O leaves —"/The touch of a leaf's edge at his throat/Guillotined further comment.' Crow has driven the wedge of himself, of his own nihilism, into the spaces of everything and paradoxically has both triumphed and killed the possibility of nature untransfigured by Crow existing anywhere. This is why Crow is the 'King of Carrion', ruling in a palace of skulls (the 'god's head' is a death's head). Even as Crow is metamorphosized into the god of his creation, within it yet inaccessible to it, we are witnessing fulfillment of the prophecy made in 'Crow Hears Fate Knocking on the Door' that he would be inside of and measure creation — even the least blade of grass or leaf. Yet nature has revenged herself by decapitating Crow and even as he triumphs he has corrupted and destroyed his life source.

'King of Carrion' is closely modelled on the last view of Trickster depicted in the Winnebago Trickster cycle as 'a deity . . . as the elemental Trickster, an aging Trickster, indeed almost a demiurge taking his last meal on earth'.[49] Crow's realm is one of corrupted flesh ('His palace is of skulls'), the emblems of his rulership are cruel instruments of torture: 'His throne is the scaffold of bones, the hanged thing's/Rack and final stretcher'. The irony is that Crow rules over a world in which life and death are indistinguishable, a bleak and barren world like a prison from which there is no escape. He attempts to leave, flapping 'hopelessly away/Into the blindness and dumbness and deafness of the gulf'. Crow has outlived everything else in the universe. His nature has corrupted everything with which he has come into contact and ironically he now cannot obtain nourishment from the world any longer; he reigns over carrion, flesh unfit for food, he is 'shrunk' but cannot die, a king of all and nothing. Having created the world in his own image, he finds that he has destroyed it as well. The emptiness, silence and blackness of Crow are now 'his palace . . . of skulls'.

The source for 'Two Eskimo Songs' is the legend of the great Raven who in Eskimo mythology is the deathless creator of the world and of man.[50] These two poems function as an epilogue, closing the circle of Crow and bringing us back to the relationship of time and eternity projected in 'Two

Legends', the first Crow poem. Within the context of these two songs man wants to become eternal and water desires to become temporal. Each experience frustration because neither can escape the condition they are fated to endure. Together their predicament mirrors Crow's dilemma, caught forever between eternity and death, heaven and earth but obtaining neither. In the first of the 'Two Eskimo Songs' man is presented as having striven since the beginning of time to touch immortality through his idealization of first the lowliest totems ('a slug', 'a trout', 'a mouse',), then dying mangods, such as Attis and Christ, and ultimately woman herself. All disintegrate under his attempt to spiritualize them. All that is, except woman. With her he creates his 'song', his ideal. In exchange for 'the song' he gives her 'eyes and a mouth', raising her levels of perception and communication. Yet by making her exchange her instinct for his intellect he has cheated her. He is both careless and indifferent ('the man laughed') and is content to use her merely as an instrument to produce a song which carries him beyond her. By this exchange man and woman have irrevocably lost what both had originally. Tormented by his mortality, the man has briefly gained access to the realm of eternity — but at a terrible price. Hughes catalogues the ascending progression of man's many attempts to escape death by seeking transcendence through identification with animals (itself an interesting echo of Hughes's earlier attempts at Shamanistic self-transcendence through merger with totem symbols) and martyr-based religions. His exploitation of women is the final outrage. The title aptly enough for this first song is 'Fleeing From Eternity'.

Although indestructible, water wants to die. This is the theme of the complementary second song 'How Water Began To Play'. Water attempts 'to live', to experience life bounded and defined by time, 'it went to the sun it came weeping back' (as rain). Water's intense desire to become finite is defeated as all plant and organic cycles reject it. 'It went to the flowers they crumpled it came weeping back' (as dew). It attempts unity with man through the watery element in man's blood but it is rejected at each turn through gestation, through menstruation and finally by man's death. Indestructible, water is always forced to return to the earth as water. In the end after repeated rejections it becomes 'utterly worn out utterly clear'. Just as man cannot move out of time, water cannot move out of eternity. 'Two Eskimo Songs' primarily are a reflection on

Crow's position — unable to live and unable to die.

'Littleblood', true to the inside-out nature of CROW, reverses tradition by having the invocation of the author's personal muse occur at the end, not as in Homer, Milton, etc. at the outset. Hughes beseeches Littleblood to help him, to deliver messages to him from the underside of things. Hughes asks for the ability to see, not as a man might see but as one 'wounded by stars and leaking shadow'. He wants to see the inside of the mountain, he wants to sing of the spaces between stars; he wants, in essence, a crow's eye view of intergalactic and intercellular space. Like Crow, Littleblood has grown wise and terrible through feeding on death. He is the sacred beast of prophecy, a strange boneless, skinless little carcass 'grown so wise, grown so terrible'. He has been 'wounded by stars' of hope and is leaking 'shadow' of despair. And so Crow's tale ends with this quietly triumphant little poem celebrating the self-realized soul, birthless, deathless, without beginning or end.

CROW is the account of a predatory bird of mythic dimensions. His birth, development and bizarre fate are told in fable form. Very few of the individual poems in the epic of Crow stray far from the Trickster cycle although certain poems take on pivotal importance in determining the themes which CROW explores. In folk mythology the crow is an animal figure predominantly associated with the twin motifs of death and guilt, a stark figure who embodies boldness, intelligence, adaptability to change and a twisted vitality. Through Crow-as-Trickster we learn of the development of the soul. We discover trembling beauty and paralyzing dread. We struggle with Crow to gain a glimpse of what lies beyond our earthly existence for Hughes is certainly one of the few writers of this century to create not merely a character but a way of looking at life that is beautiful in a grim sort of way. CROW is a series of sufferings and spiritual adventures; Crow passes through initiations, encounters monsters and is instructed in hidden mysteries. Crow is present at the creation of the world and he is present at the end of the world. His life and songs embody the history of the universe; at the same time, Crow follows the pattern set by the Trickster cycle. He is born, enjoys a brief childhood and goes about learning the why and how of things. His Trickster nature emerges in a series of 'Childish Pranks'. He observes, explores, deals with the world with both violence and detachment. His aspirations to become God-like doom him to fall, as did Icarus, and he is forced to come to terms with the powerful natural forces that frame the world: the sun, sea and stone. Although blasted to 'nothing' by truth and hammered, beaten and roasted by God, Crow is regenerated through violence and appears indestructible. In the end the world is recreated in the image of Crow: ironically, Crow inherits a diminished and sterile realm. He is immortal yet never can it be said he is truly alive. From the first Crow is associated with the faculty of sight, the pupil in the eye that peers from the crevices of the earth. For Hughes Crow is a way to explore the underside of existence, the spaces between things. The complex ironic manner in which Crow examines war, science, sex, religion strips away comforting self-deceptions to give us a 'crow's eye view' of cultural practices, sacred beliefs and natural phenomena. Crow subjects to ridicule the great meanings through which man has attempted to hide the truth from himself. Crow is both an adversary of the world as it is and a mediating force in a world that is doomed to apocalypse within a universe portrayed as indifferent. Man himself as he appears in these poems is an imperfectly created creature, insignificant and in constant danger of self-destruction. While man is manipulated by the lust for power, technology, sex and his own self-projected religions, Crow maintains his life on a more primitive level, continually scavenging for food. Simply stated, Crow's goal is the finding of a truth so basic that it cannot be undercut. He approaches life as did Thoreau who observed: 'I wanted to live deep and suck out all the marrow of life, to cut a broad swath and shave close, to drive life into a corner and reduce it to its lowest terms and if it proved to be mean why then to get the whole and genuine meanness of it and publish its meanness to the world . . . For most men it appears to me are in a strange uncertainty about it, whether it is of the Devil or of God . . .'[51] Towards this end Hughes's language is utterly simple, violent, earthy and grim. Crow's songs are like Crow, raucus, unmelodic and harsh.

Hughes's style, at once powerful, colloquial and direct, answers to his purpose of calling into question conventional ways of looking at birth and death, art and science, love and war. Through Crow, he inverts traditional mythologies, Greek, Roman, American Indian, etc. in order to more closely examine human assumptions on which they are implicitly based. The archetype provided by the North American Indian Legend of the Trickster was an inspired choice on which to base CROW. The Trickster has always been depicted as 'creator and destroyer, giver and negator, he who dupes others and who is always duped himself. . . . He knows neither good nor evil yet he is responsible for both. He possesses no values, moral or social, is at the mercy of his passions and appetites, yet through his actions all values come into being.'[52]

Alternately creator, participant and victim, Crow's triumphs contain the seeds of his own defeat. Trickster is the necessary bridge between the Shaman and the Scapegoat because Crow as Trickster can avoid bearing the responsibility for what he learns. The Scapegoat accepts and even invites his own death by embracing the responsibility for not only his actions but for those of others as well. The Trickster and the Scapegoat are clearly complementary figures; one is less accountable for the results of his actions than he should be, while the other takes on punishment that far exceeds that for which he is personally answerable.

# Part III  Scapegoat

'Nothing is more difficult and at the same time
nothing can create so much force as voluntary suffering.' In P. D. Ouspensky, *The Fourth Way: A Record
of Talks and Answers to Questions based on the
teaching of G. I. Gurdjieff* (New York: Alfred A.
Knopf, 1959), p. 375.

## Chapter Five
## PROMETHEUS: TRICKSTER REDEEMED

### PROMETHEUS ON HIS CRAG

In 1971 Hughes was invited to participate in collaborating with
the director Peter Brook and the International Centre for
Theatre Research in writing a play to be performed at the
Fifth Shiraz Festival in Iran. For the play, which was entitled
*Orghast*, Hughes composed a hybrid language which aspired
to return to the condition of chant-like rhythmically based
language characteristic of the first theatrical experience of
man, rooted in myth and archaic mystery. The central myth
he chose to elaborate was that of the Greek Titan, Prometheus
whose story is known to us in a variety of sources including
Hesiod's *Theogony* and Aeschylus's play, *Prometheus Bound*.
The nature of *Orghast* (which means 'the fire of being', metaphorically the sun, from two root words, 'org' — life, being
and 'gast' — spirit, flame) was largely due to improvisation and
was never published, although several performances of the play
in Iran were actually filmed.[2] Fortunately, Hughes also wrote
twenty-one poems since collected in *Prometheus on his Crag*
which allow us to determine and enjoy the nature of the story
he evolved in *Orghast;* they remain the external lineaments of a
drama that Hughes described as being 'enacted within the body
of Prometheus on his rock'.[3] Hughes conceived the action
of the play and the ensuing Prometheus poems as a series of
conflicting scenes in which the overall feeling was advanced
through the movement of contrasting ideas pivoting against
each other. On one hand *Orghast* is, as Hughes says, 'the story
of crime against material nature, the creatress, the source of

life', while the answering movement consists in the 'decomposition of the fallen ego among the voices of its crimes, oversights, and victims'. The revenge of the creatress, Hughes tells us is embodied in 'the vulture (the mystery of Prometheus's physical/spiritual dilemma) transformed into a woman.'[4]

It is startling to discover Hughes once again transforming the myths surrounding Prometheus in a way that displaces the eagle as the bird of Zeus with an image of the devouring feminine projected in the form of a horrendous vulture. Yet, the vulture, like the hawk in 'Hawk Roosting', has the same function and character in the emotional dialectic within Hughes's poetry. The suffering she brings is equated with Fate. The vulture has the character of an overwhelming, devouring, demonic maternal force: the principle of nurturing gone terribly wrong. With this in mind we can understand the significance of Prometheus's predicament, his suffering, his nature, the forces holding him in check and the stages of self-purgation through which he must pass in his daily war of self-renewal pitted against the vulture. Although we are told that 'the mythology that Hughes embodied in *Orghast* and the series of scenes in which it was dramatized started from Prometheus's defiance of Zeus and went on to Hercules's liberation of Prometheus',[5] the collaborative nature of the  venture allowed Hughes to build up a composite myth, centering on the figure of the scapegoat. In A. C. H. Smith's account of the months spent by Hughes, Peter Brook and the theatre company in Iran entitled *Orghast At Persepolis* we learn that Calderon de la Barca's *La Vida Es Sueno* (Life is a Dream) was one of the principal works that Hughes and Peter Brook required the actors to know.[6] The common elements between this play and *Orghast* clearly point to the direction Hughes was taking in creating the character of Prometheus. The scene in Act I of Calderon's play is set on one side of a 'craggy mountain' and Prometheus, we recall, in the account of Robert Graves is 'chained naked to a pillar in the Caucasian mountains, where a greedy vulture tore at his liver all day, year in, year out; and there was no end to the pain because every night (during which Prometheus was exposed to a cruel frost and cold) his liver grew whole again'. Like Prometheus, the central figure in Calderon's play, Prince Segismund is imprisoned as a test, so to speak, of his nature which is both vehement and irrational.[7] The prototype offered by Calderon's play held Hughes's interest principally in terms of the resemblance between Segismund and Prometheus. They are both characterized by overweaning pride, apparently unjust imprisonment and their titanic status. Segismund's nature and thoughts provide an interior dimension which allow us to penetrate, through his analogous situation, into Prometheus's mind. One thing that defines him is his extraordinary rage, while at the same time, his imprisonment objectifies an equally strong need to control that rage; thus Segismund is reduced to the status of one who must endure a living death precisely because of his nature. We have certainly seen this vicious and self-debilitating cycle again and again at work in Hughes's portrayals of rage under external restrains and the fearsome consequences of lifting controls. In the context of the Prometheus legend this trait is explored in terms of Hercules's slaughter in a fit of madness of his own family and the murderous consequences of madness when uncontrolled. Segismund, too says of himself: 'yet I, with far more life, must have less liberty?/ This fills me with such passion, I become/Like the volcano Etna'; he acknowledges he is 'a human monster . . . a man of the wild animals, a beast/Among the race of men'. As the action of the play soon makes clear he is wrong to believe that misfortune and imprisonment has curbed his 'furious rage'. The antagonism between Prometheus and the outraged creatress (whose revenge the vulture embodies) is present from the outset in Calderon's play. Segismund we learn was 'born into the world,/Giving a foretaste of his character/By killing his own mother'.[8]   And just as Zeus fears Prometheus so Segismund's father Basil understands that Segismund is fated to become a tyrant and, enraged, has him imprisoned. His fears are not ill-founded since when Segismund through the action of a drug is induced to believe himself free (hence the title, *Life is a Dream*) Segismund acts in a thoroughly bestial fashion, his irrational vehement pride spurs him to vengeance and he loses all control. Put to sleep and reawakened once more he determines to 'subjugate/The bestial side, this fury and ambition,/ Against the time when we may dream once more'.[9]

Events transpire so that he is indeed given another chance and this time, whether from his uncertainty as to whether he is in another dream or because he has learned from his past experiences, he acquits himself honourably by restraining his 'ferocious nature'. His 'inborn rage' has become 'a sheathed sword'.[10]  The depth of appeal this story has for Hughes is obvious since there are few works, notwithstanding Euripides's *Hercules Furens* (Mad Hercules), where the consequences of madness and reason totally out of control are so powerfully and poignantly dramatized. Hughes takes his cue from these works and applies not only details of external choreography and characterization but more importantly their spirit of horrified self-reproach to the Prometheus myth at hand. The consequences of loss of control are dramatized within the context of *Orghast* in a scene where a character called Krogon 'kills his wife and children, thinking they are evil birds',[11] a clear echo of Hercules's uncontrollable insanity. Hughes's notes are instructive in defining the exact nature of the forces which are oppressing Prometheus. Prometheus, Hughes notes, 'is fractured. He is the crossroads of eternal life and ecstacy and temporal doom, pain, change and death. Conscious in eternity he has to live in time. And he cannot solve his dilemma. He hangs between heaven and earth almost torn apart, an open wound, immortal. Something prevents him from solving his dilemma — Krogon.'[12] Krogon's attempt to clamp down on Prometheus and cage the light is, of course, futile. But, before realizing this, Prometheus is caused intense pain. In Hughes's notes, under the heading 'what the Vulture means' we discover that the terms by which the vulture is described have an interesting connection; the vulture is called 'the open wound', 'guilt for not having yet solved the dilemma',[13] 'a compound crime' that Prometheus 'refuses to recognize which is slowly dementing him' and again, the vulture is equated with Prometheus's 'sickness, the call to resolve the mysterious dilemma'. The action of the play and the accompanying Prometheus poems is projected as a guilt-producing dilemma which can only be solved by a radically corrected understanding. The mechanism for correcting Prometheus's understanding is also a sickness which can only be cured if accurately comprehended. The failure to do this over a period of time represents a crime for which the vulture's daily visits are the punishment. We also learn that an idea considered (but not actually used in the performance) was 'to fit the actress playing the vulture with one of the metal, beaky masks that Gulf Arab women could be seen wearing in the streets of Shiraz'.[14] Overall then, the tremendous energies embodied in Prometheus, if not held down, would quite literally mean the destruction of normality. Yet the enchained predicament that puts him at the mercy of a devouring embodiment of the revenge of the creatress is itself such an oppressive force that it is immensely difficult for Prometheus to understand his condition. His crime flows into his punishment and his punishment re-engenders, in turn, his crime anew.

The archetypal battle between Prometheus's force of desire and the cold monster of tortuous restraint reprojects what is essentially a single myth elaborated over a lifetime in the esoteric mythology propounded by William Blake. Blake's poetry plays like a blue flame about the edges of Hughes's Prometheus poems, particularly the antagonism between Prometheus and the vulture as it mirrors the strife between Urizen and the forces of energy which Blake named variously Orc or Los. In the Book of Urizen we read that Orc is taken 'to the top of a mountain/. . . they chain'd his young limbs to the rock/With the Chain of Jealousy,/Beneath Urizen's deathful Shadow'.[15] Hughes, we recall, described 'a great bird of prey, squatted on the shoulders of Prometheus blotting out the light'. Urizen's opposition to any outflow of vitality, his attempt to contain the imaginative fires over which he throws his shadow and above all, his underlying intent which, as Harold Bloom observes 'desires not an exuberant becoming but a repose of unchanging solidity',[16] all go to create a composite picture of repression which is identical to the force oppressing Prometheus. We must remember that Krogon is this force in its repressive aspect while the vulture is the actual punishment visited daily upon Prometheus.

Like Urizen, Krogon wishes to impede the natural flow of energies and gather them all to himself. The vitality of Krogon is founded on repression and on hate. As Hughes says: 'whatever transgresses his laws in this world he imprisons or destroys. Whatever lies beyond his laws, he denies. Every new birth he forbids, kills or imprisons. This is his effort to stop time . . . to hold off his death and replacement.'[17] He is the embodiment of a sickness which is not only not in harmony with the universe but wants to perpetuate that disharmony at all costs. Why this should be so is suggested by Hughes's description of the 'universal energies' in fear of which 'Krogon lives in terror.' He feels 'the energies of the whole fractured universe pressing to remove him and resume their flow of reproductions and changes and enjoyments and death'.[18] Prometheus's shout awakens the vulture who comes to rend his innards in the same way as the immolation of Orc and his outcry calls Urizen into existence. We have certainly seen this situation before in Hughes's poetry, particularly in the scenario Hughes first developed in some detail within the *Crow* poems. The scene is strikingly familiar to the portrayal of a maimed human figure in dire need of being healed from a grave psychic wound, watched over by the grinning and devilish figure of crow who scrutinizes and threatens to devour this human victim. Like Prometheus and his daily renewed agony, the man's existence (as Hughes explores it in 'Crow Improvises', 'Crow's Battle Fury', 'Crow Blacker Than Ever' and 'Revenge Fable') is the epitome of misery and a daily death that heals itself over simply to begin again. He appears crucified; he suffers the dilemma of being unable to live and yet unable to die, torn between eternity and death, heaven and earth, a predicament that clearly looks forward to the wounded plight of Prometheus. As with all of Hughes's protagonists, his need to be healed of his wound is intimately related to his profound ambivalence towards the sources of feminine nurturing. He is estranged and in violent conflict with himself. He is profoundly ambivalent towards a sacrificial communion which both inspires his profoundest hopes and equally violent aversion to the self-mutilation which is the price for a new life. Nothing less than a sacrificial death, inspired by the pattern of the Scapegoat's must precede a realignment with the life forces.

This realignment is fundamental in Hughes's poetry from this point onwards although we have seen premonitions as far back as in his Jaguar poems where the jaguar frees himself from his enslavement to his enraged condition by annihilating his rage through turning it against itself. The note of self-questioning implicit in the seesaw movement between predator and prey, Prometheus and vulture, returns us to the self-interrogation at work in 'Wodwo' where a series of questions ('What am I?') underscored the self-inquisition that sought to seek a return to an unfallen state before the dissociative split between self and world, soul and body, began. Again, Prometheus like the rat in the trap in 'Song of a Rat' finds escape impossible and refuses to accept his fate until suffering reveals new dimensions to his predicament. The stance of Prometheus is one that is reminiscent of the skylark's attempt to define itself by pitting its suffering against fate and 'the earth's centre' in 'Skylarks'. In essence, Prometheus defines his destiny by opening himself to destruction and through Prometheus Hughes realigns himself with the suffering victim, a mutilation 'towards alignment' in the words of the Prometheus poems. In Prometheus we see Hughes adopting a new strategy to resolve the emotional, spiritual and psychological dilemmas that cannot be solved by simple insistence on a monolithic stance of invulnerability.

This is the overall significance of his choice of the Prometheus figure, the first among many that stretches towards Dionysos and ultimately the Reverend Lumb in *Gaudete*. By realigning with the victim as Scapegoat rather than as we have seen before with the predator, Hughes has made the fateful choice of choosing to experience reality at the level of its victims. Only with this in mind can we truly understand the impulse behind Hughes's choice of Prometheus, his function as both rebel and creator, his mission which mysteriously entails prolonging his suffering in order to understand it and the archetypal antagonism between a human figure devoured by a bird of prey.

The scale on which *Prometheus on his Crag* is enacted is titanic, larger than life, yet Prometheus (a figure of intrinsic enormous power) is placed in a situation of utter powerlessness and passivity, shifting the level of the unfolding drama to one of understanding rather than action. The enormous disparity between the intrinsic power of Prometheus and the helpless predicament in which he is placed makes us aware of the great subjective distance that separates potency from powerlessness. What I am suggesting is that the Prometheus archetype is unconsciously chosen because it is Hughes's way of projecting, in a structural format what in reality is taking place psychologically, a projected transfer onto an outer scenario of a profound conflict between extremes of power and powerlessness first sensed internally. Other factors fall into place when we examine how Prometheus is traditionally characterized, whether in the 'poetic rendering' of *Prometheus Bound* by Elizabeth Barrett Browning, Goethe's lyric poem 'Prometheus', along with fragments of his Prometheus play, or most recently Robert Lowell's 1967 adaptation of Aeschylus's *Prometheus Bound* (Hughes and Sylvia Plath were great admirers of Lowell's poetry, dating from the days when they were teaching and writing in the Boston area). From the first, Prometheus is a compelling figure because he alone places himself in the position of being punished in order to redeem man. We cannot forget that his initial stature as a Titan, when contrasted with the torment and shameful injustice to which he was subjected for stealing fire from the gods for man, entailed a torment all the more keen for its intrinsic injustice. While various dramatizations of Prometheus's 'crime' and subsequent punishment stress this feature almost exclusively (and indeed Shelley in his 'lyrical drama' *Prometheus Unbound* utilizes the prophesied 'unbinding' of Prometheus to carry a universal message of human liberation), Hesiod's *Theogony* deepens our conception of Prometheus's nature and clearly points to both his origins and the exact nature of the punishment Zeus devised for Prometheus's rebellion.[19] Prometheus, Joseph Campbell reminds us, is 'a sublimation of the image of the self-reliant, shamanistic trickster'.[20] And indeed the various tricks that Prometheus plays on Zeus, paramount among which is of course the theft of fire through a clever ruse, show that Prometheus, far from 'knowing in advance' (which is what his name literally means) what would happen to him, is ignorant of his punishment in the form of the vulture. Hesiod identifies him as guilty of 'hybristes' or an insolence that will permit no interference; he is only apparently clever but his very cleverness is ironically the means for his own undoing.[21]

As with all tricksters his very excess of cleverness and manipulative inventiveness (which issues forth a variety of tools for acculturation) leads to his downfall. His power is tremendous, his intelligence is great but his nature is missing some vital component that ties him back to his primitive origins as a blood relation of Crow. What he does not know is that Zeus intends to punish mankind for Prometheus's trickery in stealing fire from the gods and conveying it to man. Zeus does this by giving Epimetheus (whose name means 'he who learns afterward') an idle and beautiful woman named Pandora who possesses a jar in which is contained all of the evils that plague mankind including 'Old age, Labour, Sickness, Insanity, Vice, and Passion'. Despite Prometheus's warning Pandora opens this jar and 'out these flew in a cloud, stung Epimetheus and Pandora in every part of their bodies and then attacked the race of mortals'.[22] Thus, because of Prometheus's cleverness mankind was punished with all the evils that have plagued it from the beginning. Hesiod's account in his *Works and Days* of Zeus's declaration to Prometheus makes the causal connection clear; 'I will give men as the price for fire an evil thing in which they may all be glad of heart while they embrace their own destruction.'[23] What Zeus had in mind, of course, was woman.

We must not forget, however, that Zeus was 'all-knowing'. His omniscient mind far outstrips even Prometheus's cleverness. Zeus quite clearly knows Prometheus will steal fire from the gods and allows him to do so in order that he shall legitimately have a reason for bringing woman into the world as punishment to mankind. What Hughes does is to pull together cause and effect quite literally and bring the principle of the feminine into the action as a punishing vulture afflicting Prometheus. This is unique to Hughes's own frame of reference. Even when the vulture displaces the eagle as the agent that inflicts daily injury on Prometheus it is pre-eminently a representative of Zeus, a masculine deity par excellence. Hughes alone transforms the vulture into a means of the 'revenge of the creatress', or the eternal feminine. Her victim, Prometheus, clearly suffers a magnitude of punishment that is much beyond what he has merited. The arc of his suffering moves from his early denunciations of the injustice of his position to the point where he accepts as necessary, for some mysterious reason, the suffering that had first appeared to him as an unspeakable and shameful torture.

His ability to come to terms with his suffering, a suffering that appears initially as unjust, unmerited and beyond his comprehension, clearly emerges in the course of the twenty-one poems Hughes wrote that comprise *Prometheus on his Crag*. If we ask why Prometheus's fate is the incommensurable, excessive, and unwarranted result of a trick played to bring man comfort we have missed the essential scapegoat nature of his burden. We remember that because of his sin all men must suffer the evils loosed from Pandora's 'brimming jar', as Hughes describes it in his Prometheus poems. Hence, to redeem that suffering Prometheus must become a scapegoat to assume the entire burden of all the suffering that he has unwittingly caused. This subterranean connection of cause and effect is not lost on Hughes and underscores his characterization of Prometheus. Hughes's larger-than-life protagonists, whether Prometheus or the Reverend Lumb or the Hercules based protagonist in *Cave Birds,* are confined, caught and held in peculiar circular patterns of cause and effect that are beyond their comprehension, initially, but are experienced as a fall from grace or an offence offered to a feminine deity. While seemingly innocent their guilt lies in their very natures. It is the function of suffering to force them to come to terms with a deficiency so profound and always in relationship to womanhood, at both an imminent and transcendent level, that without suffering they would never stand a chance of righting the situation. Karl Kerenyi's description of Prometheus is uncanny and accurate: Prometheus is above all 'inevitably a wounder and a wounded one' and 'the women who are associated with Prometheus in various traditions delimit his situation'.[24] These include the familiar Eve figure, Pandora, as well as Klymene who in some narratives is identified as both his wife and mother and who Kerenyi says 'points to the great goddess of the under-world'.[25] In view of this Hughes's empathy with Prometheus is implicitly connected with Prometheus's secret. Prometheus alone knows the name of the woman with whom Zeus will un-wittingly beget his own executioner and the source of Pro-metheus's secret, not surprisingly, is his mother, the earth mother of the Titans. Thus Prometheus's wisdom and defiant pride are based on the strength of a secret derived from a maternal source. The connection between the protagonist in *Prometheus on his Crag* and the Hercules based figure at the centre of *Cave-Birds* is the prediction made in the earlier play. Prometheus says: 'look for no ending to this agony/Until a god will freely suffer for you,/Will take on him your pain.' The figure that appears in the original tragedy to slay the eagle is Hercules (or Heracles) and not surprisingly Hercules then replaces Prometheus as the focal point in the sequence of Hughes's work. He becomes, in turn, the central victim and scapegoat who must consciously accept being 'a victim of in-justice, a sufferer from his own darkness exposed to unendurable torments'.[26] Thus, the wound is not healed but opened again in another context.

Among the many literary and mythological sources woven into the fabric of *Prometheus on his Crag,* we learn (from A. C. H. Smith) that Claude Levi-Strauss's *The Raw and the Cooked: An Introduction to a Science of Mythology* was a 'book which had some influence on the work in Persia'.[27] In the vulture myths and legends found in Brazil and other parts of South America we can easily identify elements which, while not present in the original Prometheus story, caught Hughes's imagination and which he incorporated in both *Orghast* and the accompanying Prometheus poems. In one Paraguayan myth, 'the origin of fire', a group of sorcerers are doomed 'to remain carrion-eating vultures . . . and never achieve the perfect life'.[28] A Bororo myth states that 'vultures consume . . . their victim — raw — and afterwards behave like genuine healers.'[29] A number of myths that explain the origin of fire have in common a belief in the idea that fire was originally stolen from the vul-tures, as Levi-Strauss says 'they attribute the origin of fire to an animal who gave it to man or from whom man stole it. In one instance, it is a vulture.'[30] One Tembe myth begins: 'In the old days the king vulture was the master of fire and men had to dry their meat in the sun. One day they decided to get possession of fire.'[31]

Another detail of these myths that makes its way into Hughes's poems is the fact that in one Bororo myth the hero is 'dressed as carrion, being covered with putrified lizards'.[32] Hughes transforms this in poem number 18 of the Prometheus sequence into the following scenario: 'the figure overlooked in this fable/Is the tiny trickle of lizard/Listening near the ear of Prometheus,/Whispering — at his each in-rip of breath,/ Even as the vulture buried its head.' These myths are tied together by a conscious desire to possess the fire of which the vulture is master. Pretending to die, to be a corpse, is in all these myths a ruse to attract the vulture, to capture it by appealing first to its carrion-eating instincts and then persuading it to relinquish the secret of fire. Since Orghast means 'the spirit of fire' and the repossession of this element is at the centre of both *Orghast* and the Prometheus poems, one can see how closely Hughes has followed these ancient myths reported by Levi-Strauss and known to most Brazilian tribes. From this important work, Hughes derives the concept of sickness versus cure which shifts his elaboration of the Prometheus myth into the framework of health and disease, putrefaction and resurrection, a series of concepts absent from the dramatizations of Aeschylus and Goethe. While it is certainly startling to discover the structural similarities between the archaic Greek myth of Prometheus and the legends that Levi-Strauss relates as being known 'to almost all the Tupi tribes of Brazil' about the origin of fire ('according to which fire was stolen from the vulture by a demi-urge who feigned death and putrefaction'),[33] it is still more startling to discover the uses to which Hughes applies these archetypal antithesises of preservation versus decay, health versus sickness, dilemma versus understanding and suffering versus release from suffering.

Hughes's work demonstrates, as does that of few other writers, the underlying affinity some artists have with archetypal and omnipresent processes (without regard to geographical contexts). This explains the diversity of sources which make their way into *Prometheus on his Crag*. For example, from the ideas concerning the shaman in Eskimo legends and myths Hughes incorporated the conception that the vulture which tortures Prometheus can be the 'helper' in disguise (a feature implicit in the Bororo myth that first sees the vulture as predator and then as 'genuine healer'). Hughes asks, through

Prometheus, was the vulture 'after all, the Helper/Coming again to pick at the crucial knot/Of all his bonds'. In the initiatory experiences of the would-be shaman the Eskimos, reports Eliade, describe 'dismemberment of the body' and 'speak of an animal . . . that wounds the candidate tears him to pieces or devours him then new flesh grows around his bones. Sometimes the animal that tortures him becomes the future shaman's *helping spirit*' (my italics).[34] Again Eliade says that Eskimo apprentices, i.e., novice shamans, display 'inexplicable terror' upon the appearance of their 'helping spirits'.[35] This relationship provides the framework within which Hughes understands the significance of Prometheus perpetually being torn apart by his tormentor.

A few stanzas further on in poem number 20 of the Prometheus sequence Hughes addresses himself to the relation between Prometheus and the vulture in language unusual for him but thoroughly familiar to readers of Yeats's poetry. Prometheus questions 'was it his anti-self —/The him-shaped vacuum/In unbeing, pulling to empty him?' In Yeats's poem, 'Ego Dominus Tuus', one character called *Ille* says 'I call to the mysterious one who yet/Shall . . . prove of all imaginable things/The most unlike, being my anti-self . . . and . . . disclose/All that I seek.'[36] Yeats's early essay *Per Amica Silentia Lunae* portrays the anti-self as permitting 'the expression of all the man most lacks and it may be dreads and of that only'.[37] In *A Vision*, Yeat's comprehensive esoteric work, he defines the 'anti-self' as a 'form created by passion to unite us to ourselves'.[38] By equating the vulture with Prometheus's 'anti-self' Hughes is having the vulture serve as a foil to enable Prometheus to discover his true self; thus, the anti-self is a means of promoting a more comprehensive level of awareness than had existed before, through self-confrontation. As Yeats said in a letter to Ethel Manning: 'to me all things are made up of the conflict of two states of consciousness, beings or persons which die each other's life and live each other's death.'[39]

The latter part of Hughes's Prometheus sequence is filled with echoes of Yeats's poetry, although so elliptically that the imagery fuses perfectly with Hughes's intent. The shout of Prometheus that awakens the vulture (an anomaly since the vulture's keen sight enables it to hunt by sight from vast distances) is modelled on both the expensive cry of the bound Orc (in Blake's *Book of Urizen*) that rouses the tyrannical stony Urizen from a sleep as deep as death and also on Yeats's 'The

Second Coming'.[40] In Yeats's poem the rocking cradle summons from stony sleep of two-thousand years a crude, slouching 'rough beast', merciless as the desert sun and associated with the circling of indignant desert vultures. The ever-enlarging spiralling movement of the desert vultures (and the falcon in the first stanza) evoke the feeling of a century out of control, suffering the loss of autonomy in all spheres, psychological, social and spiritual — each aspect of which becomes the subject of Yeats's masterful poem. Yeats's poetry makes its presence felt at a number of other points in Hughes's Prometheus sequence. For example, the image of 'the shuddering chestnut tree' which 'torn slowly open/ With its arms full' evokes Yeats's portrayal, in 'Among School Children',[41] 'O chestnut-tree, great-rooted blossomer'. While Yeats's image bespeaks wholeness, integrity and autonomy, Hughes describes the rending agony of self-immolation to reinforce the scapegoat motif. So, too, the conclusion of *Prometheus on his Crag* embodies the spirit of final release that Hercules's appearance was supposed to bring through the slaying of the vulture to Prometheus; the language and imagery are reminiscent of Yeats's 'Nineteen Hundred and Nineteen'.[42] Hughes's lines convey an exquisite sense of balance and achieved spiritual equilibrium:

> As Prometheus eases free
> And sways to his stature
> And balances, and treads
> On the dusty peacock film where the world floats.

Similarly, in the last stanza of 'Nineteen Hundred and Nineteen' the imagery of 'dusty wind' and 'peacock feathers' is caught up in a larger figure of the dancers and 'their tread' that projects the poem's central conflict, a conflict Hughes also confronts and resolves as Yeats had fifty years earlier, although in an historical rather than mythic and personal context. The issue is the same, the consequences of an uncontrollable upsurge in man's instinctual nature of an irrationality only temporarily suppressed. Significantly, Yeats's poem explores the consequences of the end of Athenian civilization by the invading Persian armies (the country we recall, that is Iran, in which *Orghast* and the associated Prometheus poems were written). The transcendent resolution portrayed in this final poem of *Prometheus on his Crag* also incorporates the scenario of one of Dylan Thomas's most beautiful poems, 'A Winter's Tale'.[43] In Hughes's sequence we read:

> Crocus evangels.
> A mountain is flowering
> A gleaming man.
>
> Cloud-bird
> Midwifes the upglare naptha,
> Opening the shell.

The conclusion of 'A Winter's Tale' witnesses a mytho-poetic consummation in which a miraculously transformed bird-woman, the 'she-bird . . . rayed like a burning bride' grasps the hero who has been seeking release and now finds it as Thomas says in a moment of revelation: 'Bird, he was brought low,/ Burning in the bride bed of love, in the whirl-/pool at the wanting centre, in the folds/Of paradise, in the spun bud of the world./And she rose with him flowering in her melting snow.' Hughes's imagery, stripped and more concise and in its own way equally evocative takes the 'spun bud' and transforms it into the flowering crocus, emerging triumphantly through the winter snow (a clear echo of 'flowering in her melting snow'). The image of the horrendous vulture recedes as the 'cloud-bird/Midwife' assumes the central place at the conclusion of Hughes's *Prometheus on his Crag*. Thus Hughes displaces the devouring feminine projection embodied in the vulture with an image of procreant, nurturing motherhood, the feminine in its most protective and beneficent aspect, a consummation in Hughes's poetry 'devoutly to be wished'.

If we telescope Hughes's initial projection of the vulture as woman at the beginning with the 'cloud-bird midwife' bird-woman at the end we have an exact image of Hughes's ambivalence towards the fearsome energy, destructive and divine that the eternal feminine, in her various guises, brings the poet. So too, the image of the peacock provides an ideal aesthetic opposite to the repulsive picture of the vulture. Hughes's notes tell us that in the resolution at the end of *Orghast*: 'the universe flows through its full circle, materialized spirit and spiritualized matter, undivided and reconciled to itself.'[44] Yet at the beginning Prometheus's self-division was likened to an illness, 'to solve this demon of disunity within himself, Prometheus descends into the warfare within himself, repeatedly.'[45] Thus from one end of the sequence to the other the emotional dialectic between these two extremes demands that Prometheus pay for his rebirth not only with his agony but with his understanding. His encounter with the devouring predatory vulture is a necessary element in his initiation process. As Hughes asks in the twentieth Prometheus poem: 'was he an uninitiated infant/Mutilated toward alignment.' Initiation can only be accomplished through the experience of dismemberment, death and resurrection; the means to this goal is clearly the vulture. Prometheus says as he 'pondered the vulture . . . was this bird . . . his condemned human ballast—/His dying and his death, torn daily from his immortality?' It is essential that Prometheus make use of the condition of his imprisonment, immovable on the crag, enduring the vulture's torture in order to burn through the disunity of his own nature and purge himself from within. The injustice of his position is a further opportunity to summon his rage to its fullest in order to turn it against itself. Prometheus submits himself to the vulture in order to earn the right to be reborn. He pays a price, in suffering and agony, in his role as a scapegoat that permits him to achieve the desired resolution.

Significantly, the final Prometheus poem presents its resolution in terms of a 'cloud-bird/Midwife' which clearly represents a rectification of the distorted, malevolent and devouring feminine forces earlier embodied as the vulture. By contrast the 'cloud-bird/Midwife' is a complementary answering image supporting and nurturing Prometheus's renewal. The 'cloud-bird' provides the sought for emotional release from his predicament; the peacock, on the other hand, provides a clue as to how he has solved the 'demon of disunity' within himself. The central feature within Prometheus's nature is, of course, pride. And the association with the peacock in popular folk lore with the expression 'as proud as a peacock' makes it an ideal choice to show Prometheus dominating his sense of innate pride, all the more keen in the light of the indignity of his unjust punishment. In Hughes's portrayal Prometheus at the end 'treads/On the dusty peacock film' and quite literally subordinates his pride underfoot.

Hughes, of course, is well aware of the sources and significance of the peacock image in myth and folklore. The peacock's tail or train and the hundreds of eyespots or 'ocelli' which give its outspread fan such a distinctive appearance is the subject of a story told by Ovid in his *Metamorphoses*.[46]

In the first book of the *Metamorphoses* Ovid relates how in the myth of Prometheus, Argus, of the 'hundred eyes', is instructed by the goddess Juno (Hera), for whom the peacock is a sacred animal, to keep watch on Io. As we discover in the story of Prometheus the hundred eyes of Argus were reputed to have passed into the tail of the peacock. Io, like Prometheus, is a victim of divine injustice having been transformed into a cow. She comes to Prometheus to learn her future from one who can supposedly foresee everything (except, ironically, his own punishment in the form of the vulture). In Robert Lowell's prose adaptation of Aeschylus's *Prometheus Bound* (and Lowell, we recall was one of Hughes's and Plath's favourite poets), Io says 'the wife of Zeus had already sent Argus, her herdsman with a hundred eyes, to watch me . . . he never harmed me and only watched but his eyes burned me like the heat of a hundred suns. . . . suddenly flies swerved and turned on me, I see them always before me and behind me now, beautiful and stinging, Oh Zeus, I am blinded by your splendour spread out before me like a peacock's tail with a hundred eyes! I shall never stop running. Prometheus, tell me where I must go and how far I must run before I die.'[47]

The significance of the peacock, like the image of the butterfly earlier in the sequence, is as a symbol of cyclic renewal. Just as the butterfly is reborn from a crysalis so the peacock loses and regains its innumerable colours every year. Hughes is characteristically senstive to the folklore surrounding the various animals, birds and insects that he mentions in ways that extend and amplify the meanings of his poems. For example, the rather unusual comparison of the vulture as 'the flapping, tattered hole—/The nothing door/Of his entry, draughting through him' and as 'the him-shaped vacuum' becomes more meaningful when we realize that vultures use pockets or 'holes' of hot air bubbles called thermals to help them soar up to a height of several miles, by circling inside the 'vacuum' of warm air as it rises in ascending currents. This characteristic method of flying is unique to vultures; their disproportionate weight makes it necessary for them to make use of thermal 'bubbles' to ascend to great heights. Consider also the superb way in which Hughes captures the characteristic glide and darting flow of the lizard in his description of 'the tiny trickled lizard/ Listening near the ear of Prometheus'. In the context of the Prometheus poems the lizard speaks of a time when Prometheus will be freed from his suffering, he carries the secret, as it were, of Prometheus's future liberation. Traditionally, because of its connection with Spring the appearance of the lizard has been considered a good omen, as numerous proverbs attest (one Bolognese proverb says that with the appearance of the lizard 'the season is beginning to improve').[48] Significantly, the lizard escapes the notice of the vulture, of which it would normally be a natural victim. It also has the remarkable habit of being able to grow another tail at a joint near the base of its spine if the first one is snapped. All these associations make it an ideal choice to suggest a time in the future when Prometheus will be freed from his condition of torment. The enormous number of sources that Hughes has woven together and repro-jected in a style thoroughly his own makes his choice of the peacock image more than casually interesting in the larger framework of the poetry Hughes writes both before and after *Prometheus on his Crag*. That is, in view of the strongly com-posite nature of the Prometheus sequence (itself almost inevi-table given the collaborative quality of the whole *Orghast* enterprise) Hughes's choice of the peacock takes on additional significance in view of its proverbial connection, in the world's folklore, with the crow. Ancient fables of the East and West (ranging from Aristotle's *History of Animals* to the great Indian work the *Pancatantram*) speak of the crow which dis-guises itself as a peacock by putting on various feathers (one proverb says 'the hasty fool takes a crow for a peacock')[49] and Hughes's reflexive sense of the ironic carries us from his *Crow* poems through the appearance of the peacock to *Cave-Birds* where the Hercules based protagonist has the unexpected experience of being swallowed by a crow. Thus, the appearance of the peacock is not idiosyncratic but part of a larger cyclic transformation from *Crow* through disguised Crow back to Crow again.

## Chapter Six
## REVENGE OF THE WHITE GODDESS

*Oedipus*

Oedipus is a recurrent figure, directly and indirectly, throughout Hughes's work. The myth of Oedipus underlies a number of *Crow* poems, including as we have seen, 'Oedipus Crow', 'Crow

Sickened', and 'Song for a Phallus'. Hughes's conception of Oedipus was developed and elaborated during the time he spent adapting the Oedipus of Seneca for production, in concert with Peter Brook.[50] The elements stressed by Hughes in his free translation of Seneca's *Oedipus,* itself vastly different from the *Oedipus Rex* of Sophocles, direct us, again and again, back to this play as a milestone in Hughes's depiction of the scapegoat archetype. No catharsis brings Hughes's Oedipus into an acknowledgment of the laws of life and nature. No sense of ineluctable yet life-affirming balance restoring principles of existence come into this play. Instead we have the world of Prometheus in yet another manifestation, and enforced submission to a malevolent destiny. Oedipus, in Hughes's version, is a character uniquely cursed, consciously innocent while unconsciously judged guilty and throughout unwittingly the cause of his own doom.

The story of Oedipus may be the world's first detective story. As the evidence mounts and Oedipus unearths clues that point to his own criminal guilt, he is compelled to realize that he is the criminal he seeks. While Oedipus's actions are violations of the basic laws of man and society and the magnitude of his crime is an offence against the gods, the peculiar twist of this story is that Oedipus did not commit these crimes intentionally. They flow from his nature. But commit them he has and the voice of vengeance, of blood guilt, the spirit of the Erinys mercilessly demands his destruction. Hughes's imagination is caught by this basic dilemma, that a man can by all rational criteria be innocent and yet held accountable. Ironically, here the differences begin since Sophocles's protagonist wishes to release Thebes from the plagues and fevers which his violation of the taboo against incest has brought. He displays a profound sense of moral obligation to the city of Thebes as its king and protector. In Hughes's version Oedipus feels no such responsibility for his city and merely wishes to escape the wholesale death which comes ever closer. He sees himself simply as one individual pursued and overtaken by a fate which he will acknowledge no complicity in creating. This in turn gives his complaints an edge of cowardly and surly petulance. Through his unwillingness to accept the moral guilt he has unconsciously incurred he makes his moral opaqueness itself the issue. The more he denies his responsibility, the greater is his sense of what is demanded of him. While Sophocles's Oedipus takes his destiny in hand and accepts the consequences as terrible as they are, Hughes portrays a man hounded, pursued and finally overtaken by his destiny — but one who never truly comes to terms with it. Hughes's Oedipus is a small man caught in a large fate, while in Sophocles's play Oedipus evokes our respect and that peculiar blend of pity and terror that Aristotle thought was the hallmark of tragedy. In Sophocles's play we feel an empathy with a human being caught in a tragic disaster; yet we are repelled by a fearful universe which can permit such events to occur. Thus, caught by pity yet repelled by terror, we experience the unique emotion which tragedy alone is capable of generating. In Hughes's adaptation we feel no empathy and no pity for Oedipus.

Other differences are significant. In Sophocles's play Oedipus strikes us as a wise, conscientious man and above all a masculine, courageous king. In Hughes's version it is primarily Jocasta who prods Oedipus to action when she says: 'a King cannot sit wringing his hands reproaching the gods weeping like a baby wanting to die.' Her character is closer to Lady Macbeth than to the Jocasta we are familiar with in Sophocles's play. Oedipus, as we first see him in Hughes's adaptation, seems principally concerned that if everyone in Thebes is in fact doomed he should not have to endure watching 'every living thing' in his country die before he does. He desires only personal release: 'Don't make me go on living . . . you have put too much onto me.' He displays no interest in trying to save the citizens of Thebes although he has been chosen by them as their king. The complexity of Sophocles's Oedipus is destroyed and the interests of the play shifted to other areas. Following Seneca, Hughes devotes an elaborate sequence to the summoning forth of King Laius's ghost and deepens our sense of archaic blood rituals involving sacrificial offerings. In Hughes's play, Oedipus is persistently characterized by extravagant gestures of self-abasement. When he first grasps his fate his reaction is: 'I should be stabbed, smashed under a rock.' But soon we are told, 'he stopped he began to reason/One little jab of pain a few seconds of death in my/Eyes and in my mouth/Can that pay for a lifetime like mine.' What is intolerable to him is not only the knowledge that others have died because of his actions but that for him death is too easy an escape for a sin as great as his. Of himself he says: 'you need to be born again suffer for everything again and die again over and over lifetime after lifetime and every lifetime a new sentence.' This scene and Oedipus's expressed desire appear again and again in a multitude of forms in Hughes's poetry. The blood-crime against the dead imposes such an intolerable and unpayable debt that one life and one death cannot possibly begin to pay what is owed. In turn this produces and is coupled with a need to re-experience suffering over and over again. As Oedipus says: 'this death has to last has to be slow find a death/Find a death that can still feel/And go on feeling a life in death a death among/the living.' Hardly has the rationalization for being reduced to the level of an object been projected with greater urgency or agony. When we last see Oedipus in Hughes's play his departing words clearly imply his resignation to his role as scapegoat: 'you people of Thebes crushed under this plague your spirits broken look I am going away I am taking my curse off you . . . the contagion is leaving your land I am taking it with me I am taking it away.'

Turning from Oedipus we notice that Hughes portrays the Sphinx in terms that suggest her role as the embodiment of a devouring, feminine force, half Medusa, half 'rough beast . . . she straddled her rock her nest of smashed skulls and bones her face was a gulf her gaze paralyzed her victims she jerked her wings up that tail whipping and writhing . . . her talons gouged splinters up off the rock saliva poured from her fangs.' Aside from the imagery Hughes's conception of the Sphinx expresses the causal belief that the plague that has descended upon Thebes is an extension of the Sphinx's revenge, a revenge that lives on after she has been destroyed; 'yet she's not dead as if I'd never solved her riddle she never died she changed I drove her off the rock and the questions stopped but her rottenness is flying her stench is a fog smothering us.' From this follows the persecution that Oedipus experiences ('that awful eye that never let me rest/And followed me everywhere hearing through every crack') and the remarkable similarity of the representation of the Sphinx, the vulture which tears at Prometheus, the vulturess which sits in inquisitorial judgement over the Hercules based protagonist in *Cave Birds* and the more naturalistic representation of womanhood revenging itself on the Reverend Lumb in *Gaudete*. Each of these figures while apparently different from each other is an extension of an instinct for pursuit and revenge that cannot be swayed or averted but must be appeased by the most elemental sacrifice — oneself. Hughes's portrayals hark back to the most ancient conception of the Erinys, the avengers of violations of the moral law, the embodied desire for vengeance and justice beyond the grave personified.

The Sphinx, as Jane Harrison reminds us, was 'a Harpy carrying off men to destruction and incarnate plague';[51] in fact, one of the Sphinx's epithets was 'the "man-snatching Ker" '.[52] This term 'Ker' has an amplitude of associations that link the Sphinx with the ancient Greek idea of the 'Kerykes, "women whose business it was to collect things polluted" and carry them off',[53] as well as the meanings implicit in 'death-angel', 'fate', and 'ghost'.[54] Harrison observes that the 'sphinx and the death-Siren' are extensions of the Erinys, 'divine beings' whose other names are the Eumenides and the Maniae.[55] Most importantly 'the Erinys primarily is the Ker of a human being unrighteously slain. Erinys is not death; it is the outraged soul of the dead' crying for vengeance — 'the Erinys are primarily human ghosts but all human ghosts are not Erinys; only those ghosts that are angry.'[56] They appear in direct response to the spilt blood and the outraged soul of the dead victim. In their most elemental form they are without pity, cannot be assuaged, put off, reasoned with, or tricked. They afflict the sufferer with unceasing torment; they hound him with madness until he dies. They are nothing less than the need of the dead to be placated and appeased by him who is held accountable, regardless of the provocation, or any subjective motivation he might claim as a mitigating circumstance.

So too, the 'winged phantoms' that escape from Pandora's 'brimming jar' in the Prometheus poems are, Harrison notes, 'indeed ghosts, but ghosts regarded rather as noisome sprights than as spirits . . . the jar of Pandora is not so much a grave as a storehouse of evil.'[57] The vengeance sought by souls escaped from the 'grave jar' is mirrored by the vultures daily visit tearing at Prometheus's entrails. In all of these cases we see the polarization between spirits, the outraged ghosts of the devouring feminine, and the scapegoat victim who places himself in a position of an expiatory sacrifice through a desire for self-purification. The most basic offering to the unslaked thirst for vengeance of these outraged spirts is the self and Hughes's *Prometheus on his Crag, Cave Birds* and *Gaudete* are part of a recurring pageant of self-sacrifice but a sacrifice offered in a very special way. In archaic purification rites 'the victim', says Harrison, 'is a surrogate for the polluted suppliant, the blood is put upon him that he may be identified with the victim, the ghost is deceived and placated'.[58] But of course, in reality things are not so simple. Seen in this light Hughes's recent major works are a series of surrogate ritual offerings that attempt to recreate the equivalence of ancient ceremonies of expiation. Each new scapegoat figure is a new offering; each self-disguised projection consititutes the laying of a new victim on the altar. The ghosts in Hughes's work, however manifold the form in which they appear, are never placated. There is always a new surrogate victim to be thrust forward, another myth to be resorted to, as the inexorable progression moves through Oedipus to Prometheus to Hercules to Dionysos and beyond. This is why the character of unaccepted sacrifice (the offering of Cain, as it were) and the repeated yet unresolved attempts at ceremonial self-purification is such a constant feature of Hughes's work. This is why we feel that suffering in his works is not at an end, that in a very real sense he must reinvoke it, re-experience it, but never achieve a final release. The dead cannot be put off; surrogate offerings just delay the inevitable. In turn this produces that deep sombre note of dread and terror in Hughes's poetry, a dread that seemingly cannot be exhausted through repeated evocation and portrayal.

Moreover, there is a very interesting progression in all of these works. The choice of protagonists, their function as initiatory scapegoats to appease the ghosts of the dead and the myths that underlie them suggest why the hoped for resolution does not occur. In his own way each protagonist is incapable of being destroyed completely. Prometheus is immortal after all and Hercules, while coming closer because of his dual status as man and god, is not destroyed but removed to the level of a deity by Zeus. While the case of Dionysos in *Gaudete* appears different since all legends and myths show him to be completely rent and fragmented, Hughes does a curious thing. He doubles him as the Reverend Lumb and allows misfortune to overtake the double while keeping in reserve the original 'polluted suppliant' (in Harrison's words) who surfaces at the end. This in turn suggests a withholding from an irrevocable commitment to paying the cost, what Sartre might refer to as 'bad faith'. The expiation is sought but cannot be achieved because the victim is unable and unwilling to completely commit himself, always keeping some portion of himself in reserve, waiting out of sight as it were in Lumb's case until the action is over.

This is but an extension of that deep survival instinct which we have seen in Hughes's earlier poetry, his unconscious identification with animals who kill but are not killed themselves.

The need to survive is so instinctive and so profound that the apparently stronger need to expiate, that is to thrust oneself forward into a variety of self-disguises within expiatory contexts must ultimately fail. This produces that ongoing subterranean warfare between the need to survive and the equally strong need to expiate, to absorb and not deflect the need for vengeance directed towards one by the spirits of the dead. Obviously the dynamics of such a dilemma cannot be resolved and forecast a perpetual ever more violent thrusting forward of the self-in-disguise to be destroyed as a scapegoat. In turn this creates a need for ever more desperate and ingenious strategems (equivalent to the doubling of Lumb) to preserve the self while seeming to put it forward for self-destruction and the hoped-for expiation. This explains the ultimately unresolved character of Hughes's poetry even at the very moment in which it seems to be rising toward conclusion ('at the end of the ritual', says Hughes, at the close of Cave Birds, 'Up comes a goblin').[59] The fact that Hughes is unwilling, or incapable of seeing his protagonists destroyed irrevocably suggests their intimate relation to his own ego. Hughes's choice of these myths can perhaps best be understood within the framework of what researchers such as Claude Levi-Strauss and G. S. Kirk have suggested. For example, myths 'set up artificial (i.e., mythical) situations that are unconsciously framed to establish some kind of mediation'[60] of problems or moral dilemmas, whether personal or cultural in nature. For the individual Kirk suggests, 'a myth might be important because it expresses something that otherwise lies repressed or dormant in the individual, or alternatively because it seems to fulfill some wish or create a desirable emotional condition. The first function would be analogous to Aristotle's idea that watching tragic drama brings about a catharsis, a kind of purgation, of pity and fear . . . the effect is quite different from that of the second category, in which a myth provides a kind of emotional consummation.'[61] Moreover, Kirk makes the valuable point that these two kinds of psychological effects, 'horror' and 'fulfillment', are not 'mutually exclusive, in fact, they often complement one another'.[62]

We see this again and again in Hughes's work as he is apparently caught and held through an empathy with his protagonists yet repelled by the fear of what happens to them so that he is forced to compulsively recreate and re-experience the same set of emotions although in apparently diverse contexts. There is only one story, omnipresent and totally compelling, beneath Hughes's choice of seemingly diverse stories. Doubtless the process at work is that first suggested by Freud: 'many myths are symbolic in that they represent a hidden attitude or preoccupation indirectly by means of concrete actions in an overtly different sphere.'[63] While the conscious mind would tend to make these preoccupations appear as insoluble problems, the function of myths as Levi-Strauss's research has shown is 'to make such contradictions bearable, not so much by embodying wish-fulfillment fantasies or releasing inhibitions as by setting up pseudo-logical models by which the contradictions are resolved or rather palliated'.[64] While specific personae or individual events may change, as indeed they do from *Prometheus on his Crag* to *Cave Birds* to *Gaudete* 'what remains constant is the relationship between one character or event and another, in short, the whole structure of the tale'.[65] In Hughes's work the fixed relationship is between male protagonists and the female furies, the Erinys, Sphinx, vulture or any of their variants. This structure and this conflict unites all of Hughes's later works although the strategy chosen to deal with the conflict changes as we have seen and as we will see in both *Cave Birds* and *Gaudete*.

## CAVE BIRDS

The inception of *Cave Birds,* one of Hughes's most complex yet compelling works, began in 1974 when he saw a group of nine drawings by the American sculptor and artist Leonard Baskin. These drawings featured a spectrum of the most incredibly bizarre, baleful and atavistic bird figures ranging from A Hercules-in-the-Underworld Bird to A Ghostly Falcon and including A Titled Vulturess, A Hermaphroditic Ephesian Owl, A Raven of Ravens and A Tumbled Socratic Cock. Based on Hughes's desire to write a series of accompanying bird poems Baskin produced drawings of an additional ten birds including among others A Death-Stone Crow of Carrion, A Flayed Crow, A Sunrise of Owl, A Monkey-Eating Eagle, A Stud Cockerel Hunted into a Desert, A Crow of Prisms and An Owl Flower.[66] Collaboration over the next year between Hughes and Baskin produced additional drawings and additional poems so that at the Ilkley Festival given in England in 1975 both drawings and poems were offered, in oratorio form, to the public. In revised form as a series of twenty-nine poems facing Baskin's drawings *Cave Birds* was published in 1978 as 'An Alchemical Cave Drama'.[67]

*Cave Birds* follows the journey of a 'guilty' protagonist who consciously feels quite innocent of any crime and is likened to a male rooster or cockerel. Yet one day while his everyday self goes about its normal business and his body moves through its customary motions, a psychological drama unfolds. His mind has been instantly transported to a different realm, a Hall of Judgment, where he is on trial for failures, guilts and inadequacies that have had a profound effect on numbers of people, especially women. He goes on trial, is prosecuted and found guilty in ceremonies that bear a marked resemblance to the 'weighing of the heart' ritual in Egyptian mythology (with side glances towards Socrates's trial, Orphism, Chaucer's *Parliament of Fowls* and Joyce's *Ulysses*). His punishment is to become a crow (for reasons that have to do with the cyclic process of alchemical transformation, as well as Hughes's own understanding of esoteric Hermetic Lore) and to attempt through various initiations (adapted, in part, from Eliot's *The Wasteland*, Dylan Thomas's sonnet sequence 'Altarwise by Owlight' and the doctrines of Orphism) and purification rites to regain his humanity. At the end of the sequence he nearly achieves this through marriage of a decidedly mystical kind with a woman who herself is half formed (an idea drawn from Jung's exploration of the mystical marriage with the *soror mystica*, or mystical sister). Each stage in his spiritual journey is designated by his equation with one particular kind of bird. When he starts out he is described as a cockerel. He then becomes a crow and aspires to be reborn as a falcon. The interrogator at his trial is a vulturess. His judge is An Oven Ready Pirhana Bird (as Baskin had originally labelled his drawing of this grotesque creature). At various points along his journey, a journey that takes him across the landscape of his own spiritual desolation, he encounters other birds who represent different points of view. On the way back to regain his lost humanity a strange hybrid creation, which Baskin called A Sunrise of Owl, offers him the easy way out: existence without the driving force of his consciousness, a non-existence of perpetual peacefulness without thought. He rejects this and instead accepts the offer of a Monkey-Eating Eagle to be punished as the price for his re-entry into the world of men. Hughes says that it is only fair that his hero suffers since he has made women — daughters, brides and mothers — suffer throughout his life. His fear and his sense of justice transform this archetypal woman into a revenging eagle. He must be punished in order, as Hughes says, 'to drive out of him a cockerel, as a scapegoat, a sacrifice to the eagles'. He must appease them and redeem himself by purging himself of that which has produced such suffering to the women in his life. Since the eagle to which his 'cockerel' self must be sacrificed is equated with the women whom he has victimized but now return as avengers, *Cave Birds* continues the central theme of *Prometheus on his Crag:* the crime against feminine nature and the subsequent revenge of the creatress. Her revenge shows itself as both the interrogating vulturess, whose intellectual scrutiny of the victim is as merciless as the sun beating down on a corpse left for vultures in the desert, and the 'monkey-eating eagle' who supervises the punishment given to the protagonist.

Hughes refers to *Cave Birds* as both 'an alchemical cave drama' and a 'ritual'. From poems as early as 'Lupercalia' we have been aware of the value that ceremonies and rituals of renewal and regeneration are given in Hughes's poetry. What Hughes intends can be gathered from what he has had to say, in a different context, about the poetry of Vasko Popa. Popa's methods, says Hughes, tend to produce 'an organic sequence of dream-visions, drawing on many sources, charged with personal feeling, an alchemical adventure of the soul through important changes.'[68] Phrases and images in *Cave Birds* ('fired with rainbows', 'cringing heat', 'rainbowed clinker', 'wind-fondled crucible', 'confection', 'crystals', and 'the gem' which is at the same time a 'seed') alert us to the alchemical framework within which Hughes is working. The project is compared to a voyage ('first, the doubtful charts of skin/Came into my hands — I set out'). As part of his journey he is consumed bodily and ingested by the Raven of Ravens. His quest is also a chemical transformation to reduce him to his essential nature. He will be purified by a 'red wind' which empties him and a 'black wind' that scourges him to disclose the quintessence of his purged self. In alchemical ritual birds of various kinds are frequently found as symbols of helping guides in the complex work of psychological self-transformation; so too, Hughes's poem 'The Guide' portrays the helping spirit as a bird carrying the hero upward.

The grave from which the hero rises has a meaning that is jointly alchemical and psychological — to rise from the grave is to transcend a state of lifelessness, or limbo, in which the soul is languishing. Ravens play a particularly important part within alchemical ritual as a symbolic stage in the initiatory process, a stage known variously as the 'shadow of the sun' or 'dead spiritual body' or simply 'Raven's head'.[69] The first stage in the process of alchemical transformation drawn on by Hughes is depicted as the act of being swallowed by a raven. Sages have referred to this 'decomposed product', notes Jung, 'on account of its blackness' as 'the raven's head'. Transferred into psychological terms the meaning of this state, says Jung, is obvious. At this point, one is 'the vilest of all men, full of griefs and sicknesses', 'despised', 'a worm and no man, the laughing stock and contempt of the people'.[70] Paradoxically, 'in the furnace of the cross . . . man . . . attains to the true Black Raven's Head; i.e., he is utterly disfigured and held in derision by the world and this is not only for forty nights and days, or years but often for the whole duration of his life.'[71] Jung draws the equivalence with the biblical figure of Job and concludes: 'evidently the *nigredo* brought about a deformation and psychic suffering equal to the plight of the unfortunate Job.'[72]

The reference to forty days stems from Genesis 8:6 ('Noah sent forth the raven after forty days') and we should not fail to overlook the fact that Hughes began using the raven/crow archetype in 1970, around the time of his fortieth birthday. The connection is quite a personal one for Hughes and stems from the esoteric symbolism associated with his astrological sign, that of Leo (Hughes was born August 17, 1930). While it is well known that the constellation Leo is represented by the ancients as the Nemean Lion which as one text says 'leaped down from the skies and was killed by Hercules',[73] it is less generally known that the third division of the sign, known as a decan and into which Hughes's natal sun falls (at twenty-three degrees) is symbolized in occult hieroglyphic writings as 'corvus, the Raven'.[74] Quoting from an ancient alchemical text which clarifies the symbolism of corvus the Raven as the third decan of the constellation Leo, Jung reports ' "with the death of the lion the raven is born" '.[75]

All ancient sources concur that this is the primordial state of benightedness and suffering, a pre-condition for self-knowledge. The symbolism of the raven or crow transcends cultural boundaries and figures in initiation experiences throughout the world. In 'The Teaching of Don Juan: A Yaqui Way of

Knowledge', by Carlos Castaneda, a novice is initiated by Don Juan under the influence of a hallucinogenic substance known as 'devil's weed' in the form of consciousness which the crow symbolizes, the art in effect of becoming a crow. To his disciples he says: 'I am teaching you how to become a crow. When you learn that, you will stay awake and you will move freely', a state symbolic of spiritual alertness and freedom. As he does what Don Juan commands he begins to feel crow legs coming out slowly from his body. But most important of all the would-be disciple 'had to learn to see like a crow'.[76] Don Juan said 'crows see straight to the side and he commands the novice to turn his head and 'look at him with one eye'. Significantly, crows seen by one who has been transformed into a crow appear to be 'silvery birds' who radiate 'a shiny metallic light'. These crows are 'emissaries' who come to summon the initiate on his spiritual journey, a journey that is likened to death. When they appear, Don Juan tells the narrator: 'it will mean you are going to die and become a crow yourself.' And, Don Juan adds emphatically, 'it takes a very long time to learn to be a proper crow.' What Castaneda is describing of course, is the archetypal encounter with the shaman, a shaman who is gifted with psychic second sight, who x-rays one's bones, holds an inquisition in order to reveal the would-be disciple to himself and illuminate the germ of spiritual nature that can guide the disciple into wholeness. A multitude of images with *Cave Birds* reflect the essential 'process of melting and recasting'[77] which is both a chemical and psychological cycle of self-transformation. Within this cycle the preliminary stage necessary for whoever would undergo 'death and resurrection and transformation'[78] was known as the *'Corvus* or *caput corvi* (Raven's head) ... the traditional name for the *nigredo*'[79] (night, or as it was sometimes translated melancholia).

This stage was of the utmost importance; 'the raven's head is the beginning of the work'.[80] It was thought of as a state of incubation necessary for self-purification, self-purgation and self-transformation. In this state one experiences the feeling of being 'shut up in a cave' and one so suffering adds: 'I am likened to the black raven for that is the wages of sin; in dust and earth I lie.'[81] This state of intractable but necessary suffering was an essential first step on the journey towards self-knowledge. It was necessary, said the alchemist, to 'face one's own darkness'.[82] Jung with characteristic insight adds that this stage was tantamount to meeting the consequences of a collision between one's own consciousness and 'the darkness of the shadow',[83] an encounter of the greatest importance and one which could not be bypassed. Even these few passages allow us to perceive how little alchemy was intended to fulfill a mercenary quest and how much it opened up areas of psychological darkness in ways that allowed man to come to terms with it. Even today, as we witness in Hughes's poetry, recourse to rituals that enable one to confront the darness within have not lost their value or purpose. These rituals, in fact, are all the more necessary. Hughes seems to say, because our society (and our world) is one where the customary 'ceremonies of innocence' are drowned, dissolved and without meaning.

Through the imagery, process and symbolism of alchemy Hughes reproduces the experience of being swallowed up and reduced to the smallest particle or mote. Hughes describes the male protagonist in *Cave Birds* first as a cockerel and then as a participant in a marriage where 'bride and groom lie hidden for three days'. In Alchemy opposites were often picturesquely described as 'cock and hen'[84] prior to their mating which the alchemist termed the *coniunctio,* 'mystic marriage'[85] or mystical union of opposites. These opposites which we have referred to variously as soul and body, or mind and body split originally Jung suggests, from 'a weakness in the hierarchical order of the ego . . . enough to set these instinctive urges and desires in motion and bring about a dissociation of personality — in other words, a multiplication of its centres of gravity'.[86] What the alchemist sensed within himself was exactly the process we see re-enacted again and again in Hughes's poetry, although in forms so apparently diverse as to conceal their common nature. Knowing, for example, that this weakness in the order of the ego is frequently sensed, Jung says, as a 'will to power' disguised as 'hunger' or 'wanting to possess',[87] we recognize these traits not only in crow's hunger and corresponding need to possess but also in Prometheus's fire theft and the Reverend Lumb's split into two protagonists precipitated by his own *sol niger* and subsequent multiplication of the ego's centre of gravity.

Essentially, this is the same phenomenon the shaman tries to deal with under the guise of 'loss of soul'. The shaman, we recall, employs methods that are basically psychotherapeutic for recapturing the soul that has 'gone astray'. In allied cases when a person is in the process of turning a new page in his life the phenomenon of energy loss is experienced as part of what

Jung called an 'incubation period'.[88] Seen in this way the hero's experience of being swallowed by a raven is a metaphorical projection of what is felt personally to be an incubation period within a cave or womb prior to being reborn or hatched from the 'egg-stone' that bursts at the end of the sequence to reveal the hero reborn. The polarization between conscious and unconscious mind results quite spontaneously in landscapes that contrast the precarious state of the ego with the threatening forces of the unconscious — for example, an island about to be overwhelmed by the ocean. Sometimes the metaphor is centred on nourishment, having to subsist on meagre food supplies 'plagued with all sorts of imaginary wants' — a condition, Jung says, that has its origins in the fact that 'too much life has been left outside'. Frequently, the weakened ego potentiates or expands out of proportion the psychic potency of elements in the unconscious as 'a terrifying monster . . . roused out of its slumbers', or 'an alarming animal that stands in secret compensatory relationship to the island'.[89] Here we have the situation of Prometheus and his vulture, the conscious mind pursued by its opposite, projected in the form of a demon. Obviously such violent disjunction or split within the personality must engender an equally powerful longing for integration, a reuniting of separated elements that alchemy calls the 'royal marriage'.[90] Seen in this light, *Cave Birds* does depict the separation into self and demon and the journey towards the ultimately hoped for re-integration within the crucible of self, as Hughes says: 'in the wind-fondled crucible of his splendor/The dirt becomes God'.

Although the joining of opposites is the central event in the entire process, highlighted as such in *Cave Birds,* the painful conflict that begins the cycle must start with what the alchemist prescribes as the *'separatio or divisio elementorum'* that is 'dismemberment of the body', a process Jung describes as follows: 'the individual's specious unity . . . breaks down under the impact of the unconscious . . . once he realizes that he himself has a shadow, that his enemy is in his own heart, then the conflict begins and one becomes two.'[91] Some alchemical texts even represent these divided pair of opposites as 'a vulture on the peak of a mountain and a Raven without wings'.[92] The most frequent form in which the opposite is represented is the *soror mystica* (the mystical sister).[93] The metaphor of union with close blood relatives, although taboo in modern societies (yet not merely permitted but encouraged to conserve family property within ancient Egyptian families) is the metaphor most favoured by the alchemists since as Jung explains 'incest symbolizes union with one's own being' and for this reason the *coniunctio oppositorum* 'in the guise of Sol and Luna, the royal brother-sister' exerts 'an unholy fascination — not . . . as a crude reality but certainly as a psychic process controlled by the unconscious'.[94] It is for this reason, Jung believed, that: 'the first gods were often believed to propogate their kind incestuously.'[95] As a result, the opposite is often represented as the *soror mystica*. Moreover, the relationship between the *soror mystica* and the White Goddess archetype, says Jung, is that 'the anima is manifested projected in the shape of the goddess but in her proper (psychological) state she is introjected; she is . . . the "anima within" which gives rise to the incestuous *hieros gamos,* the marriage of the adept and his *soror'*.[96] In one text the initiate, or adept 'Gabricus disappears into the body of his sister Beya, where he is dissolved into atoms'.[97] The meaning of this scene which would be viewed with horror as a violation of one of the most basic societal taboos (consider the outrage that followed the disclosure of Byron's incestuous sexual relationship with his half-sister Augusta Leigh) when transformed into the context of a mystical alchemical marriage becomes an accurate representation for the consolidation of the psyche. This is why Hughes describes both the hero and the earthly woman as half-formed and half-born; his language is precise, accurate and evocative 'like two gods of mud/Sprawling in the dirt, but with infinite care/They bring each other to perfection'. The deep need for wholeness within the psyche can only be brought about in the context of relatedness to the *soror mystica,* a relatedness depicted in various metaphors. One image is the grave. Jung describes how 'Gabricus dies after becoming united with his sister'[98] while Hughes refers to 'a new grave'. This grave is also a 'sarcophagus and tomb' which mysteriously holds 'the grain in the earth: it dies only to waken to new life',[99] says Jung.

Within *Cave Birds* this metaphor reappears as the image of 'a seed in its armour', a grain wrapped in mummy cloth ('bandaging') that must die in order to be reborn. This was a favourite image of the alchemists, as Jung tells us 'the stone is also called "grain of wheat" since it remained itself alone, unless it dies'[100] an idea Jung relates to a comparison with 'the egg: first it decays then the chicken is born'.[101] In Hughes's

*Cave Birds*, this cluster of images reappears as a fusion of the grain of wheat, the philosopher's stone and the egg — 'grain', 'the egg stone'. The alchemist's conception of this whole process was often pictured in the form of the rose or 'wheel'.[102] The circular, on-going nature of the work (or the opus, as alchemists called it) began with the manipulation of external reagents, chemicals and material until this process was internalized within the psyche of the alchemists. To convey this progressive internalization of the quest Hughes's protagonist journeys from a point where he claims, quite falsely, a mastery of the process, saying he mounts the 'galaxy-wheel' to a much more realistic perspective where he acknowledges he is the least significant element, a passive speck or mote at the centre of the work. He slips into the centre of a 'tightening whorl'. This is clear evidence of the increasing internalization and self-transformation, working inward towards the centre, the pretence of absolute self-sufficiency now abandoned, the role of victim and scapegoat embraced as the only path leading to self-renewal. The self so formed is achieved only with the difficulty and its rarity and objective holding in permanent relation 'both ego and non-ego'[103] are frequently represented with the symbol of a precious gem, the quintessence of selfhood.

Within *Cave Birds*, in the poem Hughes calls 'Walking bare' (a theme suggested by the drawing Baskin titled 'A Crow of Prisms') his protagonist travels into the wind, makes his way across the crystalline desert, is devastated by a "blowtorch light' and becomes crystalline, shrunk to the most permanent element within himself, a 'gem' that is also a 'seed'. 'What is left is just what my life bought me/The gem of myself./A bare certainty, without confection.' This theme appears in the mystical literature of many cultures, Hindu, Buddhist, American Indian, etc. The Oriental counterpart, observes Joseph Campbell is the ' "diamond" or "thunderbolt" body . . . which the Yogi achieves'.[104] In the reconstitution/reconstruction of the self as part of shamanic rites of self-transformation, 'the new intestines of the shaman are composed of quartz crystals . . . death and restitution . . . with a new body that is adamantine'.[105]

Yet, significantly, while shamanic rituals suggest this process of self-transformation only has to occur once, alchemists held quite a different view, one much closer to Hughes's own. They stress the necessity for a repeated pattern of suffering and death, constantly re-engaged in what they called the 'iterum mori — the reiterated death'.[106] In its entirety the alchemists' view of their work as a ritual and Hughes's conception of *Cave Birds* as 'an alchemical cave drama' that is a 'ritual' as well, appear to coincide. In fact, the scenario for *Cave Birds,* that is the external stages through which the hero passes in his quest for self knowledge, appears drawn from the letter which John Pordage, alchemist and theologian, wrote to Jane Leade, his *soror mystica,* a woman of whom Pordage says 'she is my divine, eternal, essential self-sufficiency. She is my wheel within my wheel'[107] (a metaphor Hughes extended in both the 'galaxy-wheel' and the 'stopping and starting Catherine wheel'). Pordage describes the process of being consumed and drawn into the belly of the Raven: 'bound with the chains of darkness' one 'must enter into the fierce wrathful Mars by whom (as it happened to Jonah in the belly of Hell) it is swallowed . . . and here the divine artist in the philosophical work will see the first colour . . . and it is the blackest black; the learned philosophers call it their black crow, or their black Raven.' Pordage tells Jane Leade: 'you must not despise this blackness or black colour but persevere in it in patience, in suffering . . . when the seed of life shall waken to life . . . now is the stone shaped, the elixir of life prepared . . . for now the Man of Paradise is become clear as a transparent glass.'

The distinctive nature of Hughes's contribution to twentieth-century poetry emerges quite clearly in contrast with poems in which Dylan Thomas is working with many of the same themes, if not specifically the alchemical tradition, as Hughes is. For example, in one of Thomas's poems titled simply 'Now'[108] we find, in stanza three, Thomas speaking of the 'shade' of the crow or raven in comparison with 'the cockerel's hide'. Further, this poem describes an apocalyptic 'wheel of fire' in the imagery of fire and flower petals moving towards the ultimate union of 'the two-a-vein' or fused 'we'. Thomas too conceived of the journey in one's own skin, in a series of poems called 'The Map of Love'[109] (in Hughes's poem 'First, the Doubtful Charts of Skin/Came into my hands — I set out'). This metaphor is a recurrent one in Thomas's poetry. In 1934, Thomas wrote a poem called 'Foster the Light'[110] which place 'cockerels eggs' as a contrasting image to 'cross-bones' (in essence, one's own bones, innate strengths are weapons necessary in the journey for its self-purgation; compare 'under this rock he found weapons'). Within the same poem

Thomas beseeches 'make the world of me', 'glory in the shape-
less maps'. The conception of the hero as 'cockerel' about to
embark on a voyage where he will be beset by a 'goblin-sucker'
and have to depend on his own 'bones' for rescue is the theme
of this poem. In his 1936 poem 'Grief thief of time'[111] Thomas
projects the image of a 'rainbow' which bridges 'the human
halves', a metaphor intimately related to the alchemists' belief
that the final stages in the process of self-becoming saw the
appearance of the rainbow, or as it was called the peacock's
tail ('the appearance of the colours in the alchemical vessel',
Jung notes, 'the so-called *cauda pavonis* — peacock's tail —
denotes the Spring, the renewal of life').[112]

All these elements come together in Thomas's own equivalent
of *Cave Birds*, his sequence of ten sonnets 'Altarwise by Owl-
light',[113] written at the 'half-way house' of his own life between
womb and tomb. This sonnet sequence touches on the stages
of a necessary voyage begun by a cockerel (who some have
seen as a mock Hercules) journeying towards his own crucifixion and ultimate resurrection through the reintegration of
masculine and feminine elements within his nature; he is the
'gentleman of wounds' and the 'long wounds woman' — an
event celebrated by the appearance of a 'three-coloured rainbow'. Thomas's protagonist undergoes the experience of becoming his own skeleton and instead of Hughes's 'blowtorch
light' we have the sun's 'blow-clock witness' — in both, a
penetrating vision into one's quintessential self. Further,
Thomas's conception of his poems as embalmed bodies, on
paper rag, or mummy cloth awaiting their resurrection through
publication appears transformed in the 'mummy bandaging'
imagery of Hughes. Thomas's sequence ends with an injunction
of the poet to himself not to enter the deceptive permanence
of orthodox religions but urges himself to ascend the 'rainbow's
quayrail' or Eden 'green as beginning'. Like Hughes, Thomas
sees 'Altarwise by Owl-light' as a process of ceremonial ritual.
What makes *Cave Birds* more satisfying, to my mind, is the
unfailing sense of faithfulness to the anguish, sense of failure
and consequent need to experience one's own death, symbolically and the overriding humility of the personality at the
core of these experiences. It is the nature of this failure and its
implications for the protagonist that we must next explore.

Hughes came to write *Cave Birds*, we recall, when he saw
a series of nine drawings by Leonard Baskin, the first of which
is titled 'A Hercules-in-the-Underworld Bird' (which became in

*Cave Birds,* 'The Summoner'). The multitude of iconographic, literary and mythological associations circling around the figure of Hercules made him an ideal choice as the starting point of the sequence. It was he who is represented by the ancients as slaying the Nemean Lion known today in its representation as the constellation Leo, the sign governing Hughes's birth. It was he who descended to the underworld to rescue Alcestis, the wife who died for her husband, Admetus and it was he whom the great engraver Albrecht Durer chose to represent in *Der Hercules* as wearing a cock's comb, or head of a rooster, on his head.[114] Hughes has penetrated, with uncanny insight, into the heart of the meaning of this figure and has come away with what is of use to himself, a sense of what Hercules's journey to the underworld meant in the context of his previous violence, power, and even madness, a madness that took its toll of Megara and their children. Hughes gives Hercules's descent to the underworld its true character as an initiatory ordeal, a necessary breaking of strength by the strongest of all men, a self-confrontation by him who has conquered everything and has nothing more to conquer except himself. The cycle that crested with Prometheus, of self-assertion and endurance against forces outside the self, has turned inward. The symbolism is clear and fitting; self-confrontation, in the underworld, in the cave of one's self, in the heart (in the sense of *vena cava*) has replaced confrontation and self-assertion on the crag of a mountain peak. Self-confrontation, self-transmutation through the descent and embracing of one's own death has been engaged. The 'gem' of authentic selfhood is being sought but first the splendidly feathered cockerel must see himself as he really is, a crow.

For Hughes, as for T. S. Eliot (and for Shakespeare, although for different reasons in *Hamlet*) Hercules is an archetypal figure who plays an important role at crucial moments. In T. S. Eliot's treatment of the *Alcestis* in *The Cocktail Party,*[115] Hercules is transformed into a psychiatrist, Sir Henry Harcourt-Reilly who, like Hercules, pays an unexpected visit to the home of Edward (modelled on Admetus) whose wife has died and needs the ministrations of a shamanic figure to restore her to life. Although Edward and Admetus are the focal points of both Euripides's and T. S. Eliot's plays we should not forget that Hercules appears and risks his own life in a descent to the underworld to fight Death and redeem Alcestis because he, too, albeit unconsciously, has been responsible for the death of his own wife and children. His ability to help Admetus is a crucial stage in his own self-transformation. But, before self-transformation there must be self-recognition, Hercules opposite Admetus facing each other. In *The Cocktail Party* Edward is judged guilty of sacrificing his wife to death through indifference; in Celia's eyes he has become less than human, 'dry, endless, meaningless, inhuman'.

In *Cave Birds* the protagonist is transformed as fitting existential punishment into the subhuman bestial figure of a crow. The complaints, failures and inadequacies of both Admetus and Edward echo each other and provide a framework, almost a tradition, in which to understand the self-accusations of the narrator in *Cave Birds*. These self-incriminating, inquisitorial moments, a mind flaming in the agony of self-recrimination, are interspersed within the objective framework that the alchemical process, with its inexorable cyclic progression, provided Hughes. Poems one ('The scream'), three ('After the first fright'), five ('She seemed so considerate'), eight ('In these fading moments I wanted to say'), eleven ('First, the doubtful charts of skin'), fifteen ('A flayed crow in the hall of judgment'), seventeen ('Only a little sleep, a little slumber'), nineteen ('As I came, I saw a wood') and twenty-five ('Walking bare') comprise the inner, subjective sequence most often in the first person, the heart's core of self-confrontation within and yet counterpointed to the protagonist's accusers and judges. This split, between self and world, is perhaps the most telling feature structurally and allows Hughes to place the sufferings of his protagonist in a more comprehensive mythic, alchemical and literary framework. The drama of self-estrangement becomes progressively more fitful and the intervals between these 'personal' bursts of remembered challenges that had not been met become fewer and fewer — a dwindling, so to speak, down to nothing of the old ego in a manner that is infinitely moving.

The cutting edge of Hughes's style in these poems reveals a spirit nailing itself on the cross of its own pain, an anguish so compressed and so complex in its mixture of self-mockery and self-judgment, that it quite literally requires the restraining force of the larger tableau of judgment to hold it in perspective. Shrewd insinuations of past failures, overheard comments of strangely distant participants, themselves estranged from the true nature of the suffering woman at the core of these poems, a sense of the personal indignity and humiliation that has mysteriously befallen, all are taken up and refashioned into a uniquely moving self-inquisition. As the cycle of poems within *Cave Birds* unfolds the nature of the spiritual plight plaguing Hughes's protagonist shows itself. His psychic life is divided, fragmented in a way that suggests that marriage with his *soror mystica* respresents the only way to reconcile his split self although the possibility of such a mythic fulfillment as a permanent fact is undercut by the reappearance of the 'goblin' at the end of the sequence. Seen in this way, Hughes's choice of various animals, specifically the cockerel, underscores his central purpose. What better way to parody a personality so complacent, so self-righteous, so smug and so blissfully hypocritical than to represent it as a cockerel. The metaphors speak for themselves. In the poem now titled 'The scapegoat' (previously called 'The Culprit') based on Baskin's drawing 'A Stud Cockerel Hunted into a Desert', the protagonist is portrayed as 'the beautiful thing . . . Swagged with wealth, full organed' and at the same time, 'the comedian' and 'the joker'. Yet this is but how he appears to others. From within, as in the initial poem 'The scream', he feels 'flesh of bronze, stirred with a bronze thirst'. Besides referring to that odd greenish bronze light that comes off the feathers of roosters these images suggest a constricted self, enchained, encased in a metallic bronze body. Flamboyant yet enclosed, outwardly magnificent yet inwardly constricted, his arrogance translates itself into moral insensitivity.

The choice of imagery is significant when we recall that Hercules's sixth labour, notes Robert Graves, 'was to remove the countless brazen-beaked, brazen-clawed, brazen-winged, maneating birds'[116] that flocked to the 'Stymphalian Marsh'. These birds lived in a forest near Stymphalus between Arcadia and Mycenae and were greatly feared because of their horrible beaks that could pierce metal and terrible metallic feathers and claws. Wondering what to do Hercules was helped by Athena who gave him 'a pair of brazen-castanets' whose terrible noise drove the Stymphalian birds up into the air where Hercules shot them in great numbers. Although not originally a part of the 'marriage-task sequence' (as Graves notes) Hughes has realigned this episode within a series of initiatory ordeals that precedes the marriage ritual at the end of *Cave Birds*. The numerous owls, eagles and vultures who oversee the protagonist's initiatory labours derive essentially from the figure of Athena who is present, as it were, by proxy through her totem animals. Not only is Athena always eager to aid Hercules but she often appears, Graves observes, in several 'bird epiphanies . . . in Homer she appears as a sea-eagle (*Odyssey* iii. 371) and a swallow (Ibid. xxii. 239); in company with Apollo, as a vulture (Iliad vii. 58) . . . but the wise owl was her principle epiphany.'[117]

It is startling to consider that for all its complexity *Cave Birds* is retelling an old story, perhaps the oldest in the world, a quest for love or more specifically the conditions under which it may exist and be available to the narrator — and more to the point what kind of person he himself must be, or be transformed into, to undertake such a quest. We need only recall the delightful visionary adventure described by Chaucer in *The Parliament of Fowls*.[118] On St Valentine's Day (an appropriate choice certainly) a variety of birds assemble to select their mates, a procedure they follow each year. The irony of the tale arises from the fact that the speaker to whom this lovely and unusual dream vision has occured is himself, for reasons unknown to us, exiled from participating in the experience of love. In fact, we sense the veiled self-critical irony the speaker directs against himself. The proceedings of the parliament, like those in *Cave Birds,* are equally a trial and debate and like the poem cycle of Hughes the speaker is left at the end curiously unable to attain what he has described with such passionate involvement. The profound nature of love has eluded him and his dream has remained for him but a charming exercise in futility. Instead of a hall of judgment, as in *Cave Birds* (which Hughes adapted as we shall see from Egyptian mythology) Chaucer's poem transpires within a temple of love. The diety under whose careful watch the choosing of mates takes place is the 'noble goddess nature' and true love only comes, she says, between 'perfect mates' as a balance of romantic, erotic and spiritual forces. She carefully balances arguments between contending parties who include the 'foules of ravyne' that is, eagles. We see the 'gentil faucon' (the falcon perched on his master's hand — an image Hughes returns to in the final poem in *Cave Birds*) and the 'chough' (the crow). While the criteria for choosing one's mate reflects the courtly requirements at which Chaucer was poking fun, albeit in his usual gently ironic way, the central theme of the work resides in the ironic and poignant contrast between the narrator's inability to become part of the tableau seen in his dream vision and the scenario of a nature goddess watching over, and arbitrating, various birds as they inquire into the true meanings of love. The meaning of love and the conditions under which it can be achieved by the narrator is very much the issue within *Cave Birds*.

Hughes, however, working within the framework of the mythology attending Hercules, draws this theme within a purgatorial context arising from the self-immolation of Hercules on Mount Oetna. This event occurred when Hercules's wife Dejaniera learned of Hercules's involvement with Iole. She sent him a tunic smeared with poison from a centaur named Nessus that Hercules had shot. Putting on the tunic his flesh began to be corroded and burnt yet because of his superhuman strength he was unable to die. His suffering surpassed the bounds of all imaginable pain and yet he could not die until he ordered a funeral pyre to be built and he incinerated himself on the top of Mount Oetna. The violence of his life, a violence that flows into acts of madness (although, as the story goes, supposedly motivated by the goddess Hera's lifelong hatred for him), is matched by the violence of his death. Yet it is precisely the superhuman conditions of unendurable pain and a suffering that cannot be evaded that guarantee his transcendence of himself and his entry, by Zeus's fiat, into Olympus.

What are we to make of such a spectacle? T. S. Eliot, in the last of his *Four Quartets*, titled 'Little Gidding'[119] penetrated to the essential nature of the scene in the context of self-purgation as a precondition for love. Eliot's narrator meets a spirit from the underworld who describes the enormous difficulties and the crucial role of fire, the self-engendered flames of the intellect's fiery self-inquisition, if resurrection is to be achieved. The action of the poem occurs after a dawn air raid (Eliot, we remember, wrote 'Little Gidding' in 1942 when he served as an observer to spot incendiary fires) and the speaker's relation to the ghost (a ghost who 'faded on the blowing of the horn' as Hamlet's father's ghost 'faded on the crowing of the cock' — *Hamlet* I, 2, l.57) suggests a visitation by one's alter ego. In fact, the idea of a psychic split and consequent doubling of the protagonist within *Cave Birds* may well have been suggested by the narrator's cry in 'Little Gidding': 'so I assumed a double part and cried/And heard another voice's cry: "what! are *you* here?"/Although we were not. I was still the same,/Knowing myself yet being someone other —and he a face still forming.' While it is true that the idea for having the personality of the narrator literally split is characteristic of many modern poems, some of them excellent, (as for example Eliot's 'The Lovesong of J. Alfred Prufrock' or Erza Pound's 'Hugh Selwyn Mauberley' sequence, counterpointing, as they do the inner struggling subjectivity, owning up to its own failures and inadequacies in opposition to an environment subject to the author's withering irony), Hercules is not at the centre of these poems as he is in 'Little Gidding'. Historically, we recall that when Charles I wished to find a place in which to pursue a devout reappraisal of himself, in true humility, he chose Little Gidding. We must also remember that Mrs Hughes's family were, as Edward Butscher observes, 'Farrars and Nicholas Farrar, founder of Little Gidding, was an ancestor'.[120] Thus, for any number of reasons it was an ideal choice to explore the theme that love in its most profound form entails a suffering that itself purges and tests him who would embark on such a journey. Hughes's phrase, 'her feathers are leaves, the leaves tongues, The mouths wounds, the tongues flames' as well as other references to the 'crucible . . . raw with cringing heat' and the 'bitumen of blood and smoke of tears' repeatedly return to the context of Eliot's poem, love that destroys and love that redeems, 'with flame of incandescent terror/Of which the tongues declare./The one discharge from sin and error./The only hope, or else despair/ Lies in the choice of fire or pyre —/To be redeemed from fire by pyre/Who then devised the torment? Love. Love is the unfamiliar name behind the hands that wove the intolerable shirt of flame.' In the context of *Cave Birds* the fiery purgation of self-immolation suffered by Hercules is transformed into a stripping away of illusions regarding oneself. Layer upon layer of the narrator's personality is stripped away; he slips below the threshold of man and becomes a beast. He undergoes a metamorphosis into subhumanity so that the conditions may be created within which he may regain his humanity and these conditions entail a descent into the self. Through an inexorable logic, until the process of self-purification begins his only hope of re-entering the flow of life, he fears the processes of nature: 'And when I saw new emerald tufting the quince, in April/And cried in dismay: "Here it comes again!"' These lines voice the element within himself that holds his personality apart from the rhythmical cyclic replacement which Wallace Stevens in 'Peter Quince at the Clavier' portrayed as the ultimate truth that we on earth can know, the yearly replacement of maidens, gardens and nature itself returning each Spring, in April (the quince, Graves notes, was considered sacred to Venus).[121]

Before self-confrontation Hughes's Urizenic protagonist is not only shut out from the erotic regenerating forces of nature but fears them and so suffers a diminution of his own psychic spiritual life. His self-renewal hinges on and is inseparable from his ability to strip himself bare. His personality is but a useless cockerel exterior impeding his search for truth. He is in the spiritually desolate state described by Yeats in 'The Circus Animals' Desertion', 'I must lie down where all the ladders start/In the foul rag-and-bone shop of the heart.'[122] When Hughes's 'knight' (modelled on Baskin's drawing, A Death Stone Crow of Carrion) becomes the merest remnant of himself, 'Here a bone, there a rag', we sense the brutal honesty and self-lacerating need to build again from the resources of the heart, a burning desire to refashion his life through confession. The nature of this failure can be inferred from the poem Hughes titled 'First, the doubtful charts of skin', which contains a passage adapted from T. S. Eliot's 'The Wasteland':

> I came to loose bones
> On a heathery moor, and a roofless church.
>
> Wild horses, with blowing tails and manes,
> Standing among graves.
>
> And a leaning menhir, with my name on it.
> And an epitaph, which read:
> 'Under this rock, he found weapons.'

The weapons Hughes refers to are those of self-knowledge, the values Hughes's protagonist must discover within himself in order to be reborn. In 'The Wasteland' the unseen narrator moves through a landscape of his own psychic condition, a world that reflects his own fragmented, moribund spiritual state. At moments he is identified with Odysseus or, as in the prototype for Hughes's passage, with Parzival approaching the chapel Perilous, 'Over the tumbled graves, about the chapel/ There is the empty chapel, only the winds home./It has no windows, and the door swings, dry bones can harm no one only a cock stood on the roof-tree/Coco rico coco coco rico.'[123] The questions this Parzival figure fails to ask relate to the central injunction expressed in the commands from the Upanishads 'Datta, dayadhvam, damyata', that is, give, sympathize, control. These are the true weapons. Hughes's portagonist must acknowledge his failures to give, his failures to have compassion, and above all his failures to exercise self-control (these failures, in turn are intimately related to the character defects responsible for manifestations of violence and madness in Hercules and as we shall see, Hamlet as well). The nature of the hero's guilt emerges in scenes of almost archetypal desertion, a fatal inability to rouse oneself to the urgency and implications of the moment as can be seen in the poem Hughes titled 'Something was happening'. The narrator thinks ' "Ought I to turn back, or keep going?"/Her heart stopped beating, that second.' And again, 'all the time/I was scrubbing at my nails and staring through the window/She was burning.' Originally Hughes had compared his narrator with 'Hamlet/Looking at Ophelia's corpse' but later deleted these lines while clearly keeping many traits that tie his hero's plight with Hamlet's predicament.

First of all, Hamlet consistently, if ironically, compares himself to Hercules ('but no more like my father/Than I to Hercules' *Hamlet* I, Sc.2, 1.153) and quite early in the play projects himself, despite an inital disclaimer, in a Herculean context ('My fate cries out/And makes each petty artere in this body/As hardy as the Nemean lion's nerve' I, Sc.5, ll. 82–84). The goblin that comes up at the end of *Cave Birds* to reinstigate the whole cycle yet again is drawn from Hamlet's initial encounter with his father's ghost ('be thou a spirit of health or goblin damned' I, Sc. 4, 1.40). The central issue, of course, to which Hughes draws attention to indicate its similarity to his narrator's predicament is Hamlet's treatment of Ophelia and the theme is clearly that of guilt. In Act I, Scene 1 when Hamlet's father appears before Marcellus and Bernardo the stage directions tell us that 'the cock crows the ghost disappears and Bernardo speaks'. The ghost apparently was about to speak when the cock began crowing and then, says Horatio 'it started like a guilty thing/Upon a fearful summons.' Recalling that Baskin's drawing of a cockerel faces Hughes's poem 'The Summoner' it is apparent that guilt can literally summon one to the underworld. When Hamlet learns that it is Ophelia's body that is about to be buried ('This doth betoken/The corse [corpse] they follow did with desp'rate hand/Fordo its own life' V, Sc. 1, ll.166–7) the enormous responsibility he bears for her suicide is so intolerable that he rages theatrically, pitting his love for Ophelia and affirming its greater magnitude over that of Laertes, her brother. He tries at all costs to conceal from himself, by ranting, by asserting his superior grief and by being incredibly self-righteous, the obvious causal relationship between his treatment of Ophelia and her death. Ophelia's corpse is almost a physical rebuke and his desire to shield himself channels his vehemence outward. The discrepancy between things as they are and things as they seem underlies the world of Hamlet and that of the narrator in *Cave Birds* as well.

Yet the crux of the matter and the triggering event for Hamlet is Gertrude's actions. Deep in Hamlet's nature arises a horrified aversion, a loathing and fear of womanhood that passes intermittently into madness. Ophelia, believing that Hamlet's falling out of love with her is her own fault (for no reason that she can clearly define) and subjected to Hamlet's ranting, savage and abusive harangue, in a moment of madness allows herself to be drowned. Hamlet's appearance, from the first, is ravenlike ('tis not alone my inky cloak, with mother, Nor customary suits of solemn black' I, Sc.2, ll. 77—8) and as Hughes said of his protagonist 'his crime implicates him in wider and wider responsibilites. His victim takes on a form which is progressively more multiple and serious, progressively more personal and inescapable.' One after the other, Polonius, Rosencrantz, Guildenstern, Ophelia, Laertes, Gertrude and Hamlet himself, as well as the entire kingdom succumb to the consequences of Hamlet's disastrous inability to 'suit the word to the action'. An especially sombre note is added to the poem when we realize that Ophelia's madness ('poor Ophelia/Divided from herself and her fair judgment' IV, Sc. 5, l.85), her possible motivation ('it springs/ All from her father's death' IV, Sc.5, l.75), and the occasion mentioned in her song ('tomorrow is St Valentine's Day' IV, Sc. 5, l.48) remind us that for reasons probably deeply connected with her own father's death, Sylvia committed suicide a few days before St Valentine's Day in 1963. Hamlet illustrates the tragic consequences of the platonizing mind at its most extreme. True, Hamlet is an idealist, yet his excessive intellect creates such idealized and extreme needs and demands that any real or imagined deviation from them provokes him to unwarranted physical and verbal retaliation; simply put, he kills all the wrong people, alternating long stretches of paralyzed will and spasmodic outbursts of vehement action. His madness is more than a pretence; he remains as much a mystery to himself as he is to others. Hamlet provides an insight into the character of Hughes's protagonist and illustrates the nature of the hero's crimes which must be purged through trial and judgment.

The self-to-be-purged, which Hughes represents in the form of crow (e.g. 'a flayed crow in the hall of judgment') is but the alter-ego of the Hercules based self who summons his crow self to judgment. The ancient Celtic name for crow or raven, says Robert Graves, was 'Bran'. This stemmed from the fact that 'the raven, or crow, was Bran's oracular bird'.[124] Bran is Hercules's twin or ghostly double, his 'tanist' or other self. Significantly, the sun-based hero Hercules and the crow hero Bran both have esoteric connections with Hughes's astrological sign Leo, whose ruling planet is the sun and third decan (or last ten degree division in the final third of the sign) is the raven. According to mythographers, Graves recalls, Hercules sailed 'to the west from Greece . . . and went by way of North Africa . . . and Gaul (where he fathered the Celts) . . . and ultimately arrived to do combat in a place that is famous for its bright red soil and red cattle.'[125] Here he kills an antagonist whom, by killing, Graves says, allowed Hercules to gain 'a victory over one of his own selves'.[126] Significantly, Graves hypothesizes that the place where Hercules performs his victory over himself, 'famous for its bright red soil and red cattle', may indeed be modern Devonshire, the region in England where Hughes presently lives and has for some time.[127] We must not overlook the fact that Hughes often shows a preference for heroes with whom he can establish personal and esoteric connections often in ways that are profound and mysterious.

The overriding image, the one picture, so to speak, behind *Cave Birds*, the secret dream of the self around which *Cave Birds* centres is that of Hercules's self-immolation, a fiery catharsis that is also an enduring, yet unendurable, crucifixion. Hughes's concern in *Prometheus on his Crag, Cave Birds* and *Gaudete* is principally with creating the conditions under which this sought-for crucifixion and consequent self-confrontation can take place. His heroes must be opened up, stripped bare, each impulse extracted, each motive turned over, looked at, weighed and analyzed, yet he can never release these heroes from their posture of suffering and let them slip off the cross so to speak. In fact if anything, the progression, although quite unplanned from Prometheus to Hercules to Dionysos suggests that the need to create ever more complete conditions of self-confrontation and self-purgation has become a permanent fixture in Hughes's universe of moral values, a moral stance, as it were, that must be reinvoked by increasingly violent scenes of self-catharsis. Hughes's position in these works is quite close to that of Yeats in 'A Dialogue of Self and Soul'. The Soul urges man to transcend life (to go on holiday, as Hughes might say, to one of the 'heavens' available in countless religions, East and West) while the Self is responsive to the beauty and horror of life. Paradoxically, by confronting and accepting the worst that life can inflict, the self wins the right to see life itself as the source of those spiritually transcendent values which the Soul maintains can only be achieved after death. The choice of the Self is for rebirth and the pain, agony and beauty of incarnate existence, rather than for the refusal of life and escape into eternity offered by the Soul. In effect, Hughes is depicting his own conception of self-purification which casts out guilt and achieves a kind of impassioned purity through self-forgiveness.

Numerous elements in Egyptian mythology have found their way into *Cave Birds,* especially the procedure, described in *The Book of the Dead,* which relates how the heart of the dead person is put on balance scales and weighed. In various hieroglyphs a baboon is represented sitting atop the balance beam and when the scale is perfectly balanced the judgment is ready to begin. This fact is communicated to Thoth, one of the most powerful of the Egyptian gods who describes himself, in *The Book of the Dead* as 'Thoth, the excellent scribe . . . who makes inequity to be destroyed . . . who judges right and truth for the gods'.[128] The dead person's heart was weighed against Maat, the goddess of ultimate truth and justice. The weighing ceremony took place in the Hall of Judgment into which the deceased was lead by Anubis. It was presided over by Isis and Osiris and forty-two judges who heard the deceased's so-called Negative Confessions, that is, his formal statement of the sins he had not committed during his lifetime. Significantly, Isis is often portrayed in Egyptian hieroglyphs as a woman wearing the Vulture Headress, a ceremonial raiment with a vulture figure incorporated at its base and topped by a disc of the sun surmounted by horns.[129] Each facet of this scene appears in *Cave Birds.* Vultures in Egypt were all thought to be females and were supposed to have fore-knowledge of who was to be killed and so would hover over them waiting to pick the flesh from their bones. Hughes's poem 'The Accused' describes how 'on a flame-horned mountain-stone, in the sun's disc,/He heaps them all up, for the judgment.'[130] Waiting at the bottom of the scale was a deity known as Amam, an incredible beast whose name quite literally means 'devourer'. It was the function of Anubis to not only guide the person who had died to the various levels of the underworld, into the kingdom of the dead but to make sure that Amam did not prematurely devour the dead person's heart. If the deceased's heart was found to be 'light' and the judgment went against him he was instantly seized and devoured by Amam who was often depicted sitting at the bottom of the balance beam, eagerly waiting the outcome of the judgments. The similarity between this scene and the tableau of 'The interrogator' (facing the drawing Baskin called 'A Titled Vulturess') where Hughes depicts a 'spread-fingered Efreet', or demon in Arabian mythology, sweeping 'into the courts of the after-life' is obvious. So too, Hughes's poem 'A flayed crow in the hall of judgment' depicts the narrator with his 'soul skinned, and the soul-skin laid out/A mat for my judges'. Robert Graves reminds us that in the various depictions of Hercules's visit to the underworld he is attended by a dog that Graves identifies with Anubis 'the companion of the Egyptian Thoth'.[131] Thus, for Graves there is little doubt that the Egyptian conception of the descent to the underworld and Hercules's journey through the kingdom of the dead are variants of the same myth. We have seen how Hughes's poem 'Bride and groom lie hidden for three days' embodies the alchemist's dream of a mystical marriage with the *soror mystica*. Egyptian mythology depicted this state in the relationship between Osiris, god of the underworld and Isis, his sister and archetypal symbol of the great fructifying force of womanhood, she who is mother and both sister and wife to Osiris. Specifically this poem encompasses the process by which Osiris's body, or what was left of it after it had been torn and scattered, is carefully reassembled and brought back to life by Isis. Within *Cave Birds* Hughes's complex conception of moral purgation and psychological catharsis fuses important elements drawn from Egyptian mythology, alchemy and the Orphic emphasis on the need to atone if one is to avoid repetition of the same sin and incur the same punishment endlessly.

We recall that facing Hughes's poem 'The accused' is Baskin's drawing of a somewhat disheveled cockerel whom he called 'A Tumbled Socratic Cock'. The original context, of course, is Plato's account of Socrates's last day. Socrates was tried, found guilty by his fellow Athenians, confined in prison and sentenced to die by drinking hemlock, a usual if prolonged form of execution that was quite customary. The account is from the point of view of an eye witness, Phaedo of Elis, which gives this work its name, *The Phaedo*. Hughes's antagonism to Greek rationalism as it was embodied in Socrates and conversely his imagistic allegiance to the pre-Socratic cults, including Orphism are nowhere more in evidence than in the elements he chooses to emphasise from this dialogue. During Socrates's last moments, as the numbing effect of the hemlock worked its way gradually upwards, deadening first his feet, then legs and just before it reached his heart he supposedly said: 'Crito, we ought to offer a cock to Aesclepius. See to it and don't forget.'[132] Since Aesclepius was known as the god of medicine and thus healing, Socrates's last request was a characteristically ironic gesture, thanking death, the ultimate physician for healing him of life. It was customary to offer a cock to Aesclepius in hopes of being healed. If this scene provided the cockerel metaphor then the essentially Orphic features within *Cave Birds* derive from Socrates's discussion, made more poignant by the fact he is soon to die, of the moral judgment to which the newly deceased must submit themselves and the necessary purification of those not free from sin. The underworld is conceived of as a great time of trial, a summons to judgment. 'When any man dies', observes Socrates, 'his own guardian spirit, which was given charge over him in his life tries to bring him to a certain place where all must assemble and from which, after submitting their several cases to judgment, they must set out for the next world . . . when they have undergone the necessary experiences and remained as long as is required another guide brings them back . . .'[133] Significantly, Socrates emphasises the definite need for a guide since the road there and back 'contains many forkings and crossroads',[134] a notion Hughes incorporates in his poem titled 'The Guide'. Socrates follows quite closely the Orphic doctrine in his explanation of the 'caverns and sand and measureless mud'[135] through which the dead must pass in their purgatorial descent to a judgment that demanded a scrupulously honest self-analysis as a precondition for self-renewal. Martin P. Nilsson observed that 'for the Orphics also, initiation and the accompanying purification were necessary but they added a demand for righteousness and moral purity. He who was not purified in this life will continue in his impurity in the other life. "He will lie in the mud" is the keynote of the new ideas of the other world.'[136]

This phrase forms a central metaphor in the mystical and ecstatic celebrations of Orphic cults which often took place, says R. F. Willetts, within the innermost recesses of sacred caves: 'to these sacred sites only the initiated could penetrate'.[137] In both *Cave Birds* and *Gaudete* the imagery of either a man and woman struggling in the mud ('Like two gods of mud/Sprawling in the dirt' in 'Bride and groom lie hidden for three days') or the figure of an earth goddess giving birth to the Reverend Lumb in the mud ('the rain striking across the mud face washes it./It is a woman's face,/A face as if sewn together from several faces') is derived from the imagery of the Orphic cult where, as Nilsson says, 'the old keynote, the lying in the mud, recurs constantly in many variations.'[138] This was a crucial stage in the regeneration and rediscovery of oneself and demanded an acknowledgment of one's sins. In effect, one had to 'know oneself' and it was this feature of Orphism which was so attractive to Socrates. In order to be reborn those one had injured or abused or killed had to forgive one; as Socrates says, 'they cry aloud and call upon those whom they have killed or misused . . . if they prevail, they come out and there is an end to their distress; but if not, they are swept away once more into Tartarus . . . and find no release from their sufferings until they prevail upon those whom they have wronged.'[139]

Thus, moral regeneration meant submitting oneself to an initiatory process that was a self-judgment. Significantly, the few Orphic hymns that survive connect the entombed moral state of the initiate with the image of the raven. In the text the initiate feels as if his benightedness has caused him to be 'shut up in a cave . . . I am likened to the black raven, for that is the wages of sin; in dust and earth I lie.'[140] The emphasis on admission of sin and acceptance of punishment as the precondition for a renewed life was the very heart of Orphism and in the context of *Cave Birds* chimes in with the self-immolation of Hercules as a scapegoat figure and supports this image on a mystical level. What Socrates omits from his account and Hughes, following Robert Graves and before him Apuleius in the initiatory work titled *The Golden Ass,* includes is the crucial role played in this drama of spiritual self-transformation by a figure whom Graves calls 'The White Goddess'. In Apuleius's work the experience of Lucius parallels that of Hughes's protagonist in *Cave Birds* and he is rescued from his state of bestiality and attendant 'depth of misery and spiritual degradation', says Graves, through his initiation into the worship of Isis whom Graves sees as a type of the White Goddess.[141] Hughes, as we have seen, follows the symbolism suggested in arcane tradition, making his hero crow-like to represent the undesirable character traits that render him less than human, chief among which are his indifference, his self-conceit and most importantly his power of denying to himself the truth of his condition. Since his protagonist does not understand, as Hughes says, the sequence of moral cause and effect and since he is less than human it is appropriate that cause and effect should be compressed into one existential punishment and he should quite literally become that which he is, a crow. Thus, the whole of *Cave Birds* is an exercise designed to rediscover the preliminary conditions necessary to regain one's humanity and be reborn. As such, it represents a very conscious choice for the path of guilt, suffering, punishment and atonement expressed in the poem Hughes titled 'A Riddle'. This is the path of the scapegoat who brings the whole wrath of an enraged natural world down upon him in order that he may have the chance to suffer and a still rarer chance to transform that suffering into a quality which is of permanent use to himself.

## Chapter Seven
## CLOSING OF THE CIRCLE: DIONYSUS TO PARZIVAL IN GAUDETE

Before Hughes begins the narrative of *Gaudete*[142] he cites two passages, one from the ancient Greek philosopher Heraclitus and the other an excerpt from *Parzival*, by Wolfram Von Eschenbach. The vision of Heraclitus is of two realms, life and death, Dionysos and Hades, locked in complementary embrace:

> If it were not Hades, the god of the dead and the under-world, for whom these obscene songs are sung and festivals are made, it would be a shocking thing. But Hades and Dionysos are one.

Dionysos has always stood as a symbol of the rending force of the natural instincts, a force capable of fragmenting the conscious mind, a force that is perilous to ignore. In essence, the descent into Hades, into the tumultuous vortex of the underworld restates the idea of Dionysian frenzy as a fragmentation of the conscious mind through a descent into the unconscious. Clearly, the significance underlying Hughes's reference to this passage of Heraclitus lies in the relationship between Dionysos and Hades. Through Hades we are made aware of an underworld ruled by the dead, a realm of 'terror, mystery and the inexorable'. Dionysos, on the other hand, is most often viewed as 'the god who is destroyed, who disappears, who relinquishes life and then is born again, who becomes the symbol of everlasting life'.[143] Heraclitus envisaged an ongoing, perpetual battle between these two forces. As each would weaken, in turn the other grew stronger; yet each was mysteriously dependent on the other. Two worlds existing in reciprocal relation, balancing one another are analogous to the predicament explored, although in a different context in *Parzival* (Book XV):

> Their battle had come to the point where I cannot refrain from speaking up. And I mourn for this, for they were the two sons of one man. One could say that 'they' were fighting in this way if one wished to speak of two. These two, however, were one, for 'my brother and I' is one body, like good man and good wife. Contending here from loyalty of heart, one flesh, one blood, was doing itself much harm.

The writer of *Parzival* comments that the battle between Parzival and the Moslem knight had reached a point where he cannot 'refrain from speaking up'. The life of the 'Reverend Nicholas Lumb, an Anglican clergyman' has also reached a crisis point, the point of self-confrontation that Hughes explores by transforming the two halves of the Reverend Lumb's psyche into two separate selves. In the language of *Parzival*, 'these two, however, were one.' Two separate selves, each undercutting the other, each destroying their common strength through a self-destructive interaction take the story of a battle between a Christian and a Moslem knight and transform it into the psychological conflict of two separate selves, a seesaw battle between two worlds that, at the same time, is an objectification of the philosophy of Heraclitus. The descent of the hero, whether Beowulf, Siegfried, Aeneas or Christ into the underworld to do combat with the demonic forces below the surface of the world is a recurrent feature in all mythology. By splitting Lumb into two selves, one inhabiting this world and the other claimed by the world hidden from us Hughes gives objective form to the pattern of heroic combat that psychologically entails a descent into the chaos of the unconscious. In a real sense, *Gaudete* involves the harrowing of a personal hell, a combat with one's innermost fears and traumatic obsessions. No matter how many times one re-experiences the story this frightening quality effectively communicates itself to the reader. Quite unexpectedly *Gaudete* appears as an involuntary testament to the power of the abyss, a drama of defeat by those forces that one had, as it were, volunteered to engage in combat.[144] In the death of the hero we see the conscious ego being overwhelmed and engulfed by the unconscious mind. The ego is, after all, to the psyche what the hero is to the myth he expresses.[145] Parzival is a hero caught in the pattern of the quest for a legendary Holy Grail. He does battle with demons, hideously strong opponents and demonic forces that are, in reality, projections of that within himself which he has most reason to fear.

This recurrent theme makes comprehensible the connection between Dionysos, Hades, and Parzival himself. For Hughes the secret psychological meaning of these myths is that the descent into Hades entails the dissociation and fragmentation of the ego, a war of two selves that is akin to the violent dismemberment of Dionysos as a necessary pre-requisite for his resurrection. On a mythic level the archetype of the dying and reviving god projected in the form of Dionysos provides the model for Rev. Lumb's adventures after he is removed from a rural community in the north of England 'by elemental spirits' and replaced by a changeling, 'an exact duplicate' created and entrusted with the mission of begetting a new Messiah using the women of the town.[146] We never learn the name of this isolated farming town; it seems to exist out of the mainstream of modern life. Dionysos was the god of fertility and Rev. Lumb, acting as a pseudo-Dionysos attempts to reverse the barrenness of the parish (which makes it analogous to Hades, the place of the dead) by copulating with all the women who live there. Lumb ensnares the women into joining a 'love cult' (known as the Women's Institute) by making them believe that one in their midst would bring forth a Messiah. The cult of Dionysos, similarly, saw groups of women followers (the Maenads or 'frenzied ones') abandon themselves to wild dances on hillsides clad in 'fawn skins' and carrying torches and *thyrsoi* — that is, 'staves, wrapped in grape vines or ivy stems, and crowned with pine cones'.[147] The dances usually ended with an offering or sacrifice in which a stag, bull or goat was torn limb from limb according to the nature of the ceremony. Clad in animal skins and frenzied from hallu-cinogenic mushrooms the women in the basement of Lumb's church participate in just such a ritual.

The figure of the changeling is a marionnette who, although he looks as if he's alive, (and even has the delusion that he's a real human being and tries to act as such) is actually made out of wood, a log. Hughes flattens his characterization of Lumb through the absence of any direct dialogue between Lumb and any of the other characters; we never hear him speak in his own voice. The Reverend Lumb's name derives from 'lumbar'[148] — denoting the lower back, or in a more ancient sense, the loins (a connotation which underscores his sexual function within the story). For one entrusted with the task of regenerating a community, Lumb functions in a curiously joyless manner. He is portrayed as trapped, struggling with numerous entanglements, moving in circles, enduring his com-pulsive sexuality without personal choice. When he attempts to flee he finds that his life is circumscribed by the geography of the town; he circles like a caged animal. Each time he tries to break out in dreams or through actions he encounters the lake, the river, the crater; all obstacles seem to conspire to turn him back to his destiny. Yet, his destiny is to be a wooden puppet whose strings are pulled by forces which have com-pelled him to incarnate, act, suffer, be punished and die without any choice in the matter.[149]

As we first encounter Lumb, before his abduction, he 'walks hurriedly over cobbles through the oppressive twilight of an empty town, in the North of England'. The dark shadows of buildings, the jagged outline of rooftops, the landscape itself have a hideous sense of impending doom about them. The imagery ('is it dusk or is it eclipse?') suggests the sun's occlusion. A vital principle of light has been obscured and endangered. On a psychological level the integrity of Lumb's nature has suffered an eclipse and foreshadows his abduction into the underworld. The force of T. S. Eliot's 'The Lovesong of J. Alfred Prufrock' can be felt behind this opening scene. In both *Gaudete* and Eliot's poem the journey into the streets of a city devastated of meaning parallels self-dissection of the central character. Lumb's apathetic quasi-paralyzed state suggests a personality that has become suddenly endangered, oppressed by events, grown suddenly immense, that have placed him on trial for his very right to exist. His plight is not so very different from that of Joseph K. in Kafka's *The Trial.* Lumb's entire existence rests on a precarious footing: he feels incredibly vulnerable. Thus, the image of the sun's eclipse presages the withdrawal of a rational framework and a resurgence of the irrational. Lumb's period of testing is about to begin. Significantly, when all is said and done, he fails. And this failure in turn underlies the theme of self-accusation which forms the emotional centre for the Epilogue. Simply, he is entrusted with a mission and he betrays it because of his desire to be just an ordinary person without a fateful destiny. In this sense *Gaudete* follows the logic of a dream although at a mythical level it is clear that Hughes is taking his cue from *Parzival.* The legend of the grail quest describes a maimed king, Anfortas, whose rescue and regeneration hinges on Parzival's ability to ask the right questions. Hughes follows Wolfram Von Eschenbach by suggesting that the cause of the devastation both inside and outside of Lumb is due to a canker of the spirit, a malady of the soul. In another context the Prologue is like the opening of *The Divine Comedy* as Lumb finds himself lost and not knowing which way to turn in a street suddenly littered with corpses. Innumerable sepulchral folktales begin in this fashion; the hero is first separated from the ordinary world through a ritual of initiation prior to being brought into contact with the hidden realm. Significantly, there are no physical wounds or any apparent reason for the outward devastation that Lumb has come across. This important clue tells us that Hughes is projecting a spiritual plight akin to the plagues that visited Thebes as a consequence of Oedipus's violation of the ancient taboo against incest. Indeed there are strong imagistic resemblances between this scene and the opening scene in Hughes's adaptation of Seneca's *Oedipus.* The metaphor is striking. In a landscape where no life can exist and where Lumb finds it increasingly difficult to take another step (itself a sign of his inability to continue as he was) Lumb, like Parzival, is forced to embark on a tortuous quest to redeem himself. Moreover, his self-redemption is inextricably bound to his ability to bring back to life the half-dead 'woman tangled in the skins of wolves' — a clear projection of the White Goddess.[150]

The contrast between Lumb as we first see him, haunted by visions of death, and the changeling who is fated to revive life

in its most ecstatic form and then suffer as a Scapegoat could
not be more dramatic. Rev. Lumb is a priest whose congregation has died; he presides over death. By contrast the changeling
is driven to produce a new Messiah and a new religion based on
the most elemental and primitive life force. The word Lumb,
we recall, derives from the Old English word meaning loins;
the changeling is meant to be the embodiment not merely of
sexual virility but of the life force itself.

The Prologue functions as an initiation ritual, a rite of
passage to take Lumb from his world to a mythic place where
an entire lost culture exists centred around the worship of a cult
figure, a goddess 'who seems to be alive and dead'. She is the
eternal feminine, the object of the prayers and devotion of
those who guard her and who arrange for Lumb to be abducted
and prepared for his mission that will somehow restore her to
life. The strange ceremony through which Lumb is initiated is
witnessed by figures clothed in animal skins. We feel the crushing
responsibility Lumb bears toward these mysterious figures in a
realm out of time; we sense their great need for Lumb to do
what he alone, apparently, has merely a slight chance of accom-
plishing. And ultimately we know that his failure seals the
doom of the half-living, half-dead woman as well as his own.
The way she is described, 'her face half-animal/And the half-
closed animal eyes, clear-dark back to the first creature' suggests
a mysterious continuity that returns us through her to Eve.
In a strange way, her deathly condition is similar to the state
of the world Lumb has left. It is as though Hughes was saying
that the condition of life itself in the world is quiescent, near
extinction and in desperate need of being revived. If we take
this figure in relation to Lumb himself he becomes obliged,
like the prince in the fairy tale, to revive a sleeping princess,
lingering on the edge of extinction. There is obviously a close
connection between Lumb and this female figure. Seen in this
way, she is not so much a personification of the condition of
the world but an accurate measure of a man in whom the
principle of life is atrophied, weakened and is near death.
In a Jungian context what Lumb has to rescue is endangered
and near extinction. Thus, his mission is to renew and revitalize a near-extinguished principle of life personified in 'this
beautiful woman who seems to be alive and dead'. When we ask
the difficult question as to why Lumb must go through the
horrendous experiences Hughes projects for him, suffer and die
in agony, the answer obviously points towards one inescapable

conclusion: Lumb's death and her life are intimately connected. Here, the psychology associated with the myth of the Scapegoat becomes invaluable; what happens to Lumb is intended to provide vitality, resurrection and life for the woman who lies dormant. In countless Scapegoat myths and legends it is of the utmost importance that the male be sacrificed at the peak of his sexual and virile powers so that at his death these powers pass undiminished into the earth and renew the crops and fertility of the ground. In *Gaudete,* Hughes creates Lumb as a catalyst to renew an archetypal female figure obviously identifiable with the White Goddess. This is one of the most ancient conceptions of the Scapegoat (unlike the modern conception of someone who involuntarily bears the burden of guilt); the Scapegoat has to die in order for his vital life force to pass undiminished and renew that which has been barren. Thus, the Scapegoat is destroyed in the interests of a greater destiny by forces which use him for their own purposes. In the story of Parzival the issue was the resurrection of the maimed king, Anfortas. In *Gaudete,* Lumb's purpose is the revival of the goddess who lies between life and death. The similarities are striking; a royal principle ('goddess' and 'king') is in danger of extinction and is redeemable only through the efforts of an ordinary man commissioned with an extraordinary mission.

Hughes uses the *Parzival* legend metaphorically (instead of a literal battle between Christian and Moslem combatants) to create a split personality or twin of the Reverend Lumb. Moreover, the lady for whom Parzival performs his heroic deeds is a personfication of what Jung called the Anima (and what Hughes, after Robert Graves, refers to as the White Goddess). Devotion to her teaches the hero to differentiate his feelings and behaviour towards the eternal feminine. The Rev. Lumb is offered a chance not only to redeem himself but the world through the power of love. But, whereas Parzival's loyalty to Condwiramurs fosters the regeneration of his own nature after experiences that baffle, exile and shame him, the Rev. Lumb fails to fulfill his mission. Undoubtedly Robert Graves's *The White Goddess* provided Hughes with a framework to draw upon in construing *Gaudete* at a mythical level. The doubling of the protagonist reflects the rivalry between the god of the waxing year and his other self, or blood brother (at least so Graves thought) for the affections of the Muse (whom he called the White Goddess). A true poem, according to Graves, is 'necessarily an invocation of the White Goddess'.[151] Indeed the poem Graves wrote titled 'Return of the Goddess'[152] may well have given Hughes the idea for the 'log' crowned as king, subject to the fate of victim of the goddess. The 'sacred king' is the 'moon goddesses divine victim' although, says Graves, he may avail himself of the 'privilege of sacrificing a surrogate'.[153] Seen in this light the Prologue of *Gaudete* represents a literal application of Graves's belief that 'no poet can hope to understand the nature of poetry unless he has had a vision of the Naked King crucified to the lopped oak, and watched the dancers red-eyed from the acrid smoke of the sacrificial fires stamping out the measure of the dance . . . .'[154] Hughes not only follows Graves in believing in the existence of an archetypal feminine deity whose 'names and titles are innumerable'[155] but the central theme of *Gaudete* shows Lumb and his rival both in the mysterious service of a subterranean goddess. In effect, they re-enact the seesaw battle between the poet and his rival that Graves described for the affections of the 'capricious and all powerful three-fold goddess'.[156] The profound ambivalence towards all aspects of the feminine that Hughes displays throughout his poetry explains his attraction to the diverse mixture of beauty and cruelty that comes together in the figure of the White Goddess. The central female characters, Maud and Felicity, both project and embody aspects of the White Goddess mentioned by Graves. Felicity represents the nymph or maiden while Maud is created as an extension of the hag. Not only are the poet and his rival (the dying god or scapegoat) both consorts of the fertility goddess but Maud's destruction of Felicity replays the archetypal conflict between hag and maiden. To understand the significance of this for Hughes we need only remember that Hughes repeatedly draws on myths where the hero fails to rescue the maiden from the devouring aspect of the hag. In his play *The Wound,* revengeful female furies (the Bacchae) assail the hero and it is noteworthy that he chooses the failure of Orpheus to free Eurydice as a subject for a long poem. To understand why Felicity must die in *Gaudete* at the hands of the hag figure Maud we need to recall what Jung tells us about all myths where heroes seek to liberate a single youthful feminine figure. What they have in common, says Jung, is the fear of the unconscious demonic maternal powers (of whom the Furies and the Bacchae are examples). The ability of the hero to rescue the maiden usually symbolizes the liberation of the Anima figure from the devouring aspect of the Mother image.[157] Not until this is accomplished can a man achieve his first true capacity for relatedness to women. From his earliest poetry, as for example the hawk in 'Hawk Roosting', the devouring principle of nature is identified with the feminine. Thus Felicity's death at the hands of Maud in circumstances that as we shall see clearly involve Lumb's complicity is but the latest re-enactment of this archetypal failure to rescue the maiden. It is, of course, ironic that Hughes should preface a work that centres around a failure to love with an excerpt from the story of *Parzival* — which is perhaps one of the greatest illustrations of devotion and love and the power of love to renew the world.

The rite on which *Gaudete* is specifically modelled is the initiation rite of the Cult of Attis, often called the 'taurobolium' or the ceremony of bathing in the blood of the bull.[158] This scene has the character of a baptism for the changeling. In an interesting way it suggests an instinctive re-experience of the birth and mothering condition during which Lumb comes into existence. The changeling is made of lifeless wood and needs the vitality transferred to him by being washed in bull's blood to bring him to life. The infusion is not permanent and so, in a curious way, the half-dead yet half-alive woman represents conditions of mothering or nurturing that are unsatisfactory and leave the child with a feeling of inadequate sustenance that demands constant transfusions of life energy. This theme has an obvious connection with the oral greediness and voraciousness we have seen in context with the Trickster. But here we are supplied with the archetypal scene which explains why the need for life-sustaining infusions is such a strong motif in Hughes's poetry. In this scene, Lumb as changeling is tied under a colossal white bull whose belly is slashed so that its intestines and blood pour out over him. Each element of the scene portrays an archetypal event a baby would experience. The 'domed subterranean darkness' suggests the womb and the phrase 'a drum beat, the magnification of a heart beat' evokes the world of prenatal life. In this sense the Prologue offers a glimpse into a condition of gestation and birth. Men empty buckets of hot blood over Lumb until he manages to get to a doorway that leads up to the light. He finds himself in a cellar covered with dry blood. He cannot remember what has happened to him yet he is filled with dread. He searches but there seems to be only one way out. He forces himself to move and climbs the stairs. Plato thought that each child of necessity forgot past lifetimes and each detail offers a startling parallel with the process of birth. At the same time the changeling has been subjected to a baptismal initiation implicit in the rebirth symbolism of the blood covered foetus sliding from the womb.

The white bull sacrificed over Lumb is significant because of its colour; normally sacrificial animals did not have to be any specific colour except in the case of the Scapegoat offered to God 'which must be white'.[159] Graves cites the variety of other initiatory rituals which have a sacrifice of a white bull prominantly mentioned, especially those relating to Dionysos. In fact, the later mention of Silenus (as a figure carved on a well) refers to the companion of Dionysos who has the shape of a bearded old man. We remember that an old man 'in scarecrow rags' is the one who leads the Rev. Lumb to the ritualistic bathing in the blood of the sacrificial bull. The central divinity Hughes refers to underlying Rev. Lumb is the god Dionysos whose image was often 'an upright post without arms'.[160] From the first his orgiastic activities were perceived as essential to the renewal of communal fertility. The extraordinary outbursts of sexual recklessness which Dionysos presided over were meant to underscore a common belief that intercourse was essential if the fertility of the earth was to be renewed. Moreover, the totem of the white bull was most closely associated, as Graves tells us, with both the oak tree and the god Dionysos.[161] The time of year when *Gaudete* takes place, in late May, connects the story with the countless orgiastic revels that were begun on May Day and initiated a yearly cycle that ended with the sacrifice of the oak king on midsummer day. Lumb chooses a 'young oak tree growing . . . on the summit between the rocks'. He refers to it as 'a tree of distinction'. Not only was the oak, as Graves observed, the tree of Zeus, Jupiter and Hercules, but it was the tree on which human sacrifice was most often performed.[162] In fact, the treatment of Lumb in the Prologue recalls the story related by Graves in which Hercules is led to the middle of a circle of stones arranged around an oak. The oak has been 'lopped until it is T shaped'.[163] Hercules is then bound to it and beaten until he faints. For Hughes, as for Graves, all heroes are one.

Undoubtedly, Lumb is a representative of the 'king of the wood', as he is described by Sir James Frazer in his monumental work *The Golden Bough*.[164] The conception of the king of the wood saw him as a human incarnation of a tree spirit whose life was bound up with the sacred oak. This myth projected a curious blood brotherhood between man and tree which centred around the sacred grove of oak trees at Rome. Indeed, the private meaning for Hughes's choice of the oak is that the Roman name for the oaken grove and the line of poet-priests charged with its consecration was *Silvii* — the ancient form of Sylvia's name. It survives today, although stripped of its legendary associations in the phrase, 'the Sylvan groves'.[165]

The tree-spirit was credited, as Frazer tells us, 'with the power of making the rain fall, the sun to shine, and flocks and herds to multiply and women to bring forth easily'.[166] Each phase of Lumb's existence is modelled on an aspect of the folklore surrounding the tree spirit, especially Hughes's conception of Lumb as a log, or puppet. The tree spirit is often conceived and represented as 'detached from the tree and clothed in human form' as a twin.[167] This is Hughes's source for the mutual transformation of Lumb into a tree and a tree into Lumb. But taking his cue from Graves's conception of the poet-twin who 'cannot be both of his selves at the same time'[168] Hughes transforms the anthropomorphic representation of the tree spirit documented by Frazer into a psychological reality. The conception of Lumb as a puppet is rooted in certain relics of tree worship in Europe. The tree spirit is represented 'simultaneously in vegetable form (as a tree) and in human form, which are set side by side as if for the express purpose of explaining each other'. Moreover, as Frazer says: 'in these cases the human representative of the tree spirit is sometimes a doll or puppet, sometimes a living person, but whether a puppet or a person, it is placed beside a tree or bough; so that together the person or puppet, and the tree or bough, form a sort of bilingual inscription, the one being, so to speak, a translation of the other'.[169] In certain slavic countries a figure known as Green George is both the human double of the tree and is capable of 'making rain and fostering the cattle'.[170] Hughes is representing the spirit of the tree (the oak especially is known as 'the tree of druids and the king of trees')[171] in human form.

The incarnation of the tree spirit was invariably followed by the killing, in sacrificial and ritual form, of the tree spirit as Scapegoat. In the form of an effigy or puppet the Scapegoat was ritualistically destroyed as the recipient of the evils of the community. His death by drowning and often by burning insured fertility through the transference and expulsion of death itself. Prior to the actual killing of the Scapegoat he was often allowed to be set up as a mock-king, turn the social order upside down and break all laws.[172] Hughes follows this motif in creating Lumb as a proxy or substitute priest who reigns over a feast of lust (in Roman times known as the Saturnalia) before the changeling is ritualistically pursued by incensed female worshippers (an echo of the Bacchae) and then clubbed, shot and burned. The psychology underlying the figure of the Scapegoat, whether for a community or for Hughes as an individual, offers the hope that a shadow part of the personality alien to the ego and subversive to one's conscious security can be exteriorized and subsequently destroyed. For this reason, the ritual dismemberment of Scapegoats as diverse as Dionysos, Osiris, Attis and the king of the wood are necessary before individual or collective self-renewal can take place. In this light the self-abasement and self-accusation underlying the poetry written to the nameless female deity at the conclusion of *Gaudete* is clearly a consequence of the whole Scapegoat complex.

We can see that *Gaudete* is a vision of sacrificial communion which expresses (as in all myths of the eternal feminine or Magna Mater) Hughes's ambivalence towards the profound ecstacy of union with her coupled with his equally violent aversion to the self-mutilation which must, of necessity, precede the attainment of a new life. *Gaudete* is nothing less than a sacrificial death after the pattern of the Scapegoat which must purge the old corrupt life to prepare for a new spiritual birth.

Hughes's story recounts the events that happen in the chronological sequence of one day, 'the last day of the changeling's life'. Like Joyce's *Ulysses* which also covers a twenty-four hour period, *Gaudete* is a mythical story in a contemporary setting, a dream journey that subjects the changeling Lumb to ritualistic orgies, violence and finally death. Events implausible in themselves are transformed by Hughes's approach which is both apocalyptic and sacramental into a modern treatment of the most ancient archetype of the dying and reviving man-god, the Scapegoat whose task is nothing less than the regeneration of the community. Hughes's vocabulary is elemental and raw, physical and violent. At the same time, the attitude of the unseen narrator is curiously toneless and devoid of emotion despite the violent and tumultuous types of events described. Throughout Hughes's writing characterization strongly depends on the setting so that images reinforce and clarify one another. The town in which the story takes place in the North of England is in the modern world yet seemingly isolated from it. The time is the last week of May and the lush and abundant natural environment, a time of Spring and fertility, underscores the ritualistic origins of Lumb and his function in producing a new birth. Each detail of geography is permeated by Hughes's mythic vision which transforms the arena in which the action occurs — the landscape of birds, animals, cattle pens, graveyard, tree groves and the church itself — into a larger-than-life mythical dimension. We see a world that is out of time, that has existed forever and always will — an archaic village that is timeless in its re-enactment of a prehistoric archetype. At the same time, Hughes has the uncanny ability to create a clear visual picture where each aspect of a typical country town is etched in the reader's mind: we see the farmlands with cattle and grazing bulls scattered over rolling hills in a tree 'choked' valley. The farms are situated among wooded areas separated by stone walls, barbed wire fences and rows of trees. Winding country roads connect the farms to each other. The nature of each character is reflected by the physical setting. Garten's bungalow has a garden hut where one finds cages, rabbits and ferrets. Dr Westlake owns 'an updated bleak deserted roadhouse', a house with a gate in the front, a gray sterile lounge and a dingy hall. Dunworth's house is a reflection of Dunworth himself — a 'polished modernity, the positioned furniture, in ultra colour, designed by Dunworth himself like the demoralized organs of the body'. Behind Hagan's home is a gravelled court with circles 'an old well which is surmounted by a looted silenus decorated with fan tails'. On the Holroyd place is a barn with a loft twelve feet high and an orchard. The pub in the town is called the Bridge Inn, its open door 'admits the conversation of the river and its stone'. At the edge of town is old Mr Smayle's house, the vicar's closest neighbour. 'Up the cinder path of the back garden, past the rows of trees, the spill of compost' is the Reverend Lumb's house. Next to his home is the town church with its basement. Lumb's house and the church are separated by a graveyard with squared off city-like paths, 'decayed bouquets, unsheltered stones and neglected grass'. The last grave has a round-shouldered stone and small seashells on it — 'the black stone is bare, except for bird's droppings and a lonely engraved word Gaudete'. The town also has an old quarry and a lake 'crawling with shadow, packed with reeds, snaggy with green-bronze nymphs, manned with willows'. In the background rest the tops of blue pyramid-like mountains. Beside the oak grove Hughes provides exact descriptions of rhododendrons, willows, apple trees, lilac blossoms, chestnut, poplar, white birch, fir, and sycamore trees (each of which has specific associations closely tied in with legendary attributes cited by Graves in The White Goddess).[173] The country setting provides Hughes with the opportunity to introduce a variety of animals that function both symbolically and realistically — doves, pigeons, magpies, crows, rabbits, ferrets, cattle, dogs and bulls. Throughout the atmosphere is violent and mysterious and more shocking in that something monstrous takes place within an apparently normal English country village.

The first character one meets in the context of the story is Major Hagan. He is also the one responsible for actually killing Lumb as the story circles around to its inevitable conclusion. Hughes took his name from the character of the same name in the legend of Siegfried.[174] In Gaudete, too, his role is to kill the hero and revenge the principle of outraged femininity. Hagan is described as plant-like, stolid, a soldier devoid of warmth and human personality. It is he who first sees Lumb, through his binoculars, with his own wife Pauline. Hagan has evidently understood the meaning of what he has seen and experiences 'a tremor like a remote approaching express in the roots of his teeth'. Hughes's description of Hagan as 'anesthetized for ultimate cancellations' clearly tells the reader that he is destined to ultimately cancel Lumb. At one point, he shoots a ring dove and presents it to Lumb after he has observed Lumb and Pauline together. The message is hardly subtle. It is significant that the men of the town seem to have lost their capacity to act upon the world around them. They are usually shown viewing life indirectly through binoculars, lenses, and photographs. The inability of the characters to make contact with each other is nowhere more evident than in Pauline's reactions to her husband's furious accusations, 'as if it were all something behind the nearly unbreakable screen glass of the television with the sound turned off'. Characters are either overwhelmed by emotions which totally possess them and diminish them as individuals to nothing or they are presented as so totally detached that they seem incapable of responding to outward events in a normal way. Thus, Pauline Hagan, the first woman to be described in terms of Lumb's effect on her life, is portrayed as a tiny object in the grip of a life force, a Dionysian frenzy that possesses her and strips her of her individuality. She feels guilt-striken and trapped, 'something in her is preparing a scream'. Although she does not like what has happened to her she is powerless to stop seeing Lumb. Hagan, for all his outward fury, is equally helpless to prevent the destruction of the woman he loves. His suppressed rage and helplessness even compel him to kill his dog, a black Labrador that he loves. The spiritual, emotional and sensual inertia of the townsmen is counterbalanced by the enormous life energy with which Lumb has been invested for his mission of literally inseminating the townswomen to regenerate the entire community.

Hughes's characterizations of both the men and women are vivid and each character's reaction to Lumb defines him or her clearly for the reader. After Hagan, the hunter (and executioner, following Hagan's role in the story of Siegfried), the men of the parish are described in a way that stresses their collective inadequacy. Dunworth is a weakling. He cannot grasp what he learns about his wife and Lumb; when he does he wants to shoot her, Lumb, and then himself. Yet, he cannot because 'he is hopelessly in love'. He wishes to escape, 'to lie down and sleep for fifty years in some utterly different landscape and wake up in another age'. Mr Evans has a desperate need to know why things are as they are; he beats his wife until she confesses. Yet, once he discovers the truth he views events as 'a doubtful bill which he already does not plan to pay'. Commander Estridge is the father of both Janet and Jennifer. He is afraid of losing his daughters; 'he hears something final approaching . . . and he knows his daughters are in it'. He wants to pulp Lumb's skull with an axe and his rage communicates itself to other men in the village. Mr Holroyd appears to have no interest in what is going on and when Garten, 'an agricultural pest', petty poacher and scrounger shows him the incriminating photo establishing Lumb's sexual exploits Holroyd considers it 'a questionnable picture' and wants 'to see proof'. He will not act until he is sure nor 'commit himself till he gets the facts'. Old Smayle, alone among all the men in the village, not only understands but secretly seems to sympathize with what Lumb is doing, both in terms of Lumb's sexual licence and in the new religious ethic Lumb proclaims. Smayle is both amused and amazed by the whole thing. He admires Lumb because he, too, believes that Christianity and all religions ultimately depend on women; as he says 'the church began with women . . . it was kept going by women'. In view of the one-dimensional way in which the men in the village are described he would seem to have a point. After all, Hagan and his numerous rifles, Westlake and his detached medical icy outlook, Estridge with his attic full of stuffed birds, Garten, obsessed by vicarious life through photography and the dull-witted and violent Evans hardly manifest any evidence of a capacity for communal regeneration. Not surprisingly, there are no children mentioned throughout the entire work and Lumb does appear to answer the general need for vitality and energy. Lumb's function is to revitalize the community through Dionysian excess, to reverse the village from its plight of stagnation and sterility, to serve as a channel for desperately needed vitality.

Understandably, the women of the town react, as a group, quite differently from the men. Several of them are pregnant, although the information is conveyed by implication rather than directly. Jennifer is described as being 'oppressed by the fullness of her breasts'. Janet examines 'her body, her swollen stomach'. Betty 'is trying to see herself more slender to make certain her breast is no fuller than before'. Mrs Dunworth is aware of the 'white swell on her stomach ache and Mrs Westlake is portrayed as 'gripped by archaic sea-fruit inside her'. Such is the physical situation of each of the women impregnated by Lumb. The psychological reactions of each of the women are quite varied. Pauline Hagan feels that she has been hypnotized or forced into relations with Lumb. Mrs Westlake, the doctor's wife, is painfully aware of the passage of time. She is tense and nervous and entertains the thought of suicide: 'she feels the moment of killing herself grow sweet and ripe, close and perfect'. Both Pauline Hagan and Mrs Westlake are disgusted at their relations with Lumb. Their actions go against every value they have, yet they still give in to Lumb as if possessed by some demonic force (a clear re-enactment of the possession of women by Dionysos in *The Bacchae*).[175] In quite another group are those women parishoners who are vastly susceptible to Lumb's will. Janet Estridge is in love with Lumb and is pregnant by him. She believes herself to be Lumb's only lover and cannot live with the fact she is not: 'she has made her decision and is relieved not to be suffering any more.'

Mrs Holroyd is happy and wants things between Lumb and herself to go on as they are: 'she wants nothing to change.' Mrs Walsall, the pub-owner's wife, wants to 'dedicate herself like a sacrifice to her great love'. Mrs Davies, as well as Jennifer and Betty, are not only in love with Lumb but profoundly dependent on him and utterly obedient to his will.

Felicity is the one woman with whom Lumb has not had a sexual relationship and represents something quite different from all the other women in the context of the story. She is the eighteen-year-old granddaughter of Old Smayle and her love for Lumb is genuine, not hypnotically forced or sacrificial. She represents Lumb's only chance for ordinary happiness and normality. She wants to run away with Lumb and when Garten tells her about Lumb and the other women of the parish she does not want to believe it, 'behind her face which registered no change everything changes'. Although apprehensive about attending a ceremony at the Women's Institute she still has trust in Lumb and thinks that he will not let anything happen to her. Ultimately, she accepts her fate and paradoxically feels both the vastness of her own destiny as 'a goddess' while at the same time she understands that 'she is a small anonymous creature about to be killed'.

The most important figure among the women is Maud, the Rev. Lumb's housekeeper. Hughes refrains from giving too many facts about her but she is a spectral figure full of meaning. As Lumb's housekeeper, she lives on the floor below his room, tends to his needs and is at once protector, mother and later in a mysterious dream sequence, his bride. At one point, Maud is shown bringing blossoms of lilac and apple into Lumb's bedroom. Lilac is the flower associated in classical mythology with the god Dionysos, as the first flower of Spring that brings in yearly renewal. From Robert Graves we learn that 'the silver white blossomed apple branch' was a talisman of the White Goddess and that the apple itself has always been the ancient icon of the feminine principle, from Eve onward. These associations clearly underscore Maud's mythic connections. She brings into the story another manifestation of the 'triple goddess, mother, bride, layer out'[186] — she who sees you into the world, whom you wed, and she who ushers you out of the world. Maud is loyal to Lumb as long as he remains devoted to the feminine deity 'tangled in the skin of wolves on the rock floor under dome rock', the maternal, sexual and fertile earth mother figure. Yet, on this last day she learns of Lumb's transgression, his love for Felicity and desire to run away. In her role of earthly guardian who oversees the divine plan with which Lumb has been intrusted she decides that Lumb and Felicity must die. In a mythical context she is the jealous Juno who lures Dionysos (Lumb) into an ambush after she sees him in her 'cunningly wrought looking glass'[177] (paralleled in the story by the crystal ball in which Maud foresees Lumb's destruction). Lumb must die because he cannot live out the destiny decreed for him. His 'log-like' status emphasizes his lack of free will. He is meant to be merely a puppet. In turn this reflects Graves's belief that 'in the primitive cult of the universal goddess . . . there was no room for choice; her devotees accepted the events, pleasurable and painful in turn, which she imposed on them as their destiny . . . .'[178] Lumb is destroyed by the intolerable tension between his assigned fate and his human desires.

While Lumb is projected as a rutting stag or bull he appears to function mechanically; each of his numerous sexual encounters are curiously devoid of love or tenderness. In essence, the energy and potency he embodies uses him as much for its own purposes as he in turn uses the women of the parish. Thus, on a human level, the conflict created by his impulsive promiscuity and unmet personal needs create a longing to escape which undermines and eventually destroys him. At a moral level, Lumb is guilty of producing the very conditions which he has been called into existence to reverse. The devastating human effects his actions have on the women of the parish collectively produce a condition recapitulated in the figure of archaic femininity who lies near death and whose state is clearly linked with the treatment of women in the world. This gives *Gaudete* its peculiar circular pattern and timeless quality. What happens at the end of the story is inextricably connected with the conditions which at first sight appear to have no obvious cause at the opening. In effect, *Gaudete* embodies a circular pattern of Lumb's flight from himself. Hughes draws on this pattern through his reference to the myth of Actaeon who was transformed into a stag and runs in a circle until he is brought down by the hounds that are chasing him. Maud sees Lumb in the crystal ball transfigured into a stag and later Lumb, wearing the pelt of a red stag as part of the ancient ritual re-enacted in the church basement, flees the townsmen who are chasing him and as Hughes describes it: 'Lumb realizes with nausea he has come in a circle, like a simple fool.' Hughes's conception of Lumb's character turns on Lumb's blindness to his role in producing the fatal pattern of events in which he is so tragically enmeshed.

The underlying circular structure of *Gaudete* is the basis for the title. A 'gaud' is a large bead on the rosary necklace on which the 'Our Father' is said as a prayer. Between each of the large beads are ten small beads on which 'Hail Marys' are said. Thus, a 'gaudete' is a necklace of prayers in separate scenes, strung together the way beads in a rosary are strung on a necklace. The structure of the entire work resembles a series of meditations or separate images. An additional correspondence exists in the parallel between Lumb's role as father of a new Messiah who will renew the principle of suffering female nature and the coming of Christ celebrated in the 1582 Christmas hymn that begins 'Gaudete, gaudete . . . . '[179] Moreover, the name Maud may be a derivative of Mary Magdelene, especially in view of Mary's relationship to Christ and Maud's relationship to Lumb.

Alone among all the characters in the story Felicity makes direct contact with both the original Rev. Lumb and the changeling. The fact that she encounters both sides of Lumb's nature immediately sets her apart from all the other women in the story. In this way, Hughes tells us that Felicity is Lumb's only hope. She alone possesses the capacity to return Lumb to unity through her innocence and affection. This is especially clear during the course of the scene by the lake where Felicity quite literally helps Lumb defeat his own double. Lumb is fishing and while Felicity waits in the boat she sees 'the head and shoulders of a dark shape'. It is Lumb, naked, as if he had suddenly decided to go for a swim; at the same time, she sees 'Lumb still poised on the tip of the rock sixty yards away motionless'. One of the strange things about this scene is that while the naked Lumb tries to drag Felicity into the lake, his double is strangely detached and is more intent on catching a fish than on rescuing her. The changeling is so completely absorbed in retrieving the 'good fish' he has caught that he becomes angry at having to tear himself away to rescue Felicity; finally, he abandons the fish 'with a curse'. The metaphor is clear; Lumb's insensitivity to Felicity's plight shows that he is 'a cold fish' and foreshadows his inability to save her from being killed in the church basement.

This scene presents another echo of the Orpheus and Eurydice legend where the beloved is claimed by forces of death. The meaning is obvious; Lumb is his own enemy. Not only is he powerless to prevent what he loves best from being destroyed but in some mysterious way he destroys what he loves. There is a part of him that literally appears as his double, that is immeasurably destructive to all that which would give him normal human happiness. Felicity's importance in the story increases as we understand her role as the probable mother of the new Messiah. Two scenes support this belief. Old Smayle, one of the few defenders of Lumb's actions, states that the vicar realizes that his 'religious career depends on women . . . the church began with women through all the Roman persecutions it was kept going by women . . . and now the whole thing is worn back down to its women. It's like a herd of deer . . . led by a hind.' Felicity, before being killed, makes her appearance dressed in the pelt of a hind and her relationship with Lumb is obviously meant to parallel the bond between Condwiramur and Parzival. In an allegorical sense she is his Felicitas, or happiness.

In a Jungian context of course she is the Anima aspect of himself which has been projected outward into nature as a separate character. Nowhere is this clearer than in Lumb's combat with his double. Even though Lumb, the changeling, fails to rescue her initially, together they beat off the assault of the Lumb who has emerged from the lake. Obliquely, Hughes is telling us that Lumb's true strength lies in his relationship with Felicity. Together with her he can surmount the forces opposing him; without her he is powerless. In fact, the original Lumb is becoming stronger, 'horribly strong', as the changeling begins to fail his earthly mission. To put it another way, the changeling is being pulled back into himself now that he has no reason to exist. The encounter between the two of them, 'one grinning and the other appalled' echoes the epic encounter between Beowulf and Grendel and ends when the Lumb who has emerged from the lake is defeated. His hand tears off in the grip of the changeling — 'the other rips free holding aloft his stump from which the hand has vanished.'[180] The demonic nature of the encounter turns on the fact that Lumb needs Felicity to save him. She symbolises all that is worthy of devotion; she is what Beatrice was for Dante and what Una symbolized in *The Faerie Queene*. Tragically the one woman Lumb most needs is the one whom he deserts and allows to be killed.

Ultimately, then, Lumb betrays himself. This sequence

is played over and over again in Lumb's relationships with the women of the congregation with whom he is linked by bonds of mutual love, hate and desperate need. Lumb has used every woman of childbearing age regardless of marital status or committment to other men to be the instruments of his creation. His sexual relations appear to be passionless but the enormous energies he expends in the scope of one day are beyond human capabilities. He may be superhuman but the women of the town are not and therein lies the danger. They have become so emotionally involved that they can be manipulated to perform the most violent acts, even suicide and murder. They are the priestesses of Lumb's cult of the White Goddess and the manner in which he treats them causes Janet to kill herself and Maud and Felicity to be destroyed. Ironically, the very women his new religion was supposed to honour are gravely injured. Through him, three women are dead, the entire enterprise of reviving a cult of the White Goddess has floundered. Lumb's ultimate effect is to contaminate and destroy what he was supposed to save. He has left the women of the parish languishing, neither alive nor dead in a condition that is collectively equivalent to that of the subterranean goddess. Again, cause and effect have been reversed and the circular logic shows Lumb to be guilty of the very sin of reducing womanhood to a status of the living dead which he came into the story to reverse.

In effect, the narrative of *Gaudete* displays the sin whereby womanhood has been offended and clearly reveals the reason why Lumb, as we first see him before he is abducted and doubled, is a personality obsessed with death, guilt and punishment (which he embraces through his double). Lumb, we remember, at the opening of the story is someone for whom nature is dead. At the same time his double is created to be a catalyst for the revival of a religion that depends on women for its beginnings. The changeling who replaces Lumb is defined in ways that suggest he is to be the exact opposite of Lumb. Lumb originally is an Anglican minister, guiding people through a faith centred around Christ, a male deity supported by a highly structured, restrained pattern of ceremony and ritual. In contrast, the changeling presides over a pagan ministry in which incantation, frenzied chants and drug-induced ecstacy are directed towards the worship of the most primitive forces of fertility whose visible expression is the archaic stone carving of an earth mother figure Lumb keeps propped on his mantle above the fire. Although the differences between Lumb and his double seem to suggest that the changeling is simply living out all the unrealized fantasies that Lumb has had, the changeling's apparent freedom is an illusion; both selves are equally powerless to alter their fate. If, for a moment, one withdraws the supernatural level of authorization from the story that Hughes has invested it with, and simply regards Lumb in human terms, his predicament transforms itself into a vivid dramatization of the feeling of being cursed by aspects of one's own personality.

Even as Lumb is able to control, sexually possess and totally determine the lives of the townswomen, so he himself is possessed by an increasingly oppressive destiny. Lumb's nostalgia for 'simple freedom' is not so much a desire to run away with Felicity as it is a need to escape from a life that has become unmanageable. Yet implicit in his desire to escape is a character trait that betrays the fact that if Lumb were to run away he would still be himself. He tells us that in each of the worlds waiting to be explored there is 'a bed at the centre a name a pair of shoes and a door' which is his 'to possess'. This peculiar note of possession is at the centre of Hughes's characterization. Most, given the opportunity for freedom would rather enjoy it than 'possess' it. To possess one's freedom is, as Lumb does not understand, to be possessed by one's fate. Even as Lumb would wish to limit possibilities for others so his are reduced and eliminated. Lumb's need to control invokes the reciprocal feeling that he is totally controlled by fate. He is possessed by his fate.

What happens to Lumb is a consequence of what he has done to others. He has sexually possessed and destroyed the lives of the townswomen and in one of the most powerful and convincing sequences of the book Hughes shows Lumb summoned before his accusers (in a fantasy sequence that arises from Lumb's guilt-stricken imagination). While driving along, Lumb is seized by an overwhelming hallucination that 'stubbed fingered hairy backed hands' come from behind him and wrench the steering wheel from his grip, crashing him into an embankment. While he is recovering from the shock of the crash he conceives an elaborate hallucination in which he is accused and attacked by crowds of unknown men who hand him a 'sodden paper' on which is written an illegible accusation. Lumb's guilt and fear have obviously made him perceive his own arms and hands as belonging to someone else who is trying to kill him and have caused him to crash; the theme of this fantasy elaborates his self-accusation. He imagines that he is beaten by sticks, by men 'with cudgels, with intent to kill him'. He is driven into the mud, under the hooves of cattle when suddenly his desire to be free of his pursuers makes his fantasy modulate into a terrifying vision of all of his accusers crushed and twisted under the hooves of stampeding cattle.

Then Lumb sees the women of the town, Pauline, Mrs Dunworth, Mrs Davies and all the rest buried up to their necks in the floor of a volcanic crater. Their rain-soaked heads are crying to him for help. This is a vivid symbolic representation of the predicament Lumb has plunged them into and their helplessness and dependence on Lumb to save them. But he cannot. Then suddenly a creature in the middle of the crater in which he is struggling lifts up its head 'of mud' and begins calling to him; 'it reaches towards him with mud hands seemingly almost human.' He slides down to help it and discovers 'it is a woman's face,/A face as if sewn together from several faces./A baboon beauty face,/A crudely stitched patchwork of faces.' Although his first impulse is to help her, he is suddenly seized by fear as 'her embrace tightens stronger' and 'her stitch-face grins into his face and his spine cracks./Suddenly he is afraid.' The archaic, primal figure at the heart of this experience is obviously the mythically central feminine figure, the primal earth mother at the core of Lumb's consciousness. Her face, when the mud is washed off, appears to be a stiched patchwork of all of the faces of the women Lumb has gathered for his congregation. He re-experiences his own birth from this woman: 'he can hear her whole body bellowing./His own body is being twisted and he hears her scream out./He feels bones give. He feels himself slide.' Then a mysterious transfiguration takes place. Beneath the stitched crazy quilt 'baboon face' that is the composite of all the women's faces appears the 'Undeformed and perfect' beautiful face of the goddess with whom Lumb has been locked in a life and death embrace. In being separated from her he feels as if he has been 'torn in two' — a clear foreshadowing of the first lines of Lumb's Epilogue; 'what will you make of half a man/Half a face/A ripped edge.' He sees himself 'crawling out of the river/Glossed as an exhausted otter' — again, an image that presages the emergence and communion of Lumb, after his reappearance with 'an otter up out of the lough'.[181] The implication is clear. Without her he is only half a man and since she is the embodiment of all of the women in the story, by betraying them, Lumb has betrayed her. By betraying her Lumb has betrayed himself to a severed and diminished existence devoid of any chance for happiness — the Lumb, in effect, we first meet at the outset of *Gaudete*. Whereas the women of the town cry to him from their entombed state for help, the one woman whom he does try to rescue grips him so tightly that he is afraid and so wishes to be free of her. Yet, in freeing himself from her he unwittingly tears himself in two.

Once this basic theme of betrayal is understood scenes inexplicable in themselves, such as the one where Maud wrenches the head off a white pigeon and 'sponges herself' with the bloodied pigeon's body, become clear. Innocence is a quality symbolically associated with white birds and we know that at this point Maud's perception of Lumb's innocence has been destroyed. She has decided to reveal Lumb's betrayal and is ready to sacrifice him. In effect she is killing her relationship with him, an action which mysteriously communicates itself to Lumb, resting after his car crash in the room below: 'his hands jerk./Unconscious he tries to get up/As if a soul were trying to get out of a drowning body.' He is having a dream which foreshadows the funeral pyre in which Maud, Felicity and he himself will eventually be consumed. Realistically, Lumb is incorporating the roaring flames of the fire, in front of which he has fallen asleep to dry himself, into his dream. In his dream he sees a cathedral on top of a hill as if from a great distance into which masses of women 'black as flies' continue to pour. The cathedral appears to be sinking 'with its encumbering mass of despairing women'. They cry to him to be saved in a scene which recalls the mud-filled crater filled with the crying heads of parish women. As the cathedral becomes incandescent and sinks into a 'distant volcano' the reader is being given a clear image that Lumb is aware that his religious mission is disintegrating. He is filled with guilt and remorse. Lumb sees himself dressed in 'purple and gold' priestly garments looking down on a sea of women's faces and beseeching hands that 'stretch their pleas towards him'. Suddenly, beside him appears Maud who has 'become beautiful'. They kiss, 'in a bush of flames they are burning'. At this point, it is obvious that Lumb really loves Maud rather than Felicity and the quasi-incestuous nature of this Oedipal attachment (Maud is a mother image for Lumb) produces its own penalties in the form of the bursting into flame of the cathedral. As the cathedral is consumed along with the women desperately clawing to escape from the conflagration both Maud and Lumb in their separate rooms suddenly awake from what actually is a mutually shared dream to the 'banging on the door downstairs'. Felicity has been walking in the graveyard with Garten who has shown her the photograph of Lumb's infidelity. Appropriately, the bird of the cuckhold, the faithless 'cuckoo . . . moves its doleful cry from tree to tree'. She has come to ask him to run away with her and cancel the meeting of the Women's Institute that evening.

As Maud studies the 'weak pretty face' of Felicity the reader becomes aware that Maud has established control over Lumb. She is more subjectively important as an unconscious determining force than is the 'weak pretty' Felicity. This does not explain, however, why Lumb, although given the chance to escape does not take it, although he most certainly knows that the townsmen are on to him and want to kill him. So, when we ask the inevitable question as to why Lumb does not remove himself, only one answer satisfactorily explains his behaviour. It is not that he is uncommonly self-destructive but rather his function in the story is truly that of a Scapegoat who bears a burden that can be expiated only through his own death, a death moreover, that he himself must willingly invoke. And so Lumb answers that he cannot cancel the meeting and furthermore will introduce Felicity 'to the Institute'.

That evening the women assemble in the church basement for an ancient ritual which re-enacts the archaic cult of Dionysos. Hughes is faithful to the idea mentioned by Robert Graves that partakers in the secret Dionysian cults made use of a hallucinogenic mushroom called 'flycap or amanita muscaria which bestowed . . . an enormous muscular strength, erotic power, delerious visions and the gift of prophecy'.[182] This same mushroom is referred to frequently throughout *The White Goddess* as the chief catalyst in ecstatic rites. Mrs Davies evidently has grown the mushroom in her hot house and slices the 'withered fungus' into 'each of three sandwiches'. In Part I (The Shaman) we saw Hughes frequently incorporate shamanic techniques in his poetry, and, as Mircea Eliade observed, 'shamanic ecstacy proper is obtained by intoxication with mushrooms' in order to put the shaman into a deep trance. For Eliade the use of intoxicants such as the 'preeminently shamanic mushroom Agaricusmuscarius' is but 'a recent innovation and points to a decadence in shamanic technique'.[183]

In keeping with the ancient Dionysian cult rituals each of the women in the congregation, naked and chanting, has donned animals pelts that correspond, in an uncanny yet accurate way with their natures. The 'long ragged pelt of a giant fox' hangs from Maud. Knotted over Felicity's shoulders is 'the blueish pale-fringed skin of a hind'. Around her are women who have become an owl, a badger and a hare. In the middle of it all 'Lumb bobs under stag antlers, the russet bristly pelt of a red stag flapping at his naked back.' Not only have each of the women taken on an archetypal role as an aspect of the feminine goddess but Lumb has become the shaman-priest. We recall that one prominent feature of shamanic costumes is the horns with which the shaman's caps are decorated to imitate 'stag horns'. And the shamanic costume is intended 'to give the shaman a new magical body in animal form'.[184] It is for this reason that Lumb wears the pelt of the stag as part of the ritual. Robert Graves sheds light on Hughes's choice of the stag as a ritual animal with strong connections in English folklore. One recent projection of the 'stag hero', Graves says, is 'Red Robin Hood'. We learn that 'in May (the month in which *Gaudete* takes place) the stag puts on his red summer coat.'[185] Moreover, says Graves, 'hood or hod or hud meant log . . . and it was in this log cut from the sacred oak that Robin had once been believed to reside'. Significantly, Maid Marian was originally written as 'Maud Marian' and she is another variant on Mary Magdelene, the penitent.[186] These sets of associations not only tie the story of *Gaudete* to English folklore but establish Lumb in the broader context of a suffering, crucified Christ attended by three Marys (including Mary Magdelene) who collectively, so Graves believes, are three aspects of the White Goddess.

At last Felicity understands that she is going to be killed. She willingly accepts her own sacrifice. All the women are part of some crisis that must be 'enacted/Faithfully and selflessly by them all'. She realizes that 'somehow she has become a goddess'.[187] She has become, for a moment, the White Goddess, 'the personification of all the reproductive energies of nature' and Lumb has become her lover 'divine yet mortal with whom she mated year by year their commerce being deemed essential to the propogation of animals and plants'.[188] The descriptions are those of Sir James Frazer in *The Golden Bough* and Hughes's genius lies in the utterly convincing manner in which he has created characters who become their archetypes.

The scene foreshadowed when Maud had discovered 'a glass

ball in a black velvet chamber' and gazed in it to find Lumb projected as a stag being chased by hounds[189] as well as Felicity first as a 'bride' and then struck down 'A knife hilt . . . sticking in the nape of her neck' now comes to pass. Her vision had been triggered by reading the diary Lumb kept which apparently told of his plans to run away with Felicity. Given this background we understand why Maud now plunges Lumb's sacramental knife into Felicity. In the mythical context one aspect of the feminine is at war with another; the hag destroys the maiden. Lumb is not only powerless to prevent it but is instrumental in causing Felicity to die. Throughout *Gaudete* Maud and Felicity struggle for Lumb's soul. Ironically, Lumb's weakness causes both of them to die. Maud appears as a protectress of Lumb only so long as he is faithful to her and to his mission. Maud does not perceive the other women in the parish as rivals because Lumb only gives them a purely sexual relationship. It is only when his affections are in question, his simple human preference for Felicity, that Maud desires to be revenged. Before the crucial final ceremony in the church Lumb is specifically described as having not been sexually intimate with Felicity — a clear sign that Lumb wished to set her aside from the rest of the women. This forms a domestic situation at the heart of the mythic level of the story. So that while Maud does not perceive Lumb's sexual relationships with any of the townswomen as a threat, the minute she senses his affections on a human level have gone toward Felicity, Lumb's mantle of protection vanishes. She screams that Lumb is going 'to abandon them and run away with this girl/Like an ordinary man/With his ordinary wife'. Not only has Lumb outraged the townswomen by seducing and abandoning them but he has disobeyed the goddess in whose service he has come to earth. A further irony and the most poignant one, is that Lumb through his own inadequacy and desire to escape his destiny has caused the death of precisely the one woman who might have given birth to the new Redeemer. The uniqueness of Felicity strengthens this possibility — she was to be the new Virgin Mary bearing the new Christ, not fathered by the Holy Ghost but by Lumb acting as an emissary for the life force of which Dionysos, in the story, serves as an emblem.

We recall that in *The Bacchae* on which this scene in *Gaudete* is modelled, the unbeliever, King Pentheus seeks to find out the secret of Dionysos by witnessing his forbidden rituals; 'Pentheus would take no warning . . . and determined to go himself to the scene . . . he penetrated through the wood and reached open space where the chief scenes of the orgies met his eyes. At the same moment, the women saw him and first among them was his own mother Agave, blinded by the god (Dionysos) cried out: "see there the wild boar" the whole band rushed upon him . . . in vain he cries to his Aunts to protect him from his mother. Autonoe seized one arm, Ino, the other and between them he was torn to pieces, while his mother shouted: "victory, victory we have done it. The glory is ours." '190 Lumb is no longer the god Dionysos but the unbeliever Pentheus whom the Bacchantes, seen here as the enraged women of the parish, tear limb from limb. Although the actual killing of Lumb takes place later it is clear that Maud psychologically is instrumental in disposing of him, even as Pentheus's mother kills her son and proudly displays his bloodied head thinking it is a 'wild boar'. The theme of outraged womanhood avenging itself underlies much of Hughes's work and in a very real sense his poetry has the character of an ongoing negotiation and confrontation with a brooding malevolent female deity whom he perceives as a force capable of shaping his life and fate in complex and unforeseen ways. This explains the appeal that Lumb as a character has for Hughes, his real psychological function, so to speak. On this, Lumb's last day, he feels that things are vibrant with peril. The world, for him, is out of control. He longs for simple freedom. He imagines millions of alternative worlds 'waiting for him to escape . . . to explore . . . and possess'. He cannot fully understand what has happened; he is confused and things have started to go wrong for him. Everything 'will have to be cancelled, the whole error, carefully taken apart and the parts put back where they belong'. Lumb embodies the overwhelming need to take things apart, to analyze and re-examine what went wrong. His character functions in a way that admits what Freud called the reality principle — the reality of injury done and received. He feels suddenly small and vulnerable and has now become 'ordinary and susceptible to extinction'.

After Maud murders Felicity out of an insane and cruel jealousy, the multitude of wives and villagers, the doctor, blacksmith, pub-owner, architect, poacher and farmer quickly revenge themselves on Lumb. They are ordinary people whose lives have been ruined by the engulfing, intrusive madness of Rev. Lumb. They despise him, pursue and finally kill him. Major Hagen's character, we recall, is drawn from the Teutonic myth in which Hagen murders Siegfried to avenge Brunhilde: 'Then, as Siegfried bent over the brook and drank, Hagen hurled the spear at the cross, so that the hero's heart's blood leapt from the wound and splashed against Hagen's clothes . . . . .'[191] So too, the Reverend Lumb, after being shot and killed by Major Hagen, is placed with the bodies of Felicity and Maud (who has killed herself with Lumb's dagger) 'on the narrow table,/On top of the pyre' in the church basement and all three bodies are burned.

The logic of the Scapegoat demands that, as Frazer says: 'the very value attached to the life of the man-god [who is an incarnation of the tree-spirit] necessitates his violent death.'[192] Lumb's death, replete with Hughes's concise yet detailed description of the many wounds inflicted on him, bears a striking resemblance to the ancient ritual sacrifice of the Scapegoat where he is dismembered and his blood drains into the ground. Lumb is literally bathed in his own blood: 'the blood from his burst head washes his face and neck.' Through the subterranean logic of metaphor Hughes tells us that the mystical transforming power of blood which in the Prologue had transformed a lifeless log into a living being was only borrowed and now returns to the earth. Despite Lumb's suffering we have no clear assurance that, in actuality, he has accomplished anything. In fact, it would seem because of his betrayal of the mission with which he was entrusted he has failed. The paradox that Lumb's suffering may not have benefited anyone suggests a sequence of cause and effect that underlies the story at a more profound psychological level. The scenario formulated in *Gaudete* projects a character, Lumb, into the confines of a fictional framework in order to suffer. If Lumb's suffering is due to self-delusion that he must be a Scapegoat in order to serve the cause of general renewal what we are witnessing, in fact, is an overwhelming need to suffer and consequently a need to be punished. In turn, this presupposes the commission or omission of an evil which necessitates the punishment. To take it another way, if one is suffering for no apparent reason it might prove irresistible to invent one. This quickly becomes the equation that 'my suffering will benefit someone'. Thus, the more persecuted and oppressed the individual sufferer (remembering that the person feels fully warranted in accepting the suffering imposed or sought for some real or imagined sin) the more grandiose and monumental must be the reason for which he is suffering. Extended to its ultimate outcome an infinity of absolute suffering would demand, for this individual, an absolute, consuming mission which would benefit everyone through him — in other words, a well-grounded self-delusion. So that while it might appear as if the mission calls forth the suffering, in existential terms the suffering demands the sense of having a fated mission as a Scapegoat. Thus, Lumb's feeling of being oppressed in a landscape filled with death at the outset of *Gaudete* summons into existence his chance for renewal through his abduction into the underworld.

## *EPILOGUE*

The Epilogue continues and deepens the theme of a sacrificial death that purges the old corrupt life and prepares the way for a mystical communion that inaugurates a new life. Hughes draws on the same two part structure he incorporated within his cycle of twenty-one Prometheus poems. Hughes's comments in the earlier context hold true here; while Part One contains 'the story of the crime against the creatress [the White Goddess] by the violator [Lumb] and her revenge', Part Two explores the 'self-judgment of the violator among the voices of his crimes, oversights, and victims'.[193] The archetype of the Scapegoat, whether Dionysos, Osiris or Attis, demands a ritual dismemberment before self-renewal can take place. We must keep this in mind in order to comprehend the lacerating self-accusation and profound self-abasement underlying these 'hymns and psalms', as Hughes calls them in the opening argument, composed and directed towards 'a nameless female deity' (whom we call the White Goddess). The Epilogue reveals the human face beneath the mask of the Scapegoat and provides us with a series of introspective close-ups that shift the direction of *Gaudete* to the highly personal perspective of Lumb's acknowledgment of his failure. The degree of ironic self-questionning undercuts from the outset the epic and grandiose dimension of the earlier narrative: 'what will you make of half a man/Half a face/A ripped edge.' Lumb describes himself as one who has survived an enormous tragedy that has left him incomplete, a survivor-victim. He describes himself as alienated from a society where speech 'is a fistula/Eking and deferring/Like a stupid or a crafty doctor'. The conventional wisdom of medicine and psychiatry ranges from empty chatter to vile 'sanguinary nostrums/Of almosts and their tomorrow/To a lifetime of fees'. Man alone uses speech to conceal his needs, while in the rapturous cries of birds and beasts Lumb touches on the wholeness and tranquility he so desperately wishes to repossess.

In Lumb's plight we can see the predicament of our age, deadened, secularized and searching for an integration that can reassert the wholeness of the self against the degraded condition of modern culture. Into the devastated personal environment comes the mythical, creative and profoundly disruptive force whom we have identified as the White Goddess. Lumb asks: 'Who are you?/The spider clamps the bluefly — whose death panic/Becomes sudden soulful absorption . . . . and you grab me/So the blood jumps into my teeth'. Those whom she favours experience her presence as a terrible dismemberment which Hughes expresses in metaphors of death. What she demands is nothing less than the purgation and death of the old ego, cutting through the intellectual and emotional layers of the self until one is stripped to the heart's core. Only then can the transmutation take place. All that is rotten must be cleansed and so Lumb literally dismembers himself, as he says: 'At the top of my soul/A box of dolls/In the middle of my soul/A circus of gods/At the bottom of my soul/The usual mess of squabblers'.

His self-assessment begins with an awareness that gods, for him, are but lifeless dolls. In his everyday life he acts the part of charlatan or clown and underlying it all is a growing psychological disorientation (the 'box' gives way to 'a circus' which in turn becomes 'the usual mess'). His self-analysis is presented after the pattern of a Tarot reading. This is his absolute condition. Within the framework of time his future holds 'a useful-looking world', his past reveals a cave where 'some female groaning/In labour' accuses him of foresaking her. Nature's promise for him is expressed in imagery we have seen previously in 'The Skylarks': 'Under the lark's crested head/A prophecy/from the core of the blue peace'. If he atones he will gain the miracle of personal rebirth and spirit — an idea implicit in the imagery of the sacred Egyptian scarab or 'wise beetle/Walking about inside my body'. The failures he accuses himself of are threefold: 'I neglected to come to degree of nature/In the patience of things./I forestalled God —/I assailed his daughter.' This is the essence of the crime for which he is punished: 'Now I lie at the road's edge./People come and go./Dogs watch me.'

His agony is all the more terrible because he has committed this sin in a world where absolute good and evil are not thought to exist, where truth can be disembled and where no consequences are real 'In a world where all is temporary/And must pass for 'its opposite'. Again and again he lashes himself, an unnecessary act since the powers he has offended have revenged themselves with a terrible ruthlessness. He, who like Parzival, once understood the language of the birds has descended to the lowest level of existence, foraging for spiritual food in the dim twilight of limbo. He is falling, floating like 'A kelp, adrift' in a sea 'full of moon-ghosts' — imagery which suggests an utter inability to find a secure foundation on which to establish his life. He accuses himself of improprieties and inadequacies in relation to his diminished ability to love; savagely, he confesses 'Error on error', even seeing his own insistence of guilt as one more illusion: 'Perfumed/With a ribbon of fury' of which to divest himself. His life, he feels, has been aborted by his failure 'to help/The woman who wore a split lopsided mask'. Since then he has been devoured by grief and there is pathetically little that can be done to resurrect him: 'Music, that eats people/That transfixes them/On its thorns, like a shrike/. . . or licks them . . . like a tiger/Before leaving nothing . . . is the maneater/on your leash.'

Hughes's imagery is startling and effective; music is carnivorous like a tiger, lets people forget, transfixes them on its notes (which look like barbed thorns) that Hughes compares to a shrike, a bird which, significantly, devours its mate. Together they comprise the man-eating tigress straining at the leash held by the White Goddess. But there is nothing left of himself to devour. At this point Hughes projects the possibility of a mystical re-birth using images that have appeared earlier in the story: 'I see the oak's bride in the oak's grasp', an emblem of the mysterious and all-powerful goddess who rides the earth and demands total sacrifice from those she chooses. She is the deified woman at the centre of life and death. The price to be paid for worshipping her is total; it is one's self, 'the one I hunt/The one/I shall rend to pieces/Whose blood I shall dab on your cheek/Is under my coat'.

The need to be a Scapegoat has hardly ever been stated with greater passion. To live, parodixically, he must die. He must annihilate himself through his past and the next lines are the climactic confrontation with the irrevocable death of someone who had tried to die three times before; 'It happened/You knocked the world off, like a flower-vase./It was the third time. And it smashed.' He re-experiences bestowing the last kiss on her dead 'refrigerated' brow 'in the morgue' and describes his attempt to flee his predicament to another dimension: 'I said goodbye to earth.' He arrives at a place of 'light' where he sees 'the snow flake crucified/Upon the nails of nothing'. A snowflake which scarcely exists is still able to be crucified. The law of the Scapegoat has become a virtual principle of nature in which the possibilities for suffering and atonement extend unto the most minute and transient phenomena. He literally hears 'the atoms praying . . . to be broken like bread . . . and to bleed'. He beseeches the goddess at the centre of creation to accept him although he is little better than one already dead ('And for all rumours to me read obituary'), a 'discarded foetus,/Already gray-haired'. He portrays himself as a discarded specimen, impaled yet navigating toward her; 'as for me/All I have . . . is your needle/Through my brains'. He offers himself as a Scapegoat, imploring her: 'Bite. Again, bite' to literally devour him so that she may live. The only payment that he can offer is his own pain: 'What is there left to give?/There's pain/Pain is hardest of all/It can not really be given./It can only be paid down/Equal . . . This payment is that purpose.'

These poems, in essence, proclaim his destiny as a Scapegoat, a destiny that is both blessing and curse; 'I skin the skin/Take the eye from the eye . . . I scrape the flesh from the flesh . . . boil the bones till nothing is left/But the bones/I pour away the sludge of brains/Leaving simply the brains/Soak it all/In the crushed oil of the life/Eat/Eat.' In some mysterious way his torment can benefit and regenerate the languishing goddess. The Epilogue concludes with a parodox. The dead man, Hughes says, prays that he will escape the inspired fury that a touch of the White Goddess brings with her annunciation. Yet, says Hughes: 'If you miss him he stays dead/Among the inescapable facts.' Quite literally, to have her come is intolerable because it brings a dissolution of the ego. To have her go out of one's life is more intolerable and it is in this spirit that we are to understand these final poems. The agony of revelation, the encounter with a power of transcendence so incomparably great and devastating must be experienced as a loss of self: 'So you have come and gone again/With my skin.' The reality represented by the White Goddess is too awesome and overwhelming to bear for long. Yet, without her there's no possibility of redemption and life remains choked at its source. The metaphor with which *Gaudete* closes portrays the oak tree ('your tree — your oak/A glare/Of black upward lightning') that is sacred to the White Goddess, whether she appears as Ishtar, Isis, Ashtarte or Cybele, as a guard at the doorway to another dimension, a dimension which Hughes has momentarily entered. Truly, its image is his own: 'Its agony is its temple.'

# CONCLUSION

After reading the poetry Hughes has written over the past twenty years we have the overwhelming impression of having accompanied him on a very personal spiritual journey. From the assertion of strength in the guise of the shaman to the acceptance of a permanent spiritual crisis, through the image of the scapegoat, which paradoxically calls for even greater courage, Hughes's poetry inexorably reaches this point of crisis and holds it. Loneliness, submission to the violence in oneself and moments of stark silent terror are the signposts and milestones that tell us of the complexity and depth of struggle Hughes has engaged in with himself to achieve poetry expressing the greatest mental, spiritual and emotional tension conceivable. With the poetry written in the epilogue of *Gaudete* Hughes achieves a vulnerability, an openness so complete and profound that these poems are like crystal on which a bittersweet complex design has been etched in the acid of remorse and self-accusation. The flow of Hughes's poetry moves from a shamanistic identification with powerful, violent and destructive predators like the hawk, the bear, the jaguar and the pike expressed in a style at once self-controlled, self-possessed and vehement, through a series of changes to become the poetry of the suffering victim, the self offered to the self as sacrifice, crucified, motionless, in the grip of anguish and self-purgation. Between shaman and scapegoat, trickster plays a crucial role. He is the one figure in myth and legend who is alternately both predator and victim. In the cycle of Crow poems Hughes holds the balance for a few years and writes poetry that is objective, realistic and grotesquely comic. The Crow poems are the turning point in Hughes's spiritual journey from his unspoken allegiance with the mythical life of devouring predators to the poetry of the scapegoat, a poetry of humilities that celebrates and embraces the symbolic death of his former self.

Significantly, each work after *Crow*, including *Prometheus on his Crag, Cave Birds* and *Gaudete*, re-enacts the moment of crisis in different guises, that exact moment when the intellect and the ego become aware that they must die, permonitions of which we have seen emerge intermittently in 'Snow', 'Wodwo' and *The Wound.* In these works an intellect that is accustomed to dominating events receives the first intimation of the call to submission, the breaking of the ego's stronghold. Understandably, this is felt as indescribably threatening, as if the ground has opened up beneath one's feet. Yet, this must be how the prospect of a complete psychological and spiritual transformation first appears — as the threat of extinction. We can trace this developing schism in Hughes's poetry quite clearly, from the complete identification of the self with the natural, the animal, the literal processes of nature, perceived of as the only reality, through poems like 'Wodwo' where the self and body are not split but are not in synchronization with each other to those poems beginning with 'Song of a Rat' where the schism is fully dramatized. The split first appears as the polarization between the self as victim and nature, in the guise of a demonic vengeful feminine force, as predator. Aware that it is caught in a trap from which it cannot escape Hughes's victim protagonist, replicated in many disguises, begins to attempt to locate the nature of the crime against womanhood for which it is being punished.

At this point the battle or more properly, the trial of strength, begins in earnest. One of the most unusual features of Hughes's poetry is that the nature of the enemy, the antagonist who is capable of bringing him to his knees, is obviously not apparent in the first stages of the struggle even to Hughes himself. His consciousness of who his antagonist truly is seems to lag behind his awareness that a challenge has been thrown down, his fear of the implications of what the nature of that challenge will mean for him and how much he will have to change and what he will have to give up. At first, the struggle appears senseless, as in 'The Contender' but this is simply because Hughes has not discovered its use for himself. He identifies the antagonist with the Erinys, the vengeful pursuing Furies, the vulture in her various guises and with outraged womanhood in *Gaudete.*

Yet, behind these disguises is Hughes's ultimate opponent: himself. Only in *Gaudete,* by presenting the spiritual journey in parable form as the life of Reverend Lumb do we sense that Hughes is becoming aware that the Furies are but the occasion through which the soul meets itself. The experience is similar to that projected in the 'Song of a Rat' where the rat in the trap knows that henceforward his fate is to be enmeshed in conditions not created by himself and so inescapably horrendous that it will not be possible for him to live without constant reference to them; he knows he has been overtaken by his fate, a fate he attempts to come to terms with in successive stages. In *Prometheus on his Crag* Hughes's protagonist bears his suffering for an eternity while he reviews the meaning of his suffering, point by point. Then Hercules and Dionysos, in turn, appear, each more susceptible towards self-transformation, each more successively violent and correspondingly more per-secuted by those their madness and savagery have injured. In *Gaudete* we see self-confrontation returning to the world of modern day England, returning the struggle to the sphere of the everyday world, after a temporary retreat to inaccess-ible regions of crag or cave and after a temporary withdrawal, in *Cave Birds,* using animal forms to mirror the subhumanity of his protagonist. By no slight coincidence do Hughes's pro-tagonists in both *Cave Birds* and *Gaudete* now see their lives as inseparable from the fate that encompasses them.

Now there arises that peculiar quality of silence in Hughes's poetry, as if his words have travelled enormous distances until they appear before us, like refugees from some far off war, surviving not because of their force of will but because they are utterly open and utterly vulnerable with the weakness of saints. All those forces with which Hughes's predators had been accustomed to dominate, demand and receive complete submission, have been inverted and the dominant emotion in Hughes's scapegoat protagonists is one of complete submission. In Hughes's shaman poems powerful creatures administer death and destruction to others, yet are themselves sealed off from any consequences. In the trickster poems we see a figure who both plays tricks on others and has the tables turned on himself. But in works centred around the scapegoat archetype we wit-ness Hughes's protagonists's fate as existential victims, suffering in their own persons and lives, both cause and effect, as they are compelled to experience what they send into the world. We move, as it were, from the moral universe of Francis Bacon, a world of efficiency regardless of consequences, to the moral universe of Shakespeare, a world of victims undone by their own passions.

Significantly, Hughes begins to use the cycle of poems, in *Crow,* as the most viable poetic form, precisely at that moment when the universe appears to be one of both causes and effects, where one can be either predator or prey and, horrifyingly, often both in the same lifetime. Hughes is attracted to the cyclical pattern of developing poems as the closest formal equivalent to the ongoing spiritual battle. Once generated he lets the elements within each work, whether *Crow* or *Cave Birds* or *Prometheus on his Crag,* exhaust themselves to produce that final silence, the unspoken afterbeat, beyond which the rational intellect is helpless. His critics have seen Hughes as simply being anti-intellectual, anti-rational and anti-Socratic.[1] This is not so, it is simply that for him, the intellect is no longer a serviceable or even desirable means for grasping an ultimate reality grown so distant, so unidentifiable with the usual conceptions of God that it must seem like a deity composed of silences, of emptinesses. Yet, this is but the last stage of the struggle by an extremely powerful intellect that has surveyed and has an excellent grasp of literature, history and philosophy. Indeed one has the very strong impression of a mind that increasingly must improvise, almost with every phrase or word, to capture and express a reality that is sensed but ungraspable. One feels the presence of a mind that has exhausted everything within reach, legends, myths, folklore of many nations, literature itself, a mind that now gropes, distrusting anything not under its control and strong enough to control everything except itself. This in turn produces that peculiar quality of moral alertness, the stylistic equivalent of perpetual vigilance that is so much a part of the heart-rending simplicity of Hughes's poetry, bespeaking a mind turning at great speed, but in neutral, unable to go forward, unable to return, burning itself out, exhausting itself, submitting itself to a savage self-transformation.

We see it in the plight of Prometheus torn between eternity and death, heaven and earth, unable to live, unable to die, a figure of superhuman endurance suffering his wound to be torn open by the vulture. Prometheus embodies the metaphor of self-inquisition, the need to redeem his suffering by understanding it and to be forced to endure his suffering until its meaning is burned into him. We see it in *Cave Birds* with Hughes's choice of Hercules on which to base his protagonist, the necessary breaking of strength of the strongest of all men. His image is one of self-immolation, Hercules on the pyre, a mind and consciousness stripped bare in the throes of self-recrimination. In all three major works since the Crow cycle, that is, in *Prometheus on his Crag, Cave Birds* and *Gaudete,* Hughes painstakingly creates in different contexts the conditions under which self-confrontation can take place, conditions where each motive can be weighed, analyzed and where a dominating intellect can see itself broken and where self-purification and ultimately self-forgiveness can occur. In the figure of Reverend Lumb we see Hughes's ultimate victim, modelled on Dionysos who has long stood as a symbol of the necessary dismemberment the self must experience before spiritual rebirth can take place.

The story of *Gaudete* re-enacts a fateful choice made, so to speak, before life itself began. The prologue describes the conditions of this contract, and the story shows how circumstances are inexorably created through which many women, and one woman in particular, are destroyed because of Reverend Lumb's unwitting, ruthless Dionysos-like cruelty. In turn, their destruction leads to his persecution and death. In the epilogue a new Lumb re-emerges with different values, those of humility not violence, submission of the will, not blind self-assertion. Yet, plainly this changed Reverend Lumb would not have come into existence if the preceding events in which the destructive side of his personality was projected had not occured. Lumb, like Dionysos, ultimately shares the fate of the women who have been victims in his cause. In *Gaudete* we see Hughes's awareness, rising momentarily from the unconscious, into parable form, that the circumstances of his life have been created by prior agreement between himself and a figure he represents as the ultimate goddess of nature. The nature of the agreement suggests that the only set of events in the world which could provoke him to promote a change in his nature must grow out of his being entangled in a net of circumstances so pervasive, so inescapable, that he will be forced to change. This change seen in the light of his ongoing spiritual journey is an absolute necessity since in the scheme of things the number of chances that are allowed to one diminish as one throws them away. This is what gives *Gaudete* its enormously resonant depth of meaning. In Hughes's choice of Dionysos on which to model the Reverend Lumb we see him choosing a figure who unwittingly causes the destruction of those women who share his fate and, at the end, the madness he embodies hunts him down as well. Like Dionysos, Lumb shares the fate of his women victims. He becomes the hunter who is himself hunted, the devourer of normality who is himself rent apart. He is the ultimate victim of the destroying madness he brings to others.

We must realize that Hughes seizes upon these elements of tragic savagery within his protagonists as a way of making himself aware that they are indeed their own worst enemies. Evidently, this thought would never rise to consciousness if it were not dramatized in such a terrifying extreme form. Without the full scale projection of the aggressive, violent, fanatic and unwittingly cruel traits in Reverend Lumb's nature, the new Reverend Lumb who appears in the epilogue as an embodiment of submission and humility could not have come into existence. Yet, we must not forget that ultimately the Reverend Lumb's submission is only in relation to himself, to the way he was. Seen in this light, we understand that the desire for vengeance directed against the Reverend Lumb is a disguised form of self-confrontation. The conscious intellect, the ego, the very stronghold of the personality must be assailed and brought down. Through an inexorable logic, Hughes projects situations in which his protagonists must submit to precisely that destructive violence which, in his shaman poems, he had earlier seen as the dominant feature of nature. So, too, in the work of Janos Pilinszky and Vasko Popa, East European writers to whose poetry Hughes is instinctively drawn and who have achieved a vision of victimhood analogous to Hughes's own, although for very different reasons, we see the soul *in extremis*, no longer seeking to change anything and for this reason, paradoxically, invulnerable to all temptations to transcend the conditions of its suffering.

# NOTES

## INTRODUCTION

1 A historical retrospective is provided, within Chapter 4 by Stanley Edgar Hyman, *The Armed Vision* (New York: Knopf, 1948). For what is unquestionably the best study to date exploring the effect of Frazer's *The Golden Bough* on Yeats, Eliot, Lawrence, Joyce and others see John B. Vickery, *The Literary Impact of The Golden Bough* (Princeton, N.J.: Princeton University Press, 1973).

2 A. Alvarez, *The Savage God: A Study of Suicide* (New York: Bantam Books, 1973), p. 28.

3 W. B. Yeats, *The Letters of W. B. Yeats,* ed. Allan Wade (New York, Macmillan, 1955), p. 918.

## PART I: SHAMAN

1 Mircea Eliade, *Shamanism: Archaic Techniques of Ecstasy,* trans. Willard R. Trask (New York: Pantheon Books, 1964), p. 460.

2 Ibid., p. 459.

3 Ibid., p. 460.

4 Ted Hughes, *Poetry Is* (New York: Doubleday, 1970), p. 9–13.

5 *Shamanism,* p. 44.

6 Ted Hughes, *Lupercal* (London: Faber & Faber, 1960), p. 26. See Ralph Maud, 'Last Poems', in C. B. Cox, ed. *Dylan Thomas: A Collection of Critical Essays* (Englewood Cliffs, N.J.: Prentice Hall, 1966), pp. 74–83, for an instructive contrast to Hughes's feminine hawk in Dylan Thomas's poem 'Over Sir John's hill' that begins 'Over Sir John's hill,/The hawk on fire hangs still' and elaborates the hawk as executioner imagery, filled with images of the 'gallows' and the invocation ' "Come and be killed" '; while the similarities are striking (the hawk-executioner, the hawk on fire with the last rays of the sun) the significant difference is that Thomas's hawk is set to its task by a masculine Godly Father while Hughes's hawk *is* the goddess of nature; See Vickery, *The Literary Impact of The Golden Bough,* p. 291 for discussion of D. H. Lawrence's poem, 'Autumn at Taos' which describes how Lawrence once saw 'the golden hawk of Horus/Astride above me': Lawrence too, notes Vickery, identifies the hawk, following Frazer, both with the sun and a masculine deity. Also, see Lawrence's 'Eagle in New Mexico', in Vivian De Dola Pinto and F. Warren Roberts, *The Complete Poems of D. H. Lawrence,* Vol. II (New York: The Viking Press, 1964), p. 780, for Lawrence's portrayal of a powerful predator 'erect and scorch-breasted' drawing his strength from the fire in 'the heart of the earth'; yet Lawrence never becomes, as Hughes does, the Shaman and only enters the poem as an observer. We are always terribly aware of Lawrence's overwhelming sense of loss, how separated he is from the animals he describes. With Hughes, the opposite is ture, he becomes the animal after the pattern of the Shaman. This explains the undue romanticizing of the animals Lawrence describes; we always see them through his consciousness,

never as in Hughes, as they are in themselves. In Lawrence's animal poems we are always aware of how much Lawrence is in the poem as a representative of civilized consciousness, burdened by his fear of death, tormented by his human limitations. Hughes, by contrast, submerges himself in the consciousness of the animal he is writing about.

7   London Magazine, Vol. 10, No. 10, 1971, p. 8.

8   Ibid.

9   *The Egyptian Book of the Dead,* trans. E. A. Wallis Budge (New York: Dover Publications, 1967 rpt. of 1895 work), p. CXV.

10   Ibid., p. CXIV.

11   Robert Graves, *The White Goddess, A Historical Grammar of Poetic Myth* (New York: Farrar, Straus & Giroux, 1966).

12   *Shamanism,* p. 316.

13   Ibid.

14   Ibid.

15   Ibid.

16   Ibid., p. 94.

17   Ibid.

18   Ibid.

19   Lupercal, pp. 46–7.

20   *Shamanism,* p. 182.

21   Dennis J. McKenna & T. K. McKenna, *The Invisible Landscape* (New York: The Seabury Press, 1975), p. 25.

22   Ibid.

23   Ibid.

24   Ted Hughes, *Gaudete* (New York: Harper & Row, 1977), pp. 174–75.

25   *Shamanism,* p. 215.

26   Ibid.

27   *Lupercal,* pp. 49–50.

28   *Shamanism,* p. 213.

29   Ibid.

30   *Lupercal,* pp. 56–7.

31   Angelo De Gubernatis, *Zoological Mythology* or *The Legends of Animals,* Vol. II (Detroit: Singing Tree Press, Book Tower, 1872 rpt., 1968), pp. 337–38.

32   Ibid., p. 337.

33   Ibid., p. 334.

34   Also known as the Mahabharata.

35   *Zoological Mythology,* p. 335.

36   *Lupercal,* pp. 61–3.

37   Patricia Merivale, *Pan The Goat-God: His Myth in Modern Times* (Cambridge: Harvard University Press, 1969), pp. 23–5 *et passim*; also see Graves, *The White Goddess,* p. 359.

38   Ted Hughes, *Wodwo* (New York: Harper & Row, 1967), p. 18.

39   *Shamanism,* p. 438.

40   Ibid., p. 214.

41   Ibid., p. 367.

42   *The Invisible Landscape,* p. 11.

43   Ibid.

44   Ibid.

45   *Shamanism,* p. 182.

46   Andreas Lommel, *Prehistoric Man and Primitive Man* (New York: McGraw-

Hill, 1966), p. 19.

47  Sir James George Frazer, *The Golden Bough: A Study in Magic and Religion,* abridged edition (1922; rpt. New York: Macmillan, 1963), p.627.

48  *The White Goddess,* p. 436.

49  Ted Hughes, *The Hawk in the Rain* (London: Faber & Faber, 1957), p. 12.

50  *Wodwo,* pp. 23—4.

51  Joseph Campbell, *The Mythic Image* (Princeton: Princeton University Press, 1974), p. 114.

52  G. Reichel-Dolmatoff, *The Shaman and the Jaguar* (Philadelphia: Temple University Press, 1975), p. 43.

53  Ibid., p. 54

54  As quoted in Campbell, *The Mythic Image*, p. 114.

55  Ibid.

56  Ibid.

57  Ibid.

58  *The Tibetan Book of the Dead,* ed. W. Y. Evans-Wentz (New York: Oxford University Press, 1927 rpt. 1960).

59  Ibid., p. 220.

60  Ibid., p. 221.

61  *The Mythic Image,* p. 116.

62  Keith Sagar, *The Art of Ted Hughes* 2nd edition (Cambridge: Cambridge University Press, 1978), p. 9.

63  *Wodwo,* p. 46.

64  *Sylvia Plath Letters Home Correspondence 1950—1963,* ed Aurelia Schober Plath (New York: Bantam, 1977), pp. 402—03.

65  *The Golden Bough,* p. 586.

66  Ibid.

67  Ibid.

68  Daniel 7:5.

69  *Shamanism,* p. 59.

70  Ibid., p. 44.

71  Ibid., pp. 59, 62.

72  Ibid., p. 62.

73  Ibid., p. 159.

74  Ibid., p. 163.

75  Ibid., p. 160.

76  Ibid., p. 164.

77  Ibid., p. 224.

78  Ibid.

79  Ibid., p. 266.

80  Ibid., p. 222.

81  *The White Goddess,* p. 367.

82  Anne Ross, *Pagan Celtic Britain: Studies in Iconography and Tradition* (London: Routledge & Kegan Paul, 1967), p. 375.

83  *Wodwo,* pp. 75—85.

84  Ted Hughes, *Crow: From the Life and Songs of the Crow* (New York: Harper & Row, 1971).

85  Seneca's *Oedipus,* adapted by Ted Hughes (London: Faber & Faber, 1969).

86  *Crow,* pp. 63—5.

87  *The Tibetan Book of the Dead,* pp. 161, 198; 'O nobly-born, at about that time, the fierce wind of karma, terrific and hard to endure, will drive thee . . . in

dreadful gusts.' p. 161.

88   *Shamanism*, p. 182.

89   *The Invisible Landscape*, p. 19.

90   *Shamanism*, p. 216.

91   *Wodwo*, pp. 86—96.

92   *The White Goddess*, pp. 401—02.

93   *The Golden Bough*, pp. 524—25.

94   Ibid., p. 510.

95   *Wodwo*, p. 92.

96   *The Art of Ted Hughes*, pp. 233, 258.

97   *Wodwo*, pp. 108—53; For a premonition of this theme see 'The Hawk in the Rain' in *The Hawk in the Rain*, p. 11, where the earth is hungry for the narrator and pulls him down with the ineluctable force of his intrinsic mortality.

98   *The Tibetan Book of the Dead*, p. 93, note 3, 'a bodily sensation of clammy coldness as though the body were immersed in water.'

99   See entries under Sir George Ripley in *The Collected Works of C. G. Jung*, Vol. 14, *Mysterium Coniunctionis*, trans. R.F.C. Hull, (New York: Pantheon Books, 1963), for the dissolution of the ego and its occult correspondences.

100  See entry under Erich Maria Remarque in *Cyclopedia of World Authors*, ed. Frank N. Magill (New York: Harper & Row, 1958), pp. 888—89.

101  James Joyce, *Ulysses* (New York: Modern Library corrected edition, 1961), p. 72; 'thirty-two feet per second, per second. Law of falling bodies: per second, per second'.

102  *The Tibetan Book of the Dead*, pp. xlvi, 166.

103  *Shamanism*, p. 438.

104  *The Tibetan Book of the Dead*, pp. 144—46.

105  Ibid., p. lxx.

106  Ibid., p. lxviii.

107  *Wodwo*, pp. 163—65.

108  *Prehistoric Man and Primitive Man*, p. 19.

109  Ibid.

110  Ibid.

111  *The Art of Ted Hughes*, p. 61; Sagar says: 'On 11 February 1963 she committed suicide. Later that month Hughes wrote: "The Howling of Wolves" and in March "Song of a Rat", then nothing (except a long play from which "Ghost Crabs", "Waking" and Part III of "Gog" were salvaged) until 1966, when he went to Ireland and started with "Gnat Psalm" and "Skylarks" '. Wherever Hughes uses wolf imagery, the element of self-portraiture rises to the forefront; for example, in 'A Modest Proposal', in *The Hawk in the Rain*, p. 25, Hughes describes both himself and Sylvia as wolves, locked in a too violent relationship, unable to bring down 'the stag' as greyhounds who hunt in partnership, in concord, are able to do.

112  As quoted in *The Invisible Landscape*, p. 10.

113  *Zoological Mythology*, II, 273—74.

114  See Judith Kroll, *Chapters in a Mythology The Poetry of Sylvia Plath* (New York: Harper & Row, 1976), pp. 115—26.

115  *Wodwo*, pp. 169—72.

116  See *Syliva Plath Method and Madness*  by Edward Butscher (New York: Pocket Books, 1977); *The Savage God: A Study of Suicide; A Closer Look at Ariel: A Memory of Sylvia Plath* by Nancy Hunter (New York: Steiner, Popular Library, 1973); *Sylvia Plath Her Life and Work* by Eileen M. Aird (New York: Harper &

Row, Perennial Library, 1973).

117 *Wodwo*, pp. 180—82.

118 *Shamanism*, p. 223.

119 *Wodwo*, p. 7.

120 Ibid., p. 184.

121 Ibid.

## PART II TRICKSTER

1   All references to individual poems are from the 1971 edition of *Crow*.

2   Paul Radin, *The Trickster: A Study in American Indian Mythology* (1956; rpt. New York: Schocken Books, 1972), p. 155.

3   Ibid., p. 156.

4   Ibid., p. 167.

5   Ibid., p. 166, 125—26.

6   Carl G. Jung, in *The Trickster*, p. 209.

7   Ibid., p. 164.

8   Ibid., p. 104.

9   *The Tibetan Book of the Dead*, p. 157.

10   Radin, *The Trickster*, p. 130.

11   Ibid., p. 133.

12   Ibid., pp. 138—39.

13   Claude Levi-Strauss, *From Honey to Ashes: Introduction to a Science of Mythology* Vol. 2, trans. John and Doreen Weightman (New York: Harper and Row, 1973), pp. 418—19.

14   Ted Hughes, *Gaudete*, p. 176.

15   Albert Camus, *The Rebel: An Essay on Man in Revolt* (New York: Vintage Books, 1956), p. 246.

16   Radin, *The Trickster*, p. 151.

17   'The Pardoner's Tale' in *The Works of Geoffrey Chaucer*, 2nd ed. Ed.F.N. Robinson (Boston: Houghton Mifflin Co., 1957), pp. 150—55.

18   Ted Hughes, *The Tiger Bones and Other Plays for Children* (New York: The Viking Press, 1974), p. 80.

19   Angelo De Gubernatis, *Zoological Mythology*, Vol. II, p. 254.

20   *Man and His Symbols*, ed. Carl G. Jung (New York: Doubleday, 1964), p. 237.

21   Radin, *The Trickster*, p. 76.

22   Angelo De Gubernatis, *Zoological Mythology*, p. 254.

23   Robert Graves, *The Greek Myths*, Vol. I (New York: Penguin Books, 1955), pp. 312—13.

24   Wallace Stevens, *Collected Poems* (New York: Knopf 1955, 1972), p. 64.

25   Lagarde, Andre and Laurent Michard, *Moyen Age; les grands auteurs francais du programme* (Paris: Bordas, 1967), p. 219.

26   Ted Hughes, *Gaudete*, p. 179.

27   Radin, *The Trickster*, p. 126.

28   *Portable Matthew Arnold*, ed. Lionel Trilling (New York: The Viking Press, 1949), pp. 165—67.

29   Ted Hughes, *Prometheus on His Crag* (London: Rainbow Press, 1973).

30   Radin, *The Trickster*, p. 134.

31   Carl G. Jung, in *The Trickster*, p. 203.

32   Edmund Spenser, *The Faery Queene* ed. by J. C. Smith and E. De Selincourt Vol. I (London: Oxford University Press, 1966), pp. 4—67.

33   Angelo De Gubernatis, *Zoological Mythology*, p. 258.

34   S. H. Butcher, *Aristotle's Theory of Poetry and Fine Art*, 4th Ed., (New York: Dover, 1951), p. 375.

35   Robert Graves, *The Greek Myths*, Vol. I, pp. 281—84.

36   Angelo De Gubernatis, *Zoological Mythology*, p. 241.

37   Radin, *The Trickster*, p. 78.

38   *The Complete Works of Samuel Taylor Coleridge,* ed. Ernest H. Coleridge (Oxford: Clarendon Press, 1966), p. 237.

39   Angelo De Gubernatis, *Zoological Mythology*, p. 245.

40   C. R. Ember and M. Ember, *Anthropology* (Englewood Cliffs, New Jersey: Prentice-Hall, 1973), p. 355.

41   Angelo De Gubernatis, *Zoological Mythology*, Vol. II, p. 94.

42   Compare with R. D. Laing, *The Politics of Experience* (New York: Ballantine Books, 1967), pp. 146—68.

43   Radin, *The Trickster*, p. 136.

44   Karl Kerenyi, in *The Trickster*, p. 180.

45   *Oedipus Myth and Drama,* ed. Martin Kallich et al (New York: The Odyssey Press, 1968).

46   Radin, *The Trickster*, p. 164.

47   Ibid., p. 156.

48   Frances Aurelia Yates, *Giordano Bruno and the Hermetic Tradition,* (Chicago: University of Chicago Press, 1964), p. 150.

49   Radin, *The Trickster*, p. 146.

50   E. M. Weyer, *The Eskimos* (Hamden, Conn.: Archon Books, 1969), pp. 446—47, 226—27.

51   H. D. Thoreau, *Walden,* introduction by Basil Willey (New York: Bramhall House, 1951), pp. 105—6.

52   Radin, *The Trickster,* p. xxiii; Stylistically, *Crow* is indebted to Robert Graves, *Collected Poems: 1955* (Garden City, N.Y.: Doubleday, 1955), pp. 75—6, 86—7, 179, *et passim,* especially 'The Legs' which begins 'There was this road . . .'

## PART III: SCAPEGOAT

1   An invaluable record of this experience is provided by A.C. H. Smith, in *Orghast at Persepolis* (New York: The Viking Press, 1972).

2   Ibid., pp. 50—51.

3   Ibid., p. 91; in addition to the limited edition of these poems published by Rainbow Press, November, 1973, see Keith Sagar, pp. 146—158 for a perceptive selection from key poems in the sequence.

4   A.C.H. Smith, *Orghast at Persepolis*, pp. 132—33.

5   Ibid., p. 51.

6   Ibid.

7   See the *Classic Theatre*, Vol. III Six Spanish Plays, ed. Eric Bentley, (New York: Doubleday, 1959 Anchor Books Edition), p. 409.

8   *Classic Theatre*, pp. 412—13, 423.

9   Ibid., p. 455.

10   Ibid., p. 478.

11   A.C.H. Smith, *Orghast at Persepolis*, p. 98.

12   Ibid., p. 94.

13   Ibid., pp. 96—7.

14   Ibid., p. 186.

15   William Blake, *The Book of Urizen*, ed. Kay Parkhurst Easson and Roger Easson (Boulder, Colorado: Shambala, 1978), p. 59.

16   Harold Bloom, *Blake's Apocalypse: A Study in Poetic Argument* (New York: Anchor Books, 1965), p. 180.

17   A.C.H. Smith, *Orghast at Persepolis*, p. 93.

18   Ibid., p. 94.

19   For a comprehensive discussion of literary uses of the Prometheus legend see Raymond Troussou, *Le Theme de Promethee dans la Litterature Europeenne*, 2 Vols. (Geneve: Librairie Droz, 1964).

20   Joseph Campbell, *The Masks of God: Primitive Mythology* (New York: Penguin Books, 1977), p. 279.

21   For a fuller analysis of this point, see K. Kerenyi, *Prometheus, Archetypal Image of Human Existence*, trans. Ralph Manheim (New York: Pantheon Books, 1963), p. 27, *et passim*.

22   *Robert*

22   Robert Graves, *Greek Myths*, I, 145.

23   Trans. by Evelyn White, as quoted in K. Kerenyi, *Prometheus*, p. 48.

24   K. Kerenyi, *Prometheus*, p. 55.

25   Ibid.

26   Ibid., p. 127.

27   A.C.H. Smith, *Orghast at Persepolis*, p. 91; See Claude Levi-Strauss, *The Raw and the Cooked: Introduction to a Science of Mythology* (I), trans. John and Doreen Weightman (New York: Harper and Row, 1969).

28   Ibid., p. 140.

29   Ibid., p. 141.

30   Ibid., p. 142.

31   Ibid., p. 140.

32   Ibid., p. 141.

33   Claude Levi-Strauss, *The Raw and the Cooked*, p. 187.

34   Mircea Eliade, *Shamanism*, p. 44.

35   Ibid., p. 100.

36   W. B. Yeats, *The Collected Poems of W. B. Yeats:* 'Definitive Edition with the Author's Final Revisions' (New York: Macmillan, 1956), pp. 157—59.

37   W. B. Yeats, *Mythologies*, ed. Mrs. W. B. Yeats (New York: Macmillan, 1959), p. 335.

38   W. B. Yeats, *A Vision:* 'A Reissue with the Author's Final Revisions' (New York: Macmillan, 1956), p. 82.

39   W. B. Yeats, *The Letters of W. B. Yeats*, ed. Allen Wade (New York: Macmillan, 1955), p. 918.

40   *The Collected Poems of W. B. Yeats*, pp. 184—85.

41   Ibid., pp. 212—14.

42   Ibid., pp. 204—08.

43   Dylan Thomas, *The Collected Poems of Dylan Thomas* (New York: New Directions, 1953), pp. 131—35.

44   A.C.H. Smith, *Orghast at Persepolis*, pp. 95—6.

45     Ibid., p. 95.

46     See Robert Graves, *Greek Myths* Vol. 1, pp. 190—91.

47     Robert Lowell *Prometheus Bound* (New York: Farrar, Straus and Giroux, 1969), pp. 38—9.

48     Angelo De Gubernatis, *Zoological Mythology*,   II, 385.

49     Ibid., p. 251.

50     Seneca's *Oedipus*, adapted by Ted Hughes (London: Faber and Faber, 1969) For comparison see Sophocles, *Oedipus The King*, trans. David Grene (Chicago: University of Chicago Press, 1954).

51     Jane Ellen Harrison, *Prolegomena to the Study of Greek Religion*, second edition (Cambridge: Cambridge University Press, 1908), p. 207.

52     Ibid., p. 208.

53     Ibid., p. 212.

54     Ibid.

55     Ibid., p. 214.

56     Ibid., p. 215.

57     Ibid., p. 44.

58     Ibid., p. 61.

59     Ted Hughes, *Cave Birds: An Alchemical Cave Drama*, with drawings by Leonard Baskin (New York: The Viking Press, 1978), p. 62.

60     As quoted by G. S. Kirk, *The Nature of Greek Myths* (Baltimore: Penguin Books, 1974), pp. 61—2.

61     Ibid., p. 70.

62     Ibid.

63     Ibid., p. 72.

64     Ibid., pp. 82—3.

65     Ibid., p. 83.

66     Keith Sagar, *The Art of Ted Hughes*, pp. 243—44.

67     All references will be from the 1978 edition.

68     Vasko Popa, *Collected Poems 1943—1976*, trans. Anne Pennington with an introduction by Ted Hughes (New York: Persea Books, 1978), p. 8.

69     C. G. Jung, *Mysterium Coniunctionis*, pp. 145, 290.

70     Ibid., p. 344.

71     Ibid., pp. 353—54.

72     Ibid.

73     Llewellyn George, *A to Z Horoscope Maker and Delineator*, 15th edition (St. Paul: Llewellyn Publications, 1966), p. 626; Hughes's natal chart for 8—17—30 reveals an unusual pattern of a cross in cardinal signs.

74     Ibid., p. 627.

75     C. G. Jung, *Mysterium Coniunctionis*, p. 516.

76     This episode is described in Carlos Castaneda, *The Teachings of Don Juan: A Yaqui Way of Knowledge* (New York: Pocket Books, 1974), pp. 161—76.

77     C. G. Jung, *Mysterium Coniunctionis*, p. 359.

78     Ibid., p. 510.

79     Ibid.

80     Ibid., p. 512.

81     Ibid., p. 515.

82     Ibid., p. 521.

83     Ibid.

84     C. G. Jung, *The Practice of Psychotherapy: Essays on the Psychology of the Transference and Other Subjects* second edition, (New York; Bollingen Series

XX Pantheon, 1954), p. 167.

85  Ibid.

86  Ibid., p. 173.

87  Ibid.

88  Ibid., p. 180.

89  Ibid., p. 180—81.

90  Ibid., p. 197.

91  Ibid., pp. 197—98.

92  Ibid., p. 281.

93  Ibid., p. 200.

94  Ibid., p. 218.

95  Ibid.

96  Ibid., p. 229.

97  Ibid., p. 240.

98  Ibid., p. 256.

99  Ibid.

100  Ibid.

101  Ibid.

102  Ibid., p. 260.

103  Ibid., p. 264.

104  Joseph Campbell, *Primitive Mythology*, p. 255.

105  Ibid.

106  C.G. Jung, *The Practice of Psychotherapy*, p. 266.

107  For the complete text see C. G. Jung, *The Practice of Psychotherapy*, pp. 295—99.

108  Dylan Thomas, *The Collected Poems of Dylan Thomas*. pp. 60—1.

109  Ibid., pp. 86—110.

110  Ibid., pp. 69—70.

111  Ibid., p. 76.

112  C. G. Jung, *The Practice of Psychotherapy*, p. 269.

113  Dylan Thomas, *The Collected Poems of Dylan Thomas*. pp. 80—5.

114  His drawing is reproduced as Plate 12 in G. Karl Galinsky, *The Herakles Theme* (Totowa, N.J.: Rowman and Littlefield, 1972).

115  T. S. Eliot, *The Complete Poems and Plays 1909—1950* (New York: Harcourt, 1962), pp. 295—388.

116  This labour of Hercules is described by Robert Graves, *The Greek Myths*, Vol. 2, pp. 119—21.

117  Ibid., Vol. I, p. 336; Hughes adapted the idea that Hercules welcomed, as Robert Graves says: 'the appearance of vultures, whenever he was about to undertake a new labour. "Vultures", he would say, 'are the most righteous of birds: they do not attack even the smallest living creature." ' Ibid., Vol. II, p. 93. In Hughes's poem 'She seemed so considerate' this becomes 'I am the one creature/Who never harmed any living thing.'

118  Geoffrey Chaucer, *Chaucer's Poetry*, ed. E.T. Donaldson (New York: The Ronald Press, 1958), pp. 489—514.

119  T. S. Eliot, *The Complete Poems and Plays 1909—1950*, pp. 138—45.

120  Butscher, *Sylvia Plath Method and Madness*, p. 314.

121  Robert Graves, *The White Goddess*, p. 264.

122  W. B. Yeats, *The Collected Poems of W. B. Yeats*, p. 336.

123  T. S. Eliot, *The Complete Poems and Plays 1909—1950*, pp. 37—55.

124  Robert Graves, *The White Goddess*, pp. 52, 124, 126.

125    Ibid., p. 302.

126    Ibid.

127    Ibid.

128    Anthony S. Mercantante, *Who's Who In Egyptian Mythology* (New York: Clarkson N. Potter, Inc., Publishers, 1978), pp. 189–90.; incidentally, Hughes's equation of his protagonist with a baboon not only underscores the subhuman side of his hero's personality and reflects the iconography of the Egyptian underworld but incorporates the archetypal relationship projected by writer Haggard in his book *She* (the hero is Leo Vincey and his guardian is described as resembling 'a baboon') as Leo goes in quest of 'she' who 'dwells among the tombs' and who 'is reputed to kill her lovers one by one', a fact which clearly relates her to the White Goddess, cited by Jung, *The Practice of Psychotherapy*, p. 220.

129    Anthony S. Mercantante, *Who's Who In Egyptian Mythology*, p. 75.

130    Ibid., pp. 5–6.

131    Robert Graves, *The White Goddess*, p. 51.

132    Plato *The Last Days of Socrates*, trans. and with an introduction by Hugh Tredennick (Baltimore: Penguin Books, 1969), p. 183.

133    Ibid., p. 170.

134    Ibid.

135    Ibid., p. 173.; Socrates provides a description of the earth as a ball 'made of twelve pieces of skin' sewn together, surely an uncanny image. This same stitched-together metaphor is later used by Hughes in *Gaudete*, p. 104, to describe the earth mother deity. Hughes characteristically inverts the metaphor to apply to the underworld goddess with a stitched patchwork face, a natural enough extension of Socrates's earth metaphor, since for Hughes, the earth is always mother earth.

136    Martin P. Nilsson, *Greek Folk Religion* (Philadelphia: University of Pennsylvania, Press, 1940 rpt. 1972), p. 116.

137    R. F. Willetts, *Cretan Cults and Festivals* (London: Routledge and Kegan Paul, 1962), p. 55.

138    Martin P. Nilsson, *Greek Folk Religion*, p. 120.

139    Plato, *The Last Days of Socrates*, p. 178.

140    C. G. Jung, *Mysterium Coniunctionis*, p. 515.

141    Robert Graves, *The White Goddess*, p. 70.

142    All quotations are taken from the 1977 edition.

143    John Middleton, *Lugbara Religion;* Ritual and Authority Among an East African People (London: Oxford University Press, 1960), p. 165: see Walter F. Otto, *Dionysus: Myth and Cult*, trans. Robert B. Palmer (London: Indiana University Press, 1965), pp. 49, 50, 65–6, 73–4, 75, 76, 79, 86, 90, 104, 107, 109, 113, 114, 117, 142, *et passim*, for specific traits, incidents, and characteristics relating to Dionysus that Hughes incorporated in his portrayal of the Reverend Lumb; for example, Hughes transforms the pair of sisters, Procne and Philomela, who are associated with Dionysus into the sisters Janet and Jennifer, cf. p. 173. Yet, again, Otto relates, on p. 133, how 'the daughters of Minyas, who wish to remain faithful to their household duties and attend their husbands were driven out by Dionysus' because 'his fury ripped them loose from their peaceful domesticity'. Duality is the essence of Dionysus, a trait celebrated in the 'two-fold nature' of 'a large mask of the god' which was his symbol, cf. p. 86.

144    Otto, *Dionysus: Myth and Cult*, p. 113 observes that 'No single Greek god even approaches Dionysus in the horror of his epithets which bear witness to a savagery that is absolutely without mercy . . . correspondingly we hear not only of human sacrifice in his cult but also of the ghastly ritual in which a man is torn to

pieces.' In Hughes's story, Lumb quite literally becomes the object of the hunt, the one who is to be torn into pieces.

145    Sigmund Freud, 'The Relation of the Poet to Day-Dreaming," trans. I. F. Grant Duff, in *On Creativity and the Unconscious,* ibid., p. 45. First published in Neue Revue, I, 1908.

146    See Katharine Briggs, *An Encyclopedia of Fairies:* Hobgoblins, Brownies, Bogies, and Other Supernatural Creatures (New York: Pantheon Books, 1976), p. 70, for the folklore backgrounds of the changeling: 'This "changeling" was of various kinds. Sometimes it was a STOCK of wood roughly shaped into the likeness of a child and endowed by GLAMOUR with a temporary appearance of life which soon faded, when the baby would appear to die and the stock would be duly buried.' Also, see entries under 'fairy trees' for the importance of the oak, and her discussion of the 'Separable soul, or external soul'.

147    Michael Grant and John Hazel, *Gods and Mortals in Classical Mythology* (Springfield, Mass. G. & C. Merriam Co., 1973), p. 148.

148    vide OED sv. 'lumbar'.

149    From Robert Graves, *The White Goddess,* p. 446 we understand why Hughes made use of the dramaturgy of the puppet to describe the split of Lumb's personality; as Graves says 'he is himself and his other self at the same time, king and supplanter, victim and murderer . . . and his right hand does not know what his left hand does . . . in order to simplify the myth he was represented as twins . . . poets are aware that each twin must conquer in turn in an age long and chivalrous war fought for the favours of the White Goddess.'

150    This scene reflects an archetypal encounter common to the Eskimo shaman, as portrayed by Eliade, *Shamanism,* pp. 289, 294—95; the Eskimo shaman visits the bottom of the sea where 'the mother of the sea beasts' dwells, a great goddess of the animals upon whose good will the tribe depends and whose condition suffers in direct proportion to violation of community taboos. On reaching the bottom of the ocean the shaman sees that 'the goddesses's hair hangs down over her face and she is dirty and slovenly'. This is the effect of men's sins which have almost made her ill. To restore her the shaman demands a 'public confession of sins' a collective purgation if she is to be restored to life. Hughes highlights the intimate connection in the scene where small seashells, which otherwise might seem to be out of place, are placed on the mysterious grave bearing the name Gaudete.

151    Robert Graves, *The White Goddess,* p. 24.

152    Ibid., p. 486.

153    Ibid., p. 489.

154    Ibid., p. 448; Hughes is drawing on the ascensional rites known in ancient India as well, cf. Eliade *Shamanism,* p. 403: 'the sacrificial post . . . is made from a tree that is assimilated to the cosmic tree. The priest himself accompanied by the woodcutter chooses it in the forest. While it is being felled the sacrificing priest apostrophizes it . . . the sacrificial post becomes a sort of cosmic pillar.'

155    Robert Graves, *The White Goddess,* p. 24.

156    Ibid.

157    C. G. Jung, *Man and His Symbols,* p. 178.

158    In the chapter 'The Myth and Ritual of Attis' (Sir James Frazer, *The Golden Bough,* p. 408) describes the annual ritual enactment of the death and resurrection of Attis. A bull was stabbed to death and its 'hot reeking blood poured in torrents . . . was received with devout eagerness by the worshipper on every part of his person . . . till he emerged from the pit drenched dripping and scarlet from head to foot . . . as one who had been born again . . .' This ceremoney was carried out near the spot

where St Peter's Basilica now stands.

159    Middleton, *Lugbara Religion*, p. 98. In Frazer, *The Golden Bough*, p. 173 we learn that 'the flesh of the white bull sacrificed on the Alban Mount' was consecrated admidst the oak forests in Rome.; Robert Graves, *The White Goddess*, p. 105 describes a rite called the bull feast in which a 'white bull was killed and the man who ate of his flesh and drank of his blood' would see 'in a dream the shape and appearance' of a man who 'should be made king'.

160    Sir James Frazer, *The Golden Bough*, p. 449.

161    Graves, *The White Goddess*, p. 134.

162    Ibid., p. 176.

163    Ibid., p. 125.

164    Frazer, *The Golden Bough*, p. 189.

165    Ibid., p. 172.

166    Ibid., pp. 135—36.

167    Ibid., p. 144.

168    *The White Goddess*, p. 125.

169    *The Golden Bough*, p. 144.

170    Ibid., p. 147.

171    Ibid., p. 298.

172    See John B. Vickery, *The Scapegoat: Ritual and Literature* (New York: Houghton Mifflin Co., 1972), p. 39. Walter F. Otto, *Dionysus*, p. 49 reminds us that Dionysus was known as 'the raving god whose presence makes men mad', whose arrival brings the toppling of the powers that be and leads to madness and the mockery of law.

173    *The White Goddess*, pp. 165—205.

174    *The Nibelungenlied*, trans. A. T. Hatto (New York: Penguin, 1965), pp. 130—31.

175    *Three Plays of Euripides*, trans. Paul Roche (New York: W. W. Norton & Co., Inc., 1974), pp. 100—04; see Vickery, *The Literary Impact of The Golden Bough*, pp. 287—93 for discussion of D. H. Lawrence's poems 'Under the Oak' and 'Late at Night' where Lawrence asks: 'tall black bacchae at midnight, why then, why/Do you rush to assail me? . . . Have I profaned some female mystery.' Both Lawrence and Hughes share the belief that acceptance of a sacrificial communion must precede the attainment of a new life.

176    *The White Goddess*, pp. 254, 256.

177    *The Golden Bough*, p. 451.

178    *The White Goddess*, p. 464.

179    I am indebted to Sagar, pp. 188—89 on this point: the first lines from this Christmas hymn, taken, as Sagar notes, from the *Piae Cantiones* announce: 'Gaudete, gaudete Christus est natus/Ex Maria virginae, gaudete.'

180    The struggle is strikingly similar to the scene in *Beowulf* where the hero battles a demonically devouring figure in the middle of a lake. Also, the choreography of the scene in which Lumb appears and re-enters the lake is due to the fact that, as Otto, *Dionysus*, p. 162 observes, 'the cults and myths are as explicit as they can be about the fact that Dionysus comes out of the water and returns to it' especially 'the lake of Lerna'.

181    The otter we recall was characterized by Hughes as a 'king in hiding', an ideal animal totem for the split existence, in and out of water, for the Reverend Lumb.

182    *The White Goddess*, p. 45.

183    *Shamanism*, p. 400.

184    Ibid., pp. 155—56.

185    *The White Goddess,* p. 318.

186    Ibid., p. 397.

187    Ibid., p. 110 informs us that 'Dionysus has epiphanies as Lion, Bull and Serpent, because these were calender emblems of the Tripartite year. He was born in winter as a serpent . . . he becomes a lion in the spring; and he is killed and devoured as a bull or stag at midsummer.' These, in fact are the stages through which Lumb is depicted: as the story opens, Lumb is intertwined with a tree branch, serpentlike, then he falls, literally and metaphorically, 'chews earth and loses consciousness'; before the story is over he is linked with the kingly lion and rutting stag. Maud is the human parallel of Hera, the jealous wife-sister of Zeus. Several times she attempts to kill Dionysus, who escapes and miraculously revives. Like Hera, Maud is not only Lumb's housekeeper but a mother figure and high priestess. As in the myth when Hera discovers that Zeus has chosen Semele, a mere human and has begotten Dionysus so Maud, having read Lumb's diary, is overcome with anger and jealously and makes her plans to destroy Lumb and Felicity. Just as Lumb rescues Felicity at the lake, so Dionysus reaches Hades by diving into Lake Lerna and recaptures Semele. Thus the antagonism between Hera and Semele reflects in the hostility between Maud and Felicity; see Graves, *The Greek Myths,* Vol. I, pp. 103—11.

188    Frazer, *The Golden Bough,* p. 385.

189    See Graves, pp. 216—17: Graves tells us that 'in Ireland during the Bronze Age as in Crete and Greece both stag and bull were sacred to the white Goddess.' Lumb is cast in the mould of the antlered king and on May Day 'stag mummers' re-enacted the chase of a man dressed in deer skins. Underlying the imagery of Hughes's description is the Greek myth of Actaeon who was changed into a stag by Artemis and hunted to death by her dogs.

190    Thomas Bulfinch, *Bulfinch's Mythology* (New York: Modern Library, 1934), p. 164; see *The Bacchae,* trans. Paul Roche, pp. 112—24.

191    *The Nibelungenlied,* p. 130.

192    Frazer, *The Golden Bough,* p. 344.

193    *Orghast at Persepolis,* pp. 96—135, *et passim.*

## CONCLUSION

1    For a brilliant account that takes Platonism to task, see 'The Greek Ghost Dance' Chapter in Weston La Barre, *The Ghost Dance: The Origins of Religions* (Garden City, N.Y.: Doubleday & Co., Inc., 1970), pp. 517—553.

## BIBLIOGRAPHY OF WORKS CITED

Aird, Eileen M. *Sylvia Plath Her Life and Work.* Harper and Row, Perennial Library, 1973.

Alvarez, A. *The Savage God: A Study of Suicide.* New York: Bantam Books, 1973.

Arnold, Matthew. *The Portable Matthew Arnold.* Ed. Lionel Trilling. New York:

The Viking Press, 1949.

Bentley, Eric, ed. *The Classic Theatre.* Vol. III. New York: Doubleday, Anchor Books Edition, 1959.

Blake, William. *The Book of Urizen.* Ed. Kay Parkhurst Easson and Roger Easson. Boulder, Colorado: Shambala Press, 1978.

Bloom, Harold. *Blake's Apocalypse: A Study in Poetic Argument.* New York: Anchor Books, 1965.

Briggs, Katherine. *An Encyclopedia of Fairies.* New York: Pantheon Books, 1976.

Bulfinch, Thomas. *Bulfinch's Mythology.* New York: Modern Library, 1934.

Butcher, S. H. *Aristotle's Theory of Poetry and Fine Art,* 4th ed. New York: Dover, 1951.

Butscher, Edward. *Sylvia Plath: Method and Madness.* New York: Pocket Books, 1977.

Campbell, Joseph. *The Masks of God: Primitive Mythology.* New York: 1977.

. *The Mythic Image.* Princeton: Princeton University Press, 1974.

Camus, Albert. *The Rebel: An essay on Man in Revolt.* New York: Vintage Books, 1956.

Castaneda, Carlos. *The Teachings of Don Juan: A Yaqui Way of Knowledge.* New York: Pocket Books, 1974.

Chaucer, Geoffrey. *Chaucer's Poetry.* Ed. E. T. Donaldson. New York: The Ronald Press, 1958.

. *The Works of Geoffrey Chaucer.* 2nd ed. Ed. F. N. Robinson. Boston: Houghton Mifflin Co., 1957.

Coleridge, S. T. *The Complete Works of Samuel Taylor Coleridge.* Ed. Ernest H. Coleridge. Oxford: Clarendon Press, 1966.

Cox, C. B., ed. *Dylan Thomas: A Collection of Critical Essays.* Englewood Cliffs, New Jersey: Prentice Hall, 1966.

*Cyclopedia of World Authors.* Ed. Frank N. Magill. New York: Harper and Row, 1958.

De Gubernatis, Angelo. *Zoological Mythology* or *The Legends of Animals.* 2 Vols. 1872; rpt. Detroit: Singing Tree Press, 1968.

*The Egyptian Book of the Dead.* Trans. E. A. Wallis Budge. 1895; rpt. New York: Dover Publications, 1967.

Eliade, Mircea. *Shamanism: Archaic Techniques of Ecstasy.* Trans. Willard R. Trask. New York: Pantheon Books, 1964.

Eliot, T. S. *The Complete Poems and Plays 1909—1950.* New York: Harcourt, 1962.

Ember, C. R. and M. Ember. *Anthropology.* Englewood Cliffs, New Jersey: Prentice-Hall, 1973.

Euripides. *Three Plays of Euripides.* Trans. Paul Roche. New York: W. W. Norton, 1974.

Frazer, Sir James George. *The Golden Bough:* A Study in Magic and Religion. Abridged Edition. 1922; rpt. New York: Macmillan, 1963.

Galinsky, Karl G. *The Herakles Theme.* Totowa, New Jersey: Rowman and Littlefield, 1972.

George, Llewellyn. *A to Z Horoscope Maker and Delineator.* 15th ed. St. Paul, Minnesota: Llewellyn Publications, 1966.

Grant, Michael and John Hazel. *Gods and Mortals in Classical Mythology.* Springfield, Mass.: G. & C. Merriam Co., 1973.

Graves, Robert. *Collected Poems: 1955.* Garden City, N.Y.: Doubleday, 1955.

. *The Greek Myths.* 2 Vols. New York: Penguin Books, 1955.

. *The White Goddess: A Historical Grammar of Poetic Myth.* New York:

Farrar, Straus & Giroux, 1966.

Harrison, Jane Ellen. *Prolegomena to the Study of Greek Religion.* 2nd ed. Cambridge: Cambridge University Press, 1908.

Hughes, Ted. *Cave Birds: An Alchemical Cave Drama,* with drawings by Leonard Baskin. New York: The Viking Press, 1978.

⸻. *Crow: From the Life and Songs of the Crow.* New York: Harper and Row, 1971.

⸻. *Gaudete.* New York: Harper & Row, 1977.

⸻. *The Hawk in the Rain.* London: Faber & Faber, 1957.

⸻. *Lupercal.* London: Faber & Faber, 1960.

⸻. *Oedipus,* adapted from Seneca by Ted Hughes. London: Faber & Faber, 1969.

⸻. *Poetry Is.* New York: Doubleday, 1970.

⸻. *Prometheus on His Crag.* London: Rainbow Press, 1973.

⸻. 'Ted Hughes and Crow,' *London Magazine,* 10 (January, 1971), 5–20.

⸻. *The Tiger Bones and Other Plays for Children.* New York: The Viking Press, 1974.

⸻. *Wodwo.* New York: Harper & Row, 1967.

Hunter, Nancy. *A Closer Look at Ariel: A Memory of Sylvia Plath.* New York: Steiner, Popular Library, 1973.

Hyman, Stanley Edgar. *The Armed Vision.* New York: Knopf, 1948.

Joyce, James. *Ulysses.* Corrected Edition. New York: Modern Library, 1961.

Jung, C. G., ed. *Man and His Symbols.* New York: Doubleday, 1964.

⸻. *Mysterium Coniunctionis.* Trans. R. F. C. Hull. Ed. Sir Herbert Read, Michael Fordham, and Gerhard Adler. Bollingen Series XX, Vol. 14. New York: Pantheon Books, 1963.

⸻. *The Practice of Psychotheraphy.* 2nd ed. Trans. R. F. C. Hull. Ed. Sir Herbert Read, Michael Fordham and Gerhard Adler. Bollingen Series XX, Vol. 16. New York: Pantheon Books, 1954.

Kerenyi, K. *Prometheus: Archetypal Image of Human Existence.* Trans. Ralph Manheim. New York: Pantheon Books, 1963.

Kirk, G. S. *The Nature of Greek Myths.* Baltimore: Penguin Books, 1974.

Kroll, Judith. *Chapters in a Mythology:* The Poetry of Sylvia Plath. New York: Harper & Row, 1976.

La Barre, Weston. *The Ghost Dance: The Origins of Religions.* Garden City, New York: Doubleday, 1970.

Lagarde, Andre and Laurent Michard. *Moyen Age; les grands auteurs francais du programme.* Paris: Bordas, 1967.

Laing, R. D. *The Politics of Experience.* New York: Ballantine Books, 1967.

Lawrence, D. H. *The Complete Poems of D. H. Lawrence.* Ed. Vivian De Dola Pinto and F. Warren Roberts. New York: The Viking Press, 1964.

Levi-Strauss, Claude. *From Honey to Ashes: Introduction to a Science of Mythology.* Vol. II. Trans. John and Doreen Weightman. New York: Harper & Row, 1973.

⸻. *The Raw and the Cooked: Introduction to a Science of Mythology.* Vol. I. Trans. John and Doreen Weightman. New York: Harper & Row, 1969.

Lommel, Andreas. *Prehistoric Man and Primitive Man.* New York: McGraw-Hill, 1966.

Lowell, Robert. *Prometheus Bound.* New York: Farrar, Straus & Giroux, 1969.

McKenna, Denis J. and T. K. McKenna. *The Invisible Landscape.* New York: The Seabury Press, 1975.

Mercantante, Anthony S. *Who's Who in Egyptian Mythology.* New York: Clarkson

N. Potter, 1978.

Merivale, Patricia. *Pan The Goat-God: His Myth in Modern Times.* Cambridge: Harvard University Press, 1969.

Middleton, John. *Lugbara Religion.* London: Oxford University Press, 1960.

*Nibelungenlied.* Trans. A. T. Hatto. New York: Penguin, 1965.

Nilsson, Martin P. *Greek Folk Religion.* 1940; rpt. Philadelphia: University of Pennsylvania, 1972.

*Oedipus Myth and Drama.* Ed. Martin Kallich *et al.* New York: The Odyssey Press, 1968.

Otto, Walter F. *Dionysus: Myth and Cult.* Trans. Robert B. Palmer. London: Indiana University Press, 1965.

Plath, Sylvia. *Sylvia Plath Letters Home: Correspondence 1950–1963.* Ed. Aurelia Schober Plath. New York: Bantam, 1977.

Plato. *The Last Days of Socrates.* Trans. Hugh Tredennick. Baltimore: Penguin Books, 1969.

Popa, Vasko. *Collected Poems 1943–1976.* Trans. Anne Pennington with an introduction by Ted Hughes. New York: Persea Books, 1978.

Radin, Paul. *The Trickster: A Study in American Indian Mythology.* 1956; rpt. New York: Schocken Books, 1972.

Reichel-Dolmatoff, G. *The Shaman and the Jaguar.* Philadelphia: Temple University Press, 1975.

Ross, Anne. *Pagan Celtic Britain: Studies in Iconography and Tradition.* London: Routledge & Kegan Paul, 1967.

Sagar, Keith. *The Art of Ted Hughes* 2nd ed. Cambridge: Cambridge University Press, 1978.

Smith, A. C. H. *Orghast at Persepolis.* New York: The Viking Press, 1972.

Sophocles. *Oedipus The King.* Trans. David Grene. Chicago: University of Chicago Press, 1908.

Spenser, Edmund. *The Faery Queene.* Ed. J. C. Smith and E. De Selincourt. London: Oxford University Press, 1966.

Stevens, Wallace. *Collected Poems.* New York: Knopf, 1972.

Thomas, Dylan. *The Collected Poems of Dylan Thomas.* New York: New Directions, 1953.

Thoreau, H. D. *Walden.* New York: Bramhall House, 1951.

*The Tibetan Book of the Dead.* Ed. W. Y. Evans-Wentz. 1927; rpt. New York: Oxford University Press, 1960.

Troussou, Raymond. *Le Theme de Promethee dans la Litterature Europeenne.* 2 vols. Geneve: Librairie Droz, 1964.

Vickery, John B. *The Literary Impact of the Golden Bough.* Princeton: Princeton University Press, 1973.

———. *The Scapegoat: Ritual and Literature.* New York: Houghton Mifflin, 1972.

Weyer, E. M. *The Eskimos.* Hamden, Connecticut: Archon Books, 1969.

Willetts, R. F. *Cretan Cults and Festivals.* London: Routledge & Kegan Paul, 1962.

Yates, Frances Aurelia. *Giordano Bruno and the Hermetic Tradition.* Chicago: University of Chicago Press, 1964.

Yeats, William Butler. *The Collected Poems of W. B. Yeats:* 'Definitive Edition with the Author's Final Revisions' New York: Macmillan, 1956.

———. *The Letters of W. B. Yeats.* Ed. Allan Wade. New York: Macmillan, 1955.

———. *Mythologies.* Ed. Mrs. W. B. Yeats. New York: Macmillan, 1959.

———. *A Vision:* 'A Reissue with the Author's Final Revisions' New York: Macmillan, 1956.

# INDEX

233